PHILOSOPHY
AND
POLITICAL
CHANGE
IN EASTERN
EUROPE

THE MONIST LIBRARY OF PHILOSOPHY

PHILOSOPHY AND POLITICAL CHANGE IN EASTERN EUROPE

J. C. NYÍRI
TIBOR HAJDÚ
G. M. TAMÁS
ERNEST GELLNER
WOJCIECH ŻEŁANIEC
JAN WOLEŃSKI
JÁN PAVLÍK
WILLIAM McBRIDE and IVANKA RAYNOVA
EDWARD M. SWIDERSKI
BARRY SMITH

Edited by Barry Smith

The Hegler Institute
Monist Library of Philosophy
La Salle, Illinois
1993

First Edition

ISBN: 0-914417-06-1

The Hegeler Institute
publishers of *The Monist,*
an International Quarterly Journal of General
Philosophical Inquiry
and of the Monist Library of Philosophy
Box 600, La Salle, Illinois 61301

CONTENTS

FOREWORD

The papers which follow were presented at an international conference which was held in the Hungarian Academy of Sciences in Budapest in March 1992. The conference, the first in a series of Monist Colloquia sponsored by the Hegeler Institute, was directed by G. M. Tamás and J. C. Nyíri, both of the Hungarian Academy of Sciences, with the collaboration of Todd Volker (Hegeler Institute) and Barry Smith.

Among the participants in the conference were included, in addition to those represented here: György Bence (Budapest), Jörgen Habermas (Frankfurt), Aladàr Madaràsz (Budapest), Josef Novák (Munich), and members of the Carus family (Illinois). The organizers are grateful to all these individuals for their contributions to the success of the conference as a whole.

For generous financial assistance we should like to express our thanks also to the Lynde and Harry Bradley Foundation (Milwaukee), the Soros Foundation (Budapest) and the Hegeler Institute.

Barry Smith

July 1992

TRADITION AND BUREAUCRATIC LORE:
LESSONS FROM HUNGARY

Of the three defeated revolutions by which modern Hungary was afflicted, two—those of 1848 and of 1919—gave rise almost immediately to some remarkable products of political philosophy. József Eötvös began to write his *Ruling Ideas* in 1849; Zsigmond Kemény's major essays were published between 1850 and 1853. The essays making up Georg Lukács's *History and Class Consciousness*[1] were written between 1919 and 1923. Gyula Szekfű's conservative manifesto *Three Generations*[2] appeared in 1920; Dezső Szabó's novel *Az elsodort falu* in 1919, making its nationalist-populist, anti-semitic author into the most influential intellectual figure of the following years. Indeed these revolutions had been partly *brought about* by the very ideas which were then subsequently applied to analyze them. The "ruling ideas" investigated by Eötvös were, after all, those of *liberty*, *equality*, and *nationality*; while the collectivist eschatology of the communist revolution was foreshadowed not only by Lukács's notes on Dostoevsky written in 1914/15,[3] but also, for instance, by Dezső Szabó's essay "The Bankruptcy of Individualism".[4] "The individual by itself," Szabó here wrote, "is a nonsensical being and exists only to the extent that the community endows it with sense ... Only the institution, in which the community as it were becomes embodied, can be the criterion of truth."

To the revolution of 1956 there has been no philosophical aftermath. This was a spontaneous uprising, with a markedly left-wing outlook, striving to realize radical demands of democracy and socialism. It was from the very start, as Bill Lomax puts it, "the masses of working people, not the élite of writers and politicians" who were responsible for the birth and development of the movement[5]—a movement, the underlying theoretical paradoxes of which remained hidden for quite some years due to the traumatic effect of the Soviet invasion. The political thinker István Bibó, a minister of state in the last coalition government of the revolution, whose left-wing democratic ideas achieved considerable underground prominence after 1956, did not, characteristically, draw any theoretically significant conclusions from the events of that year. His ideas, becoming especially influential by the late 1970s, had been formulated and published, in all essentials, between 1945 and 1948.[6]

But now, with the radical changes experienced in and around 1989, with this most recent revolution we have had: why does one encounter here again no philosophical responses whatsoever? Perhaps because the revolution was not defeated. After all, the overriding aim seems to have been to get rid of the Russians, and we *did* get rid of them. Or perhaps because there has been no revolution. After all, there were no rebellious masses, no subversive political forces to speak of, no social aims demanding to be realized. What happened was that the Soviet Union collapsed. Or perhaps there were no philosophical reactions — because whatever had really happened, it happened entirely without a philosophical *prelude*. It came, philosophically, as a complete surprise; there were no concepts there to handle it.

What really happened was, of course, that the Soviet Union lost the Cold War. The centralized economies of the so-called socialist countries proved unable to keep up with Western developments in technology, in particular in microelectronics. As a consequence, the faith in the continuing military supremacy of the Soviet Union over the West wavered. Eastern European products became, for reasons of quality and price, increasingly difficult to export. Attempts at a decentralization of the economy with no democratization of the political system failed. Liberalization at home and a new *détente* in foreign policy were the results.[7] In Hungary, the communist leader Kádár was in effect removed at the Party conference of May 1988, and formally disposed of—by then a human wreck—in May 1989; in October 1989 the—nominally still ruling—communist party, leaving behind the orthodox, reconstituted itself along social democratic lines and received something like 10 percent of the votes in the first free parliamentary elections of March/April 1990. In June 1991 the last units of the Red Army—an army defeated by the ultimate impotence of socialist economics—left the country.

How can one explain the fact that Hungarian philosophy, ostensibly dominated by Marxism for over four decades, turned out to be utterly incapable of coping with these developments—even though the story as here told is a perfectly intelligible one from the point of view of technological determinism, and even though technological determinism is of course an important part of the Marxist orthodoxy? The answer is threefold. First, the dominance of Marxism in Hungarian philosophy had become, by the early 1980s, a merely apparent one. Marxists came to constitute an oppressed majority, still in power at the numerous smaller universities, as well as at the schools of higher instruction belonging to the—very extended—party network; but they were fighting a rearguard battle at the centers of research and learning in the capital, in the editorial offices of the major journals and publishing houses, and in higher academic committees. At these places all the usual currents of Western philosophy were represented—hermeneutics and analysis, philosophy of science and philosophy of language, modern logic, Heidegger and Wittgenstein, Popper and Merleau-Ponty, Husserl and Rahner, Gadamer and Kuhn. Leftism was not fashionable. Philosophers came to be interested in the power of ideas—not in the effects of technological change.

Secondly, orthodox Marxists of the dialectical/historical materialist sort had been an oppressed majority within Hungarian Marxism ever since the late 1960s. One of the main reasons for this was of course the presence of the philosopher Georg Lukács. A great thinker and an ardent communist, Lukács could maintain a certain level even during the intellectually or morally less brilliant phases of his career. Even his most maligned book, *The Destruction of Reason*,[8] succeeds in conveying philosophical vision and quite a significant amount of historical knowledge.[9] Except for perhaps two or three years in the early 1950s, philosophy in Hungary never quite came to be equated with Soviet textbooks on Marxism-Leninism, or indeed with the latest resolution of the Party Central Committee. With the bloody repercussions after 1956, political pressure again, for a time, grew; ideological pressure, however, lessened—a consequence of Kádár's strange compromise with the country. By the early 1960s it was possible, at the University of Budapest, to study philosophy in an almost scientific manner, with members of the circle around Lukács providing the most important impulses. In 1963 Lukács's *Die Eigenart des Ästhetischen* was published, a Hungarian translation appearing in 1965. The first three chapters of the book, analyzing the relations between science, art, and everyday life, did, its somewhat *ontological* tendencies notwithstanding, much to lessen the influence of dialectical materialism. But while the master went on to work out the implications of just these tendencies,[10] his students, and the students of his students, some sooner, some—under the impact of the year 1968—later, discovered for themselves a very different Lukács: the author of *History and Class Consciousness*. The Marxism of that early work is an activist and voluntarist one; the emphasis is on *changing* the world by changing political *attitudes*.[11] At the time, then, when Marxism reached its most creative phase in post-war Hungary, it acquired a distaste for the idea that underlying technological processes could essentially influence political history.[12]

Thirdly, technological determinism pursued in a spirit of historical materialism would of course never have sufficed to foretell the collapse of the Soviet Union: the insight would also have been necessary that *technological progress is impeded by the absence of a free market*. Now the rudiments of this insight were certainly there in post-1956 Hungary. The promise to permit a minimum level of economic well-being was, after all, the most important element in the Kádár compromise. Within severe limits, private production, prices and profits, were, very gradually, allowed to play a role. A scientific reflection upon this practice of employing market mechanisms was, at the same time, neither encouraged, nor indeed seriously attempted. A singularly important exception is the—still unpublished—book *Is Critical Economic Theory Possible?*, written between 1970 and 1972 by three members of the Lukács school,[13] a book G. M. Tamás appropriately characterizes as the "greatest achievement of post-war

Central European Marxism".[14] The authors here on the one hand formulated a very detailed argument showing that the suppression of market mechanisms invariably leads to social effects incompatible with Marxian humanism—with the idea of socialism; on the other hand they upheld the aim of effecting a "rational-social control" over the spontaneous economic processes of the market. Between these contrasting tendencies the vision of a participatory democracy of workers served to ease the tension, with genuine socialism depicted as pluralistic and tolerant, a "revolution of everyday life". No wonder that the book provoked immediate repercussions—the attack mentioned in note 12. Leading representatives of the Lukács school lost their jobs; some were forced into exile. Marxism would, henceforth, not play a role in weakening communist rule in Hungary.

Nor did, of course, any other ideology play such a role. During the 1980s a kind of liberal-democratic oppositional movement came into being, made up of a handful of intellectuals groping their way from Marx to Bibó. An element of ferment and a moral signal, this movement hardly meant a threat to the establishment. Even less of a threat was another, quite blurred, group of intellectuals, mainly writers, harboring vague reminiscences of a nationalist-populist ideology which, beginning with Dezső Szabó, became rather important in the interwar period. Through the ideas of Bibó they had points of contact with the democrats; through the person of the writer Gyula Illyés, with the communists. As the regime retreated, these two still lingering oppositional currents, gradually and hesitantly, developed into political parties. In the 1990 elections the Free Democrats obtained 91 parliamentary seats out of 386, becoming the major party in opposition; the Hungarian Democratic Forum won 165 seats, becoming the major party of the government coalition. These were almost entirely random results, since neither party succeeded in coming to represent specific social interests, or indeed in really articulating a particular ideology of its own.

Once established in power, the Forum began to act out the pattern the peripheral position of Hungary invariably seems to force upon its political elites. As Andrew C. Janos puts it in his *The Politics of Backwardness in Hungary*, "one of the most outstanding features of Hungarian history" is "the periodic rise and decline of political classes living by and off the institutions of the state".[15] This feature became especially pronounced with the onset of the age of liberalism, in the second half of the nineteenth century. As Janos writes:

> In the core area of Europe where it was born, liberalism did indeed originate with a class of... entrepreneurs and merchants who, in their historical moment of success, wanted to be free to pursue their affairs without any outside protection or interference. The result was a doctrine built around the idea of personal freedom and the emancipation of the individual from the authority of the state. Not so in Hungary and in other societies of the European periphery, where liberalism became the ideol-

ogy of a class desperately searching for alternatives to economic entrepreneurship. This class ... wanted to strengthen rather than weaken the modern state, so that it could afford protection against the vagaries of the market, and, as a last resort, provide ... security of employment in its bureaucracy and political institutions.[16]

With no powerful middle class to counterbalance the political elite's interest in a strong state, a "symbiotic relationship" between the administration and the governing parliamentary party inevitably came into being,[17] "administrative leverage was quickly transformed into political leverage"; the party and the bureaucracy were "welded into a single, powerful machine" in which the bureaucracy was charged with perpetuating the parliamentary majority, "while parliament and party would lend an aura of legitimacy to bureaucratic policies and provide a forum to articulate bureaucratic interests".[18] In backward Hungary the attempt at modernization, "instead of leading to political democracy, a capitalist market economy, and a society based on equal rights", resulted "in a bureaucratic polity, a pseudo-market, and a neo-corporatist society in which rights continued to be commensurate with social function".[19]

This pattern, characteristic of Hungarian political conditions throughout the decades before and after 1919, re-emerged unchanged in 1990. With it, the need for an appropriate ideology arose. One obvious component of such an ideology, proclaimed by a governing elite ostensibly intent on catching up with, indeed joining, Western Europe, had to be *liberalism*. Another obvious component had to be *étatism*. As just indicated, in Hungarian politics these two components had been brought together again and again under the idea of the *modernizing state*. They were now meant to be representative of the *national-liberal* wing of the Forum. For a governing party determined to perpetuate its hold over the electorate the building up of powerful and loyal Church organizations, the launching of an aggressive clerical propaganda, must appear to be a rewarding policy. The verbiage surrounding this policy was now said by members of the Forum— may God forgive them—to be representative of a second current within the Forum, the *Christian-Democratic* wing. It is a third wing, however, that came to be the bearer of the main ideology of the Forum: the *popular-national* one. In Hungarian this is "nép-nemzeti"—"nép" meaning people; the compound expression standing for the fuzzy mixture of nationalist-populist ideas I have already alluded to. The function of this ideology is to *intimidate*: it suggests that the opponent—oppositional politicians, the press, complaining schoolteachers, etc.—is *not genuinely Hungarian* (the implication not necessarily being that he is a Jew—he might be a communist, or a liberal, or an entrepreneur, or an intellectual, or a pop-music fan). The implication is that he is *not rooted* in the Hungarian people, does not have a Hungarian *character*, does not conform to the national *traditions*.[20]

What prehistory does this blend of ideologies have in Hungarian philosophy? The combination of liberalism with étatism had mostly been a matter of
political practice here, not of political thought. As a possible exception one
could mention, perhaps, the ideas of the so-called *centralists*, a group around
the young Eötvös in the 1840s. To them the establishing of a modern, centralized, parliamentary state appeared as the essential step towards a liberalization
of Hungarian society. However, these ideas did certainly not add up to a system
of political philosophy; and by the time they did, in Eötvös's *The Influence of
the Ruling Ideas of the 19th Century on the State*,[21] they have been transformed
into a liberal-conservative *criticism* of centralization. Eötvös there contrasts the
French democratic with the English liberal view; the latter envisages the possibility of a plurality of sovereign powers—King, parliament, the courts, cabinet,
even the church and private associations—each limited by the others in such a
way that there is no absolute power within the state and in such a way that the
rights of individuals are clearly guaranteed. Eötvös's main idea in the *Ruling
Ideas* is that of regionalism or territorial self-government. Not only individual
liberty but also historical continuity are threatened by centralization. A system
of territorial pluralism, of municipalities, on the other hand, will defend the
freedom of minorities (and ultimately those of the individual) against centralist
absolutism. Another guarantee of civil liberties in a liberal state is the separation
of the spiritual from the temporal power. Eötvös's philosophy certainly does not
lend support to the idea of a liberal state striving to imbue its citizens with religious values. Nor does it bolster the idea of specifically Hungarian traditions. A
nation capable of development will always be open to foreign influences; and
indeed all those much-revered ancient Hungarian customs and institutions have
been, Eötvös stressed, in reality taken over from the West during the centuries
when this nation was not yet a backward one; they are by now, in the West,
obsolete and forgotten—while in Hungary falsely believed to be unique and
authentic.

   That Christian philosophy in Hungary, during the communist era, did not
show any great creative brilliance, can hardly be explained by the fact of
oppression. After all, higher centers of religious learning did not cease to function, Catholic and Protestant professors of philosophy continued to lecture, to
pursue research, to publish. But then it is perhaps significant that original works
of Christian philosophy had not been written in inter-war Hungary either.
Szekfű's political philosophy of course, as formulated in his *Three Generations*,
had a markedly Catholic intonation. Early Hungarian history, as Szekfű sees the
matter, is essentially moulded by Christian values. As he puts it:

> Ever since the Hungarians, forced by St. Stephen, have been converted to
> Christianity and have organized their state after the great Christian model, the

Carolingian empire, they have not ceased to be a member of the Central European Christian community which we ... designate as Christian-Germanic. In the political system of this community the principle of Christian authority is united with the idea of Germanic freedom and has given rise, in contrast to the unboundedness of the idea of liberal freedom,... to the political principle of *suum cuique*, alloting recognition to each one according to his merit.[22]

With the departure from this principle in the nineteenth century there begins, Szekfű says, the fatal decline of Hungarian history, and hence of Hungarian national character. Szekfű's hero in *Three Generations* is Count Stephen Széchenyi, a politician and political writer, whose conservative reform program had played a substantial role in Hungary's pre-1848 development. Széchenyi, Szekfű suggests, was the first to achieve a combination, into a complete and perfect system, of *nationalism, Christian morality,* and *individual perfection*.[23] Széchenyi created a synthesis which is "genuinely Hungarian", yet resting "on universally European foundations": "With Széchenyi a new bough has branched off from the Christian-Germanic trunk, the Christian-Hungarian one."[24] Immediately after Széchenyi, however, decay sets in: "The liberal recent past has been a period of deviation, from which we can emerge only through organic work, the cultivation of national traditions."[25] Szekfű nowhere really succeeds in defining *what*, specifically, Hungarian traditions are; but in *Three Generations* he at any rate makes it clear that whatever they consist in, they become diluted through the Jewish presence in Hungary.

The position of *Three Generations* no doubt exerts an influence on the Forum's ideology today; Szekfű himself however began to move away from that position by the mid-1930s. His idea of a Christian-German cultural unity faded into the background; with regard to Hungary, he tended to speak of "an amalgamation of the national with the European spirit";[25] he became increasingly critical of the state's omnipotence; of anti-Semitism; and, in particular, he developed a less one-sided view of liberalism.[27] And at no stage did he have sympathies for the nationalist-populist current. Peasant culture, for Szekfű, was but an element of a nations's overall cultural make-up;[28] for the populists, peasant culture was the ideal.

Now although they offered false solutions, the *problem* the populists saw was in a sense real. In Hungary and in East-Central European countries in general there was a wide gap, especially in the nineteenth and the early twentieth centuries, between high and low culture. As Tamás Hofer puts it in his "The perception of tradition in European ethnology",

> East European countries, in the continental system of Europe, belonged to a peripheral zone, which means that at least since the beginning of the modern age (from the sixteenth century on), the ruling classes have been connected to cultural forms and patterns of behaviour developed in the centre. As a consequence, the gap between

the rulers and the rural peasant segment of these societies ... became deeper and deeper.[29]

Hofer points to the Eastern European "peasants' isolation and exclusion from the tight network of cultural transmission established in the core areas of the continent"—in France or in England, for instance—"where the existence of a great number of small cities and the peasants' involvement in market and cultural relations brought them into contact with other segments of society", and quotes the Hungarian composer Zoltán Kodály referring to the " 'happy people of Europe', whose 'development was undisturbed and [who] use a homogeneous language'. In the tunes of Verdi, an Italian peasant 'can recognize the presence of his own musical mother-tongue'".[30] Adopting the explication of the term "people" given by Karl W. Deutsch—"membership in a people essentially consists in ... the ability to communicate more effectively, and over a wider range of subjects, with members of one large group than with outsiders"[31]—one could say that the lower and the upper classes in nineteenth-century and early twentieth-century Hungary did not belong to the same people. The populists' fallacy was: not to recognize that the difference in ethnic origins was merely an aspect, not the essence, of the problem. Their program of *replacing* the urban culture of a middle class of ethnically heterogenous origins by building upon the traditions of a supposedly pristine Hungarian peasantry was not only politically dangerous; it was, also, scientifically unfounded.

An adequate theory of traditions and traditionality was of course not available in inter-war Hungary[32]—indeed it was hardly existent anywhere else at the time. By 1990, however, a vast body of literature on the subject has appeared,[33] with some of it reviewed in Hungarian. The present author attempted a traditionalist interpretation of Wittgenstein in 1975,[34] gave a brief survey of some English and American liberal-conservative theories, with an emphasis on the work of F. A. von Hayek, in 1981,[35] occupied himself, throughout the 1980s, with reconstructing a liberal-conservative succession within Austro-Hungarian intellectual history,[36] and stressed the importance of the Hayekian idea of *a tradition of liberty* in 1988.[37] Today I believe that the traditionalist stance of these writings rested on delusions; but no harm was done, my thinking had no impact whatsoever. G. M. Tamás's conservative turn, with the publication of his "Farewell to the Left" in 1988,[38] had of course been a momentous event; but it was the party of the Free Democrats that Tamás then became a prominent member of; I cannot detect any signs, in the rhetoric of the Forum, of an influence of his arguments.

Traditionalism—the attempted revival of extinct traditions believed to recapture the genuine history of a people having lost contact with its past, seen as uprooted and degenerated—is a misdirected, and dangerous, attitude because it fosters irrational thinking in an epoch when belief in authority has ceased to play a cognitively functional role. The *handing down of traditions* is a specific institution for preserving knowledge under conditions such that collective memory can find no support in *written documents*, and is therefore dependent on the oral repetition of texts the truth of which is not allowed to be called into question. The indubitability of the transmitted text is legitimated through the fiction that it has been passed on *unchanged from generation to generation*.[39] With the rise of literacy, this fiction becomes unnecessary, and indeed impossible. In a literate culture the functionality of traditions is confined to the sphere of face-to-face communication between the individual and his primary groups. The concept of *national traditions*, in particular, is misleading, since only with the spread of literacy, in the age of the printed text, did modern nations come into being. So-called national traditions are ideological instruments for facilitating monopolistic competition in the era of modernization.[40] The material out of which national traditions are fabricated is provided by *folklore*. As Richard M. Dorson has put it:

> Far from being an antiquarian hobby, folklore has throughout the history of its study been connected with national issues and concerns. The appearance of folkloristics as a discipline coincided, not by chance, with the heightening of nationalism in a number of countries, since folklore traditions could help reinforce the sense of national identity, once the intellectuals and policymakers become aware of their existence.[41]

Dorson specifically refers to the Nazi's use of folklore,[41] as well as to the connection between folklore research and the rise of nationalism in Finland. This latter topic has since received a detailed analysis in a book by William M. Wilson, a book which, as the author says, focuses

> almost exclusively on Finland, but the aim has been larger—to trace thoroughly in one country the history of an idea that has borne fruit in many lands, the romantic nationalistic idea that in order to survive and to maintain its independence, a nation must continually re-create itself in the image of its noble and heroic past and that it must seek that past in folklore.[43]

The politically dominant Hungarian ideology today is a romantic nationalism of precisely this sort. As I have tried to show in the foregoing, this ideology is a reflection of political pressures, rather than of philosophical influences. And as far as there is room for oppositional politics at all, it too is moved by entirely pragmatic considerations. Philosophy does not play a part in contemporary Hungarian politics. But politics is becoming, once more, a *topic* for Hungarian philosophy. For this politics, caught between modernization and backwardness, is burdened with antinomies; embodies paradoxes; gives rise to conceptual tensions. Our latest, non-existent, revolution now seems to turn into a creeping counter-revolution. Obvious answers have become, once more, doubtful; unequivocal words have become, once more, deeply ambiguous. In Hungary, there seems to be a foretaste of philosophy in the air.

J. C. Nyíri

Hungarian Academy of Sciences
Budapest

IDEOLOGY AND TECHNOLOGY: A COMMENT ON NYÍRI

Professor Nyíri has stated correctly that the main factor in our so-called revolution or change of regime was the collapse of the Soviet state as a result of its own inability to keep up with Western developments in technology. However he forgot to mention the historical fact that Soviet ideology stopped developing first, and Soviet microelectronics only later. Now I do not claim that political ideology alone was responsible for the growing distance between high-level technology on the one hand and Soviet technology on the other. There were and are inherent factors hindering the latter's progress. But political ideology acted as a double break. By anathemizing cybernetics, genetics, etc., and by hindering the free circulation of scientific information, Soviet personnel departments and the KGB did more harm to the cause of Soviet science than did the COCOM list. The creation, for ideological reasons, of a Bloc market stimulated only the black market; it did not stimulate, but rather even blocked, the development of technology and production. And when, after the Second World War, Stalin ordered a campaign against underestimating Soviet power, Soviet culture, etc., the easiest response was simply to suppress information concerning new foreign achievements instead of propagating them.

If, on the other hand, we compare Hungarian governmental policy towards scientists and scientific institutions in the early 1980s with what prevails now, in the early '90s, then we do not see any striking differences; we see, rather, similarities—in slowness, clumsiness, bureaucracy, in the frittering away of energy and money. The ideology and the reasoning differ greatly; the methods rather less. This may seem to contradict what I stated earlier, and surely it does; but it is a contradiction inherent in the fact that Soviet and Hungarian state ideology were derived not so much from Marxian ideas as from a home-made mixture of backwardness, slowness, impatience and xenophobia—in a phrase, from the Eastern European mentality.

Perhaps some would say that I overestimate this nebulous East-Europeanism. To make it more precise: at least in Hungary after the seizing of power by the communists, dogmatic Marxism initially prevailed in ideology, though in a Sovietized or Stalinist form. This Stalinism was born fighting Easternness—slowness, anarchy, bribery, xenophobia—all of which Stalin and Beria sought to suppress in the Caucasus, where they are now enjoying something of a renaissance. But of course Stalinism itself was Eastern enough. When the dogmatical fanatics failed in '56, "Kadarism" came, and grew year by year less Marxist and more eastern-pragmatic-possibilist. And the less dogmatic it was, the more successful it became, but in the process of developing from dogmatism to total pragmatism it lost its original, socialist aims, replacing them with nothing, a ship without compass and destination.

Seen from outside, this regime could seem dogmatic enough even in the '70s and '80s. However this was rather a pseudo- or post-dogmatism. The old Marxian ballast had been thrown out piece after piece, though always, as it were, under cover of darkness. This is the reason why a follower of Wittgenstein or of old Hungarian liberals was less alarming than those, like Kis, Bence and Márkus, who were trying to help modernize the edifice of Marxism in their "Is Critical Economic Theory Possible?", etc.

Now Eastern-European backwardness is very different from the backwardness of the Third World, all the more so on the western fringes of the east, i.e. in Hungary, Bohemia and Poland. Here we are far from reaching western standards of wealth and technology, yet we have an intelligentsia that is not below the western level and a common people knowing of and wishing for a western standard of life. This is why some of our economists are dreaming in vain about accelerated development after the fashion of the Asiatic "little tigers". Rákosi or Ulbricht were tigers enough, but when they tried to make their people work hard while living on the level of the Taiwan or Korea of the fifties, the people answered with June '53 and October '56. And what turned out to be impossible under the dictators seems to be even more impossible in our new democracy.

After the Second World War there were two real ways forward as far as Hungary was concerned: extreme nationalism or some sort of socialism. No possibility presented itself for a conservative polity, even without Soviet domination, for not enough remained to be conserved. As Prof. Tamás has correctly stated, the last regime worthy of being conserved (or restored to life) seemed to be the Austro-Hungarian Monarchy; but her faithfuls like Cardinal Mindszenty waited in vain for the consent of the Great Powers (to say nothing of the Slavic and Rumanian peoples who also had a certain interest in this regard). Nationalism remained a strong force, but it was made impossible for Hungary when at Paris the old Trianon decisions were renewed. To conserve the Horthy regime would have been no less impossible then as it would be now. A nationalist government would have led to open conflict with all our neighbors. In this connection it is significant that our first elections after the collapse of "real socialism" led to the emergence of a nationalist government which soon succeeded in worsening our contacts with most of our neighbors. Its members claim, too, to be conservative—but they have even less to conserve, reducing their conservative aims to the prohibition of abortion and the changing of the names of all the streets. And while the present government is sincerely anticommunist, it has nevertheless preserved rather a lot of socialist bureaucracy, industry, centralized financial redistribution, etc.

And why was socialism tolerated by the people? Partly because of the terror, the presence of the Russian Army, but not only for that reason: even in the late seventies there were still no serious common feelings against socialism in principle—even throughout the 1956 revolt. Producing the necessary capital for a capitalist economy was impossible without great capital investment from the outside or a regime of industrial slavery of a type that has become impossible in the Europe of the 20th century. Indeed, the strongest popular feelings in '56 and for some years after that were directed not against utopian levellers but against the existing differences between minimum and maximum salaries.

As for ideology, Marxist philosophy had an advantage in postwar Hungary which it never had in Western Europe; most of the modern thinkers of the first half of our century—even the Hungarian emigrées Mannheim and the Polányi brothers—were little known in Hungary. Marxism was confronted not with modern philosophy but with an outdated, conservative-dogmatic ideology, to say nothing of *völkisch* and other Ruritanian tendencies. Even later, in '56 or '68, Marxist revisionism was still confronted with century-old ideas. Almost the same applies in the field of sociology, with things only a little better in economics. Only later was there formed a generation conversant with and able to apply 20th-century western ideologies, including modern conservativism.

The party leadership itself cleared the way for the new (for Hungary) ideas when around 1973 it made its ideological offensive against revisionists, thereby helping Márkus, Bence, Kis, Szelényi and the others in getting rid more swiftly of their Marxist and other utopian heritage.

In my own field of historiography, finally, we were confronted with quite different forces from those faced by philosophy or economics. While the leading Hungarian historians were conservative-legitimists, the history-telling of the nationalists remained more popular. Marxist history bosses like Révai, Andics and Mód tried to adopt the nationalist-populist, anti-German (*"kuruc"*) historiography, at one and the same time fighting against both cosmopolitism and Habsburgism. Only in 1956 were they awakened to the fact that they were riding a tiger. Therefore the new ideological bosses in the 1960s gave way to revisionist, social-democratic and even *"labanc"*, i.e., pro-Habsburg ideas in Hungarian historiography: on the condition that the proponents of such ideas would fight against nationalism, which we were happy enough to do. Whether we were right or wrong politically, and whether we wronged or helped other fields of science, are complicated and much-debated questions. However, this compromise made possible the forming of a realistic, post-Marxist historiography which met and collaborated, strangely enough, not only with the young liberals, but also with the old bearers of anti-nationalist, even conservative historical ideas. What resulted out of this might seem like a very eclectic mixture, but it had powerful results; some nationalistic historians not very successful in historiography changed academic career for the field of politics—in some cases not without success. Ideas obsolete in historiography seem to be very useful for the realization of nationalistic political ends.

Tibor Hajdú

Institute of History, Budapest

CONSERVATISM, PHILOSOPHY AND EASTERN EUROPE
TO THE MEMORY OF ELIE KEDOURIE

Der Revolutionär flieht vor dem, was am schwersten zu ertragen ist, vor der ziellosen Vielfältigkeit des Lebens nämlich, in die Richtung der Vollkommenheit, was in der Welt seiner Untertatsächlichkeiten jedoch bestenfalls Vollständigkeit bedeuten könnte. Volk, soweit es das noch ist, wird wohl augenblicklich rebellieren, revoltieren gegen unerträglich gewordenen gegenwärtigen Druck der Herrschenden; nie aber wird dieses Volk revolutionär sein: eben wegen seiner allzu großen Vertrautheit mit der Zähigkeit, der Wucht, dem Zwang der organischen Lebenszusammenhänge. Deshalb kommt auch hier etwas ganz anderes bei ihm bald zum Vorschein, nämlich seine natürliche Skepsis. Damit endet das euphorische Stadium jeder Revolution. (Heimito von Doderer, *Die Dämonen*, II, i)

It is a remarkable fact that the most conspicuous conservative writers have always been rather fond of paradox and satire—think of Chesterton and Karl Kraus. The style most frequently associated with modern conservatism is fragmentary and ironical; it is given to speaking in riddles as in Wittgenstein or it is notoriously reluctant to come to the point, as in Oakeshott. Why should this be so?

The indirectness, the allusiveness, the genteel stammer of conservatism is caused, I believe, by the politically plausible but intellectually difficult conservative task of defending a rag-bag of mutually irreconcilable states of affairs, considered worth defending by the simple virtue of their being already there. In a more high-minded way this is called, of course, Upholding Tradition. For if we consider Tradition as something good, or at least as better than reform, futuristic planning, revolution or whatever, then we have, of course, substantive criteria circumscribing Tradition which is, therefore, not praised by us simply because of its originating in the venerable past, but because of its goodness. Professor Kedourie warns us in a recent handsome article[1] that conservatism, historically, was never an ideology with specific content. Indeed the conservatism that stood for the divine right of kings now stands as the staunchest standard-bearer of libertarian modernity. Nevertheless we are still justified in calling both "conservatism" for the apparently technical reason that both are trying to preserve the status quo ante against new-fangled utopias of any sort.

This shows conservatism to be the quintessentially modern phenomenon that it really is. So-called traditional societies do not defer to Tradition as such. What we regard as Tradition, traditional people regard as Truth. The collection of true ideas and stories bequeathed by the ancients, the canon, is respected, but not only because of its antiquity; it is believed because of its veracity.

Veneration of tradition does not inspire discussion. Tradition as moral custom is an institution: one tries to illustrate and defend an institution rather than to establish its truth. Traditional people thought otherwise. The respectability of a canon is dependent on whether it is believed or not. The critic of canon is a heretic, the critic of Tradition is a cultural adversary. Disbelieving truth is heresy. Heresy is mortal sin. Consequently establishing the truth of the canon is of paramount importance for every good man. The body of theses and stories deemed to be true by the community was debated in a few well-ordered institutions like churches, monasteries, colleges and universities. The mere veneration of Tradition, especially the veneration of a plurality of traditions, is inimical to debate, most particularly to institutional debate in a university. The critic of Tradition being a cultural adversary, we should bear in mind that adversaries fight, win and lose, but are not proven right or wrong. Modern "debates" therefore must ascertain the continuity of conflict and preclude intellectual triumph, that is, a final agreement concerning the truth or falsehood of a thesis or of a story. Conservatives can get around this problem by silently disregarding other traditions (other than their own). This tactical move presupposes some faith in one's tradition, a faith that in this case is little more than voluntary blindness.

Syncretism or eclecticism is excluded only by a judgment of taste. Good-mannered Western conservatives do not become Buddhists. This is indeed a question of manners, not of orthodoxy. Traditional people had institutions for debating the truth or falsity of a canon. Modern conservatives conceive of Tradition as an institution and are attempting to defend it. For a modern conservative the question whether a given traditional story is true or not, betrays incomprehension, lack of initiation, poor taste. His defence is institutional and aesthetic rather than moral or philosophic. This contrast at the same time is the difference beween politics old and new.

As a result conservatives had better be good at the art of improvization and even better at the art of critical invective. Conservative critics can be recognized by their routinely castigating rational invention; exposing the presumption of Reason is the poor man's (or the poor grandee's) theory of society. Radicals can hardly keep down the overwhelming feeling that conservatism is nihilistic, that it is merely carping at "ideas", lacking same itself. Nor is this feeling completely groundless. It is not wholly unfair to describe conservatism with the aid of the ancestral wisdom of the Viennese café: Nie kommt 'was Besseres nach. Conservatism is described in Michael Oakeshott's immortal essay[2] as distinctly unadventurous, quietistic and enamoured of humanity as it is—in other words, as being at peace with imperfection. With characteristic cunning, Oakeshott leaves open the question whether the conservative disposition is always his and, indeed, his magna opera scarcely bear out this contention. Conservatives can point out the ever-disappointing result of change, but they expose themselves to the charge of being at least accessories after the fact of preserving obsolete social circumstances in sore need of improving.

Thus conservatives have intellectual strategies and stratagems rather than theories. These strategies have been winningly described by a liberal critic of conservatism, Professor Hirschman.[3] His picture, though less dark, is quite similar to that painted by Sir Isaiah Berlin in the latter's essays on Count Tolstoy's and Joseph de Maistre's philosophy of history.[4] According to Professor Hirschman, conservatives or reactionaries oppose change, especially revolutionary change, on the grounds that change will (1) bring about results opposite or strikingly dissimilar to those intended or (2) in spite of immense sacrifices will achieve nothing in particular or (3) though successful, might have such unintended side-effects disrupting the precious fabric of society as will render the change at least not worth our trouble. Perversity, futility and jeopardy are the main types of conservative counter-argument which, if frozen into a rigid doctrine, may indeed prevent any sensible improvement of our lot. This is why, it will be remembered, the late Professor von Hayek hesitated to call himself a conservative.

I think we can accept Professor Hirschman's description as basically sound, although incomplete. It also offers the opportunity to approach our main subject less obliquely than heretofore. The question we should address, I think, is: Is conservative philosophy possible? The well-known English conservative, Professor Scruton, says in his book, *The Meaning of Conservatism*,[5] that conservatism is inarticulate and that it is in need of dogma, not philosophical theory. This is, indeed, the essence of the British conservative tradition: it sticks to attitude, disposition, experience, custom, skill, and it is reluctant to go further. We cannot deny, though, that the encounter of philosophy and conservatism has happened—on the Continent (in France, Germany and Russia)—and this encounter is what needs to be analyzed.

Modern philosophy, in contradistinction to ancient philosophy, is a rival of Revelation. It is, in very important respects, a critique of religion, not excepting theistic philosophies. Ancient (pagan) philosophy played a role quite similar to revealed religion in the Judaeo-Christian world, since it tried to elucidate the supernatural, the divine, the good, the eternal. The philosophical discourse of the ancients—particularly the Socratic one—presented an alternative to the barely human and social. The incompleteness of the human and of the social is not less forcefully expressed by Plato than by the Prophets, although here the similarity ends. Leo Strauss—of whom more later—said in an early work on modern philosophy that "if one wished to refute Orthodoxy, no other way remained but to attempt a complete understanding of the world and life without the assumption of an unfathomable God. This means that the refutation of Orthodoxy depended on the success of a system. Man had to prove himself theoretically and practically the lord of the world and the lord of his life. The world he created had to make the world that was merely 'given' to him disappear. Then Orthodoxy was more than refuted, it was 'outlived'."[6]

Briefly put, this is the image of Enlightenment Leo Strauss presented later in his books on Spinoza, Hobbes and Machiavelli. The fundamental idea of the Enlightenment is a doctrine of independence and this doctrine, according to Strauss, informs the standpoint of modern philosophy. Modern philosophical inquiry might discover that Man is dependent on the divine, but this can only be a finding at the end of that inquiry, the starting point is always Man in himself and human reason in itself. Man's independence is presupposed by the independence of the modern philosopher. There is at least one subject—the philosopher—who can at least try to think independently of traditional presuppositions. This minute fact, the hypothetical Cartesian starting point—doubt—is all that is required. The privileges of the philosopher as shown by Milton, Spinoza and Locke (extended into a theory of free expression) are philosophically prior, not ulterior, to the Enlightenment view. The switch here is not simply from blind faith to critical thought. Critical discussion of the grand European canon had taken place before the Enlightenment. But the critique of the canon was institutional, limited to scholars in holy orders regimented hierarchically in organizations such as chapters, faculties and colleges. Their privilege was to be conferred to scholarly lay gentlemen of independent means as well. This social novelty of extra-institutional, that is, extra-hierarchical discussion of the canon, in full view of a secular audience or public, needed arguments in its support, like all extension of privilege. The train of thought started by Milton's *Areopagitica* was captured most perfectly in Kant's *Was ist Aufklärung?*, still an openly political statement.

The old-fashioned contrast between "philosophic" and "secular" had been replaced by the difference between the public and private use of Reason and between private and public argument. In other words, this was the ideological foundation of a lay or secular university and academy. This change in the social climate caused Revelation to be discussed in ways respectful of Tradition by gentlemen in holy orders, and the Truth of the canon by lay gentlemen within or without university walls. The possibility of a non-ecclesiastical, stricto sensu non-academic critique of Revelation has made the problem of Tradition and the problem of Truth appear as separate matters. This divorce is the true basis for free speech. The universalistic principle of free speech is to be understood historically as the dissolution of a peculiar institutional demarcation that used to ensure the scholarly guardianship of the Jewish and of the Christian-Aristotelian canon. The discovery of logical and narrative inconsistencies in biblical Revelation, the dispassionate reflection on the worth of other civilizations (other than Christian, that is), the systematic mathematical construal of natural phenomena, are consequences of the acceptance of the possbility of independent inquiry. I think Leo Strauss is right in stressing that "Averroism", that is, the vindication of the freedom of philosophizing which is the main point of Spinoza's *Tractatus*, is of crucial importance here.

Freedom of philosophizing and independent inquiry are not the same, but the connection is strong. "Averroism", of course, means assuming that the freedom of philosophizing will not endanger the tranquillity of the City. The allegorical or historicist explanation of biblical Revelation will ensure that no substantive criticism, however radical, of revealed religion will jeopardize the prevailing institutions. "Averroism" offers a strange pact to the princes of the Church and of the State: truth will be divorced from the necessities of the social peace, the latter being based (or not, as the case may be) on the belief in a peculiar religious doctrine. There will be one type of man, the modern philosopher and savant, who will follow specific rules in the specific realm of the quest for truth. These rules will be different and separate from vulgar beliefs that guarantee tranquillity and harmony or social peace.

The political project of incipient Enlightenment is thus a moderate doctrine of freedom of thought. However moderate, this doctrine, by its implicit consequences proved revolutionary. For at the pinnacle of the hierarchy of different orders of human existence the ancients had placed life according to contemplative wisdom. Now that philosophy has become both independent (institutionally) and free (theologically and metaphysically), contemplation, wisdom, the quest for truth have withdrawn either into the garden of Epicurus or into the Republic of Letters (see the Strauss-Kojève debate[7])—and human society has to fend for itself guided by something which in the most charitable view is little more than mere prejudice and the this-worldly technical *virtù* of the Prince.

Aided and abetted by religious tolerance, modern philosophy has become the vehicle par excellence of change, for the simple reason that philosophy has to judge any proposal for political arrangements on its merits and, since every human society is by necessity imperfect, improvements are always called for. The "Averroist" promise of tranquillity could not be kept.

The advent of modernity—Enlightenment, liberalism, popular government, extension of franchise, natural science and the like—has forced those who wanted to reaffirm the pre-eminent merits of the Old Order to seek radical new foundations for the old ways. The philosophers of Restoration—de Maistre, de Bonald, Don Juan Donoso Cortés and, in this century, Carl Schmitt—may very well have been traditionalists in their sympathies, but they were by no means traditional. I shall have to explain why the doctrine of reaction has become a revolutionary philosophy and what are the consequences of this regarding both philosophy and conservatism.

The noblest version of Enlightenment, Kant's philosophy of morals, had posited Man's maturity, his coming of age, a tense theory based on the contradictory symmetry of freedom and responsibility. The philosophers of Restoration countered with a hard dogma of man's inborn and perpetual immaturity expressed by sombre theologoumena of complete sinfulness. Carl Schmitt is right in calling to our attention the profound disgust for human nature exhibited by the Restoration philosophers and their dark and acid pessimism.

De Maistre, de Bonald and Donoso Cortés have learned the cruel lessons of the French Revolution. They had to be, in Burke's words (*Thoughts on French Affairs*, December 1791) "not... resolute and firm, but perverse and obstinate" because they were seen "to resist the decrees of Providence" rather "than the mere designs of men". While Burke thought that French democrats were perverting the idea of liberty, the Restoration philosophers contended that liberty was perverting the body politic. Curiously for people associated with "Restoration", they did not really believe that the Old Order could be restored in its traditional shape. After the rupture or anomaly of the French Revolution they, as one particular sect engaged willy-nilly in independent philosophical inquiry, refused point-blank to play by the rules of modern philosophers. Their pre-emptive answer to the not yet pronounced counter-arguments of their putative critics was "just so"—the answer of pure Tradition to any critical upholder of the canon. If the main ideas of the Old Order had been incapable of being preserved as universally recognized "truth", they were ready to accept that those were superstitions and declared themselves ready to die and—what is more important—to kill for them. It is well-known that de Maistre considered the Pope more essential than Christ, and de Bonald thought that the hangman was more necessary than the Prince. Authority was not accepted as good, but with deliberate irrationality as a mere cause for unthinking obedience. The sword was not only considered as a proper instrument of a good policy arranged according to the precepts of the ancient sages, but good simply because it could chop off heads. The humility of the subject for them was little more than languid acquiescence in institutional rape. The ideal social link for them was the military solidarity of nations at war, the bloodier the better, their school the scaffold, their culture automatic ritual and the obliteration of learning, their simpleton's theology a terrible God's unremitting wrath. At the heart of this frightening doctrine was nevertheless a truly conservative idea: that tradition was venerable because it was tradition, any questioning thus betrayed sheer incomprehension and lack of metaphysical flair. Or was it? British conservatism was unphilosophical enough to include doubt of tradition into tradition. This view of course is self-contradictory; but then British conservatism is inconsistent and proud of it.

Let us dwell for a moment longer on Restoration theology, more courteously called "Continental conservatism". This is best summarized by a few apophthegms from Wittgenstein's *Vermischte Bemerkungen*, jotted down presumably in 1944. They are a tiny, indeed, shrivelled manifesto of anti-individualism, remarkably similar to Simone Weil's jottings from the same period and from the same exile.

> No cry of torment can be greater than the cry of one man.
> Or again, no torment can be greater than what a single human being may suffer.
> A man is capable of infinite torment therefore, and so too he can stand in need of infinite help.
> The Christian religion is only for the man who needs infinite help, solely, that is, for the man who experiences infinite torment.
> The whole planet can suffer no greater torment than a single soul.
> The Christian faith—as I see it—is a man's refuge in this ultimate torment. ... Someone who in this way penitently opens his heart to God in confessions lays it open for other men too. In doing this he loses his dignity and becomes like a child... A man can bare himself before others only out of a particular kind of love. A love which acknowledges that we are all wicked children. (Tr. Peter Winch.)

All this is heart-rending, but nevertheless poor theology. The Christian religion is not solely about confession, but also about justification and redemption. Wicked children surely deserve punishment, but this is only the first half of the story. The second half is that justification can confer dignity—at a price, yes, but all the same it can. "Continental conservatives", i.e., Restoration theologians will exclude justification and redemption, even the perspective of them, from the social realm. The function of the social is humility, blind and willing submission to authority. The subject of religiosity is the child, the non-citizen (however grown up socially), religion is equated with *Unmündigkeit*. This is, alas, irreconcilable with Pauline dogma, irreconcilable with Tradition. "Continental conservatism" is deeply subversive and rebellious when it hesitates to identify the nature of authority out of fear of irreverent criticism. The failure to identify the source and nature of authority makes conservatism unthinkable, for without it establishing a hierarchy is wholly impossible. Thus "Continental conservatism" is not only self-defeating, it will always degenerate into a masochistic worship of the whip, the result of infantile obedience pushed beyond morals.

No accusation of British inconsistency can be levelled against Carl Schmitt, the only true heir of Restoration political philosophy. Let me consider briefly two of his fundamental ideas developed in his *The Concept of the Political*[8] and *Political Theology*.[9] The first is that of the primacy of the political (which is of course shown by Leo Strauss to be a perverse, but nevertheless evidently moral-critical idea[10]) based on the famous friend/foe dichotomy; the second is his teaching on sovereignty as the decision of exception. Carl Schmitt thinks that there is one way of excluding the state of nature setting in a liberal society (though presumably for him variety and competition, these mainstays of liberal society, are exactly the prerequisites for such a disaster to happen)—and this is to declare a Hobbesian natural state obtaining between States. Subjects subsumed under the authority of one State are friends of one another and enemies of the subjects of another State (exclusion of civil war). Apart from a curious variant of the idea of the internal neutrality of the State and a criterion for the sovereignty of the nation-state as opposed to the imperial idea, Schmitt's theory serves a more important purpose, namely, that it undermines the classical doctrine of civic patriotism.

If the goal of human life is the attainment of moral wisdom as the Grand tradition believes, then in borderline cases the wise man will side with the good policy and the just cause, regardless of his origins, because loyalty binds him to the Law, not to a territory, to a tribe or suchlike. Since wisdom is divine, it is superior. This thought is necessary to make the moral criticism of a régime possible, and this is exactly what Schmitt is desirous of preventing. This is a very significant instance of the Restoration philosophy of obedience being sharply anti-traditional. Schmitt's second idea is slightly more intricate. Deciding on exceptions seems a very seductive criterion of sovereignty since it shows the sovereign deciding the boundaries of law which is of course in harmony with the doctrine of the primacy of the political (a primacy, that is, before the State self-evidently defined and regulated by law). Contradicting liberal constitutionalism, Schmitt believes that only that ruler can be considered sovereign, who can suspend or supplement the law of the land at will. Schmitt is harking back here to the idea of personal power. If the ruler is able to decide what constitutes a state of necessity or emergency, then no legal arrangement or abstract entity can be called truly sovereign. Since there is no independent or external criterion determining what a necessity or an emergency may be, again, there is no possiblity of passing any moral or political judgment over the (exceptional) decision of the sovereign ruler, therefore the traditional question as to whether the state is good or bad becomes naturally immaterial.

The reestablishment of unconditional authority makes the ascertaining of the rectitude (or "legitimacy") of that authority unworkable: the authority is there because it is there—but in my opinion this is confusing authority with mere power, a more than common mistake in contemporary political thought. Still, at the heart of this doctrine there is this truly conservative idea, the willing suspension of rational criticism regarding authority. Or is it? British conservatism silently presupposes (since it is based on an institutional tradition), that authority is subordinated to law and that exceptions are made into law by legal authority. This is obviously less clear-cut than Schmitt's doctrine, but then British conservatism is inconsistent and proud of it.

Leo Strauss's bold and simple solution is quite different from all this: he does not think that ancient wisdom is venerable because of the antiquity of that tradition. He does not think at all that it is venerable: he thinks that it is simply right and that the moderns are mistaken. However this is not conservatism, but classicism. In a recent interesting study, Dr. Aaron Rhodes[11] criticizes Strauss from a quite unexpected angle. Dr. Rhodes appears to believe that Strauss's famous critique of Max Weber is guilty of subjectivism. The reader will remember that Strauss has attacked Weber for his "value-free" treatment of, inter alia, charisma and of the "routinization of charisma". Strauss said that the use of such a religious notion for explaining political authority without stating what religion is, is a scandal, mainly because this might mean the conferral of sacral qualities to possibly evil deeds. In other words, Strauss thought that Weber's detached *a*-moralism was immoral. But since Strauss did not develop a political-theological dogma himself, Dr. Rhodes thinks that he is committing the same fallacy as Weber with the added disadvantage of denying himself the austere delights of observatorial detachment.

This is a remarkable conservative critique of classicism, for if a conservative does not believe that Tradition could supply the apparently missing criterion for deciding between true and counterfeit charisma, who will? Leo Strauss's silence about his positive beliefs can be explained by his historical opinion on the state of modern learning. If I was right in emphasizing that Enlightenment, modern philosophy, free speech, etc., had become possible as a result of a redefinition of the institutional limits of the interpretation of Tradition, then it should become clear that a true believer in the truth of Tradition such as Leo Strauss must have found himself in an extremely odd spiritual and institutional quandary. Since the old division of literate people into scholars and gentlemen had long become obsolete, a traditionalist cannot possibly define his own place in a university. A layman in a chair bequeathed to him by distant ecclesiastical ancestors cannot really tell who he is and whether he has still the right to impart esoteric knowledge (non-public arguments) or not. Should the modern liberal state's nominal ideological neutrality be extended to the university and to the academy? I tend to believe that both Max Weber's detachment and Leo Strauss's strange silence have the same source, which I might call *illimitation*.

Illimitation means a lack of precisely delineated institutional guardianship of Tradition (or if you wish, high culture), which of course would mean censorship and imposition of orthodoxy. Nobody can propose this in good faith in an organization founded intellectually on the assumption of free expression. The old presumption of the concomitantly true and edifying character of learning had to be abandoned. Anybody nowadays speaking to the public ought to refrain from resisting free expression since their ability to speak to the public is founded on the selfsame free expression. Whatever the truth of the matter, it would be dishonest of any public speaker (including philosophers) to do so. So conservative (and classicist) arguments have to be perverse, futile and perilous or otherwise put: negative and critical. Thus conservatives will resemble more and more their adversaries, the men of Enlightenment. Illimitation makes the scholar into a critic and little more. Unlike the silence of Leo Strauss, the positive theories of Restoration philosophies cannot be traditional. They naturally can be, as it were, "pro-tradition", but the authority that might have made their arguments edifying has been undermined by illimitation.

I hope I have shown that strictly conservative philosophies in the end tend to be anti-traditional. Is then conservative philosophy possible? I think not. Conservatism and philosophy are best kept apart. I think someone can be a conservative and a philosopher at the same time, but this will not make him into a conservative philosopher.

This is arguably the case of Michael Oakeshott, who was a man of conservative disposition and a liberal philosopher. (His idea of the "conversation of mankind" was *avant la lettre* contemptuously rejected by Carl Schmitt in his *Political Romanticism*[12] as liberal nonsense.)

The case of Restoration philosophy shows that "constructive" re-creation of tradition within a system of deliberate irrationality will blend nicely the disadvantages of extreme relativism with those of an extreme dogmatism. To a certain extent this seems to be the case in the most heroic attempt at a Continental conservative philosophy: that of Ludwig Wittgenstein. On the one hand, following rules is just following rules. There are no "better" rules; the prevalent ones will presumably be "naturally" selected by trial and error or suchlike. On the other hand, examining rules of behavior (i.e., moral reflection) is sinful rebellion against a vacuous, ineffable *Deus absconditus*. One of the lessons of Wittgenstein's superb failure is surely that, since philosophy has irrevocably become an independent inquiry, it is not well equipped to defend tradition as such, partly because it has its own traditions (therefore it is conditioned to defend one particular shaft of them, not any old cultural material encountered no matter where) and partly because reverence and deference are silent endeavours, and philosophy is talk. One cannot, now, be silent and be Socrates.

The prevalent political doctrines in Eastern Europe are of the Restoration kind, and it would be a grave error to mistake them for conservatism. The dominant mythologies of "lost" and "interrupted" Tradition allow authoritarian political forces to construct ideologies of power exempt from moral criticism and to use warlike solidarity (not ours the gentle commercial society beloved of Burke and Benjamin Constant) to prevent diversity, variety, pluralism—to use all the weapons of modernity to prevent modernity from happening. At the same time,

East European societies have their own tradition of modernity: state socialism and the modernizing reforms that went on under its aegis, reforms that are profoundly compromised. The great historical paradox of our region is that the liberal and modernist critique exercised by dissidents, reformers and "deviationists" over socialist dictatorship is used to disrupt both our particular subset of modern traditions and the continuity of the Grand Tradition in the spirit of a *passéiste* fervour, resulting in "constructivist" dictatorship based on spurious nationalist myth. The ideologies of artificially re-created (that is, imagined) solidary communities that never existed within that other artefact, the modern authoritarian state, with its militancy, boorish intolerance and moral indifference, seem only to add to the number of ruins we are anyway liberally provided with. Our new political régimes manage to look both pathetically obsolete with their Ruritanian trappings and wretchedly lacking in historic nobility and dignity. Continental conservatism was relatively successful only when linked to the imperial idea (as in the case of the *ci-devant* Austro-Hungarian Monarchy), but it does not appear to be suited to the needs of ethnic nation-states.

Professor Gellner once observed that Third World intellectuals and politicians speak Marxism as they speak prose. East European politicians are the Messieurs Jourdains of nationalism. Both kinds depend on their definition of the alien. Both have found that definition in what they think fit to believe is Western (elements of this "critique" supplied courtesy of the Western academic New Left: greed, lack of compassion, dissolution of organic communities, the familiar combination of Bob Dylan and Rousseau). The critique of the West parroted by the East European nationalist "Right" is *marxisante* in the extreme: it is based on suspicion. Law equals group interest, state equals domination by an elusive minority, economy equals oppression, political controversy equals foreign conspiracy and so on. There never was such a faithless revolution. The *bien-pensant* liberal commonplaces recited for the benefit of credulous (and therefore despised) foreign audiences can hardly mask the political reality of a body politic that does not believe in anything other than naked power and material advantage while hating this moral misery. The most courageous utopia of this unhappy part of the world is a bit of common decency; but even the chances for this seem hopelessly remote.

It is a well-worn cliché of the history of ideas that Robespierre and Joseph de Maistre had many things in common. This we know only too well. Our culture is neither conservative, nor reflective or philosophical. For the former it lacks reverence and for the latter it lacks moral faith. It is a surreal intellectual desert where anything can happen to instruct, elevate and amuse adventurous travellers in search of the weird.[13]

G. M. Tamás

Institute of Philosophy
Hungarian Academy of Sciences
Budapest

AN IDEOLOGICAL MIGHT-HAVE-BEEN

The study of ideologies is liable to concentrate on success stories: belief systems which have made a powerful impact. But negative examples perhaps also deserve investigation. There may be clusters of ideas which have all the merits required for success, but which have, perhaps because they saw the light of day too soon or too late, or in the wrong place or context, failed to make the impact which was their due on merit.

I believe that the work of Yuri Semenov belongs to this category. It is relatively unknown outside the Soviet Union, and has had but a limited impact inside it. The historical circumstances were not propitious to it. Yet there is a good deal to be learnt from it.

Yuri Semenov is a Marxist philosopher and social anthropologist (or what would, in Western terminology, be described in these terms). He has combined teaching Marxism-Leninism in a technological institute, with being a member of what had been the Institute of Ethnography of the Academy of Sciences of the USSR, and of what is now the Institute of Ethnology and Anthropology. Within this Institute, he was a member of a section known as the section of Primitive Society, other members of which are scholars such as I. Pershitz, V. Schnirelman and O. Artumova. Semenov may be described as a general theoretician of Marxism with a special interest in that part of Marxist theory which deals with early society and the early history of mankind. But he is also much involved with what in the West would be called comparative historical sociology or macro-sociology, with issues such as the typology of societies, historical periodicization, the acceptability or otherwise of the notion of an Asiatic Mode of Production and its place in the Marxist scheme. He is not, and as far as I know never has been, a field anthropologist; nor has he been specifically concerned with the internal organization of any one society. He is primarily a theorist. He is very much at home in the tradition of Marxist classics and its predecessors, but at the same time, is very familiar with Western social theory and in particular with social anthropological theory. For instance, he has written a summary of the debate, in Western economic anthropology, between "formalists" and "substantivists", between those who would uphold the usefulness of formal economic theory in studying the economy of simpler peoples, and those who, by contrast, prefer to focus on the actual institutions found in such societies, without interpreting individual economic behaviour in terms of a supposedly universal economic theory. His account of this debate is a model of lucidity and objectivity, and its translation has appeared in English.[1]

Something should perhaps be said of the history of the Institute of Ethnography (as it was) and its role. It has had, successively, three directors: Tolstov, Bromley, and Tishkov. These correspond more or less neatly to three stages of Soviet history, to Stalinism, Stagnation, and Perestroika. The fate of Perestroika is undecided at the time when these lines are being written, and I shall refrain from speculating about it here. Tolstov was a hard-line Stalinist and his reign ended in the late '60s, after the fall of Khrushchev, and he is not relevant to our theme. Bromley expressed the relative tolerance of the period of *Zastoi*.

There are two features of Yulian Bromley's reign at the Institute which deserve note. One is the *relative* liberalism of the atmosphere at the Institute during the period, which was the object of envy amongst members of neighbouring institutes (neighbouring both in terms of subject matter and of physical location—I have in mind, for instance, the two institutes of history). I do not mean that the place was liberal by Western standards and that discussions occurred in public in which Marxism was questioned. What I do mean is that a high proportion of people who by the Soviet standards of the day had multiple black marks against them (Jewish background, a period of incarceration in the camps, a habit of "taking their mouth for a walk", questionable orthodoxy, a tendency to be willing to have contacts outside the socialist world) did find employment at the Institute, sometimes after failing to obtain it elsewhere or losing it. Internal debates, sometimes bitter, about fundamentals of social anthropological theory, with possible implications for Marxism, were not unknown. A member of the Institute who applied to emigrate and became a refusenik was treated with great leniency by the Soviet standards of pre-Perestroika days, being kept on at his previous rank for quite a time, and, when dismissed, reappointed, albeit at a lower rank. No attempt was made to harass other members of his family. Members of the Institute active in spheres not then much approved (revival of the Jewish communal institutions in Moscow, or teaching Hebrew), though not receiving the promotions which were their due on merit, were nevertheless kept on. More orthodox members of the Institute certainly felt that Bromley was taking a risk by adopting such a tolerant attitude (an attitude which might be considered normal in liberal societies, but which was unusual and possibly risky in the moral and political climate prevalent in Moscow at the time). A cynical or hostile observer might well say that a double game was being played, one securing for the man in question the approval of the outside world for his relative liberalism and tolerance, and yet also securing him Brownie points from the local establishment for restraining a bunch of potential dissidents. The contract which seemed to operate between the Director, and the dubious characters (by the standards then prevailing) seemed to run roughly as follows: "*you lot* don't rock the boat too visibly and produce a lot in the scholarly line, and perhaps help me a bit with writing my books, and *I* will do my best to ensure that you can get on with your work, without undue harassment. Who knows, some of you might even, in the fullness of time, travel a little, though this perk, in the nature of things, is severely rationed."

The second feature of the Bromley period was that Bromley gave the Institute a new direction, namely that of the study of *ethnicity*, i.e., the study of ethnic culture and ethnic relations, and hence, by implication, that he made a bid for "ethnography" to become the science specializing in the problem of nationalities.[2] This was an interesting move from a number of viewpoints. Social anthropology in the Soviet Union (under whatever name it happens to be practiced) is facing the same problem which it faces the world over, namely, that with the rapid diffusion of modernity, primitive communities are rapidly disappearing, so that the discipline is quickly losing its distinctive subject matter. Distinctive ethnic cultures, on the other hand, are not disappearing, and by making *ethno*graphy the study of ethnic culture—Bromley was rather given to using this verbal argument—the subject was assured of a sphere of activity. By turning the discipline into the study of ethnic culture, the field of structure was by implication left to other disciplines, and the likelihood of conflict with Marxist theory diminished. Above all, the orientation of the Institute in this direction made it possible to claim that it was dealing with something supremely important, namely the problem of nationalities and ethnic diversity, and even conflict, in the Soviet Union. When the problem exploded with the liberalization under Gorbachev, it was of course possible to say both that the Institute had focussed on the problem long before its importance had again become manifest, and equally, that it had been unduly complacent about it. At the time, of course, it would have been impossible to publish findings to the effect that conflict and disharmony were rife.

It would be difficult to defend the publications of the Institute on this topic against the charge of complacency, if this means the failure to spell out the explosive nature and force of irredentist nationalism, and of national conflicts, in the Soviet Union—but one can only add that the publication of such conclusions, at the time, simply is not imaginable. Granting this weakness, which given the political realities of the time could not have been remedied, the work of Bromley and his Institute must be credited with certain merits. It asked what seem to me the right questions about modern nationalism, namely, what are the relative life-chances of members of various ethnic categories, and what is the relationship between ethnicity, educational opportunity, and career prospects. In other words, ethnic sentiment is not an atavism emanating from members of primordial *Gemeinschaften*, but, rather, a sentiment of urbanized, educated, mobile members of an industrial society. Secondly, Bromley was clear about the *social* nature of the modern ethnic group, as opposed to any kind of biological definition of it, and his debate with the romantic erstwhile dissident Gumilev (geographer, and son of the poetess Akhmatova) concerned this point.

However, notwithstanding the fact that his public stance was primarily that of a theoretician of ethnicity, Bromley was not really, for better or for worse, by temperament or calling a theoretician. Though he considered himself a Marxist (sincerely so, I think) I do not think he deeply internalized the elaborate structure of Marxist thought, or found it of absorbing interest. He was not a man of either theoretical or dogmatic temper, and in conversation was liable (as a heretic in the Institute privately observed with amusement) to make quite het erodox statements, not because he wished to defy orthodoxy, but simply because he had not noticed that he was doing so. Now the age of stagnation was not an age of faith (on the contrary, it was the age of the erosion of faith), but it was certainly not the age of open dissent either. The Marxist decencies were observed. But in order to observe them, you need to know what they are. As in Václav Havel's excellent play about the role of unintelligible Marxist jargon in running a socialist enterprise, you need to have someone about who really understands how the language works, all its nuances and flexibilities as well as its rigidities—someone who is, by temperament and by intellectual equipment, a theoretician. Yuri Semenov was such a man. To describe him as an ideological watchdog of the Institute sounds unpleasant, and it is most certainly not my intention to do so. Rather, it is my intention to describe him as a man with a deep and thorough understanding of Marxism, who had sincerely embraced it, who had a fine sense of its problems and potentialities, and knew how to play with the intricate conceptual system it contained.

At an international conference at which they appeared together, Bromley and Semenov gave the impression of being a team. Theory and praxis were not united in a single person, as perhaps might be ideal according to Marxism, but they were present in this two-man team, one of whom embodied great political skill and energy, and the other supplied theoretical refinement and depth.

So this perhaps was Semenov's effective role: at a time when ideological zeal and conviction were in marked decline, when the concrete work of the Institute was oriented towards a field in which Marxism was hardly relevant (or an obstacle), but when open dissent was not yet tolerated, to help supply that element of theory which was still de rigeur. He may not have been the only one to help perform this task, but he did it well, with ingenuity, depth, scholarship and (I am persuaded) with sincerity. Had history gone in a different direction, had the climate been different, his theoretical output might have received great acclamation. Were this a just world, which it is not, we might yet have heard of Marxism-Leninism-Semenovism: the adjustments and interpretations which Semenov brought to Marxism would have been so appropriate, and at the same time so inherently plausible, if only the world had gone in a direction in which it still seemed to be going, shall we say, in Khrushchev's day, and in which it perhaps still might have seemed, without absurdity, to be going for quite a few years after that.

There are two problems within Marxism to which Semenov seems to me to have made interesting, ingenious and suggestive contributions. One is the problem of origins: how did the human race, and human society, begin, and how do these beginnings fit into the overall Marxist scheme? The other is the problem of the basic typology of human societies and of the periodicization of history. Let us call these the problems of Genesis and of Entelechy.

GENESIS[3]

Marxism crystallized in the mind of its founder in the 1840s. At least one commentator, Richard Tucker, believes himself capable of locating almost the moment at which Marx invented Marxism, in a fit of Hegelizing, when he suddenly saw that the philosophy of Hegel contained, in coded form, the economic history of mankind.[4] This early formulation of Marxism, however, suffered from at least two handicaps: it preceded the publication of Darwin's ideas, and it also preceded, by a greater span, the publication of H. L. Morgan. In other words, there was as yet neither evolutionary biology nor the beginnings of modern anthropology. These elements went into the later formulations of Marxism, but obviously, they could not enter the earliest crystallization of the system, prior to their own existence. This being so, what exactly did the Founding Fathers of Marxism think about the very beginning of human and social things? The main answer, as far as I can see, is that they did not think about it much, or perhaps at all. They were not merely Eurocentric, they were also history-oriented. They were not much given to looking at man against the backcloth of biology. History was enough.

Still, the question does have to be faced. There must have been a beginning, and an overall theory of the development of human society cannot avert its gaze from the question of how it all began. But Marxism has a special need to face this problem. In the way it finally crystallized, it attributes "primitive communism" to human beginnings, and attribution is of great importance. It helps provide crucial evidence that communism is feasible, and also helps answer the question—why is it desirable? Marx operated with the concept of *Gattungs-Wesen*, somewhat awkwardly translated as "species-being", or perhaps as "species-essence". Why is communism desirable, why is man alienated from his true essence when he lives in non-communist, class-endowed social formations? One answer, once fashionable amongst some at least of the adherents of Marxism and also proposed by its most eloquent critic, Karl Popper, ran as follows—Marxism eschews moralizing, it merely preaches, in the wake of Hegel, the recognition of necessity.[5] It predicts what *must be*, and because it must be and will come, it has the only kind of goodness which scientific thinking permits, and Marxism is nothing if not scientific—or so at one time its adherents liked to think. The trouble with this simultaneously scientistic and Hegelian interpretation is that it most certainly did not correspond to the real state of mind of ardently believing Marxists in the days when the faith still was ardent (which perhaps would not matter too much, could not a measure of false emotional consciousness be enlisted on the side of history?), but it also does not seem to correspond to the actual convictions of Marx, at any rate during his youth. He does seem to have believed that man did have an essence, and that this was in conflict with class society in general and with capitalism in particular, and that the true essence would come into its own again under communism, and that this validated communism.

Now this is all very well, but it raises some problems. It may be all very well for the young Karl Marx: for him, as Heinz Lubasz has insisted, Aristotle was not a classical text, but a living scientific authority, and one has to take Aristotle as seriously as Hegel if one is to understand how Marx's mind worked.[6] In other words, there were species, and they had essences. But this is not a view easily acceptable to the modern mind. For one thing, many of us are nominalists, and do not believe in essences. (Some, like Quine, may not be too sure of their nominalism, but are quite sure they do not believe in essences, and see the repudiated ghost of Aristotle behind the very notion of meaning.) But, quite irrespective of any general nominalism, there is the problem of Darwin, whose doctrine establishes, if it establishes anything, that there are no stable, given species. So, even if there were things in the world which did have essences, species, being unstable, cannot have them. So where is *Gattungs-Wesen* now?

So if mankind is to start its career with a generic essence from which it can then be painfully alienated, it must first of all be endowed with an essence, and with the essence which this theory requires. That is the problem, and, in a volume produced under the auspices of the Institute of Ethnography, with the Director as one of its three authors and Semenov as another, the problem is answered. The volume was clearly intended to supply Marxism with its missing Book of Genesis, missing in part because Darwin had published so late. The part of this volume which answers this question—how did mankind acquire its essence, and what was its essence—is Semenov's work, as the volume itself specifies.

Theoretically, it would be possible to credit communism not merely to early man, but also to his prehuman ancestors, and to legitimate communism not as something specifically human, but as something belonging to life as such.

The idea is not inherently absurd. The one great philosophy primarily inspired by Darwinism, namely Pragmatism, does precisely this. It claims that the correct procedure in the acquisition of knowledge is not something distinctively human, but something practiced by all life: trial and error, elimination of mistaken theories or interpretations by life itself. Amongst contemporary philosophers, the two who are widely held to be the best—Popper and Quine—believe versions of this theory.[7] Popper has acclaimed similarity of the method deployed by the amoeba and by Einstein.[8] The only difference between life in general on the one hand, and humanity on the other (or perhaps, more narrowly, literate or scientific humanity) is that the process of elimination of error in the first case has to use the brutal procedure of eliminating the carrier of the error, whereas amongst us, the error can be eliminated, whilst its carrier can live on to err another day. But that is a mere detail, though perhaps one of some importance to the carrier in question. The basic point is, that the recipe for cognitive salvation, according to these theorists, remains the same throughout the history of life.

So this continuity of salvation-procedure *might* be a way out of the problem. But it really is rather more difficult to apply this doctrine in the sphere of morality and social organization, than it is in the sphere of the theory of knowledge. For one thing, it simply does not appear to fit empirically. Some animals are gregarious and some are not. Communalism is not endorsed, as you might say, by the consensus of all life (whereas the cognitive method of trial-and-error perhaps is, or at any rate, it is not wholly absurd to claim that it is). Some species which seem to exemplify that communalism most perfectly—notably the social insects—seem exceedingly unattractive as moral-social models for emulation. Invoking them would hardly strengthen the appeal of communism. So, whatever the pragmatists may have done in epistemology, in socio-political theory at least, this option would seem to be out.

Semenov adopts the other strategy. Something special happened on the way to becoming human, in the course of anthropogenesis, which differentiates man proper from his proto-human ancestors. What was it? It is natural for Marxism to look at man as the tool-using animal: it is the deployment of tools which really differentiates him. It is *work* above all which lies at the heart of humanity, productive and intelligent work. But tools need to be invented, used, maintained. And here we come to the heart of Semenov's theory of why early man *had* to be communistic, why he could not progress along the path of tool-using production unless he became such.

Proto-human gangs or bands were both cohesive and haunted by domination and violence. The strong dominated the weak. These bands had to be cohesive if they were to survive in a rude environment, and above all if they were to survive inter-band competition and conflict, but the only method of ensuring internal cohesion open to them was domination. Cohesion was present, but it was *enforced* cohesion. But this kind of social order, rule by thugs, was not propitious to technological innovation and advance, to the invention and deployment and development of tools. The innovating intellectuals, as we know from our own society, are not always or generally also physically strong and aggressive. Perhaps they become thoughtful because they are gentle, or they become gentle because they are thoughtful. Whichever way it is, the thugs will take the fruits of their innovation from them, and thus the rule of thugs is not propitious for the advancement of early technology. What to do?

Answer: an egalitarian, sharing, communistic ethos emerges. This doesn't ensure that the innovators get a special reward for their innovation (such a theory might suit a laissez-faire enthusiast seeking vindication in the history of early man, but it wouldn't suit Marxism), but at least it ensures that those paleolithic or whatever innovators benefit in some measure, alongside the other members of the band. Without a communistic ethos, no advance into toolmaking and humanity proper!

The problem is on the way to being solved, but is not yet solved properly. We see why communism was *needed*; we do not yet see how it came about. Do needs engender their own satisfaction? To say that they do is brazenly teleological thinking, incompatible with true science. Things do not happen in this sad world because they are required, because their occurrence would be of benefit to someone, even to mankind at large. Believers in a benevolent deity who had a beneficent Design for his creation might argue in this way, but such teleology has been exiled from science.

However, it has come back thanks to that widely used deity-surrogate, namely Natural Selection. And indeed, Semenov uses this. (Note that if this is the correct interpretation of Marxism, its full formulation was not possible till after Darwin.) Semenov invokes natural selection, operating not on individuals but on bands, in such a way as to favour those which happen to develop a communistic ethos, one which insists on sharing, so that technological innovators benefit at least as much as their fellow band members. Bands which, on the other hand, persist in using violence-based domination as the main agency of cohesion, thereby lose in the technological race and are, in the end, eliminated thanks to their economic inferiority. Elimination of bands does not necessarily mean the elimination of their members; a band may disintegrate and its members, or some of them, may find a place in a better endowed, more survival-worthy gang. It is important to note that the elimination operates on social communities and their spirit, not on individuals.

So we have seen Semenov find the theory which explains why mankind had to acquire a communistic ethos which then becomes part of its species-essence, *and* avoid the trap of teleological reasoning by means of invoking a version of natural selection. However, he is not yet out of the wood. Natural selection has been used to avoid the danger of teleology, but it is itself not acceptable as a basic principle of sociology, as the mechanism which determines and governs the fate of human societies. If *that* is all there is to it, if that is the main thing which rules history, what has happened to Marxism, to the doctrine that the internal conflict of classes is the main motor power of history? If natural selection propels or selects societies, are we not close to some form of biologism or even fascism?

This danger in turn is avoided. Natural selection did indeed play a crucial part in the first stage of human history proper, in the endowment of mankind with its communistic ethos, but thereafter it is no longer essential, perhaps hardly present at all. How so? The communistic *ethos* works internally, through internal compulsion, through *will* and *consciousness*. A new mechanism has been introduced into the world, indispensable—a tool-using species evidently cannot manage without it, for it needs to be communistic and social, and there is no way of achieving this other than through an internal constraint. This defines society, and once it is present, a new and properly social mechanism operates, different from merely external selection by nature.

This line of thought is fascinating and dramatic. Semenov encounters danger after danger—first teleology, then biologism—and avoids each only by falling into the next, which seems worse than the fate it is intended to avoid. Certainly, this last solution—intended to avoid biologism—may succeed in its aim: but is not the price worse than that which it is meant to avert? We are now clearly in the presence of a marked form of *idealism*: humanity is defined in terms of the presence within it of consciousness and will, which endows it with its truly human character and determines its subsequent development! Semenov's language here clearly evokes Rousseau and his General Will, and Durkheim and his collective representations. It is presumably in order for a Marxist to echo Rousseau (who had after all exercised an influence on the Founder), but Durkheim is a different matter. (Semenov quotes neither by name, but there can be no shadow of doubt about the resonance of their ideas in his argument and his prose.)

But fear not: the danger of idealism is, in turn, avoided, once again. The invocation of will and consciousness would indeed condemn the position to idealism, were they the prime movers, or the ultimate, irreducible explanation. But, most emphatically, they are nothing of the kind. They do not initiate anything, nor do they terminate the chain of explanation. They are *at the service of* an economic imperative: the need to engender, enhance, develop, protect the invention and deployment and maintenance of tools! Consciousness and will, inner conceptual and moral constraint, in the style of Kant and Durkheim, are indeed brought in to explain how morality and humanity are possible—but only as servants, as instruments, of an economic need. The decency of historical materialism is respected and observed.

But is that not a teleological argument? Is not a need invoked to explain the emergence of the thing which satisfies that need? Is that a permissible line of reasoning? We have of course been at this point before: teleology is avoided, by the time-honoured, traditional method of using natural selection; and then, biologism, by invoking inner compulsion; and then ... and so on.

The circle is neat, complete, and tight; but not, as far as I can see, vicious. This does not mean that the position is necessarily valid; but it is not inconsistent or incoherent. However, its elegance and coherence are not its only virtues. The position is presented with considerable eloquence and literary verve, and it is most moving, it seems to me, when it describes the inner condition of the early man caught up in this process. The new communistic inner compulsion is operative within him, but its nature and purpose is not yet fully clear and it may cause bewilderment; moreover, it is not yet fully effective perhaps, and must needs on occasion be supplemented by the earlier instrument of social cohesion, namely *external* compulsion, mediated or sanctioned by menaces, fear, perhaps even terror. Given that the newly humanized hominid band is still surrounded by nasty enemies, whose cohesion has not been weakened by the transition to humanity so that the old mechanisms are still working to the full, humanity-in-a-single-band may need to be reinforced, in extremity, by the use of the old methods, which in any case may have a tendency to survive, as old habits do. ... In the fullness of time, the new inner compulsion and its economic fruits will be sufficient both to ensure the cohesion of the newly human band, and to protect it from external enemies who have not made the transition; but that happy time is not yet, and one must wait, and in the meantime, the newly-humans may be haunted both by prehuman survivals (violence, domination) and by the unintelligibility and merely partial effectiveness of the new, inner sanctions.

Such is Semenov's account of the inner condition of very early man, pained by the survival of oppression and inequality in his own band, puzzled by the incomprehensibility of the new ethos and its dubious hold over himself and his fellow members. What a striking parallel with the mental state of at least some Soviet citizens (prior to Perestroika of course), pained by the survival of oppression and intimidation, puzzled by the ineffectiveness of the new socialist morality, disappointed by its material fruits, at any rate so far. ... Of course, as long as humanity is present only in one band, as long as socialism is present in only one country, or merely a set of them, as long as the fruits of a technology-friendly ethos have not yet fully arrived, it is all bound to be a bit painful. Patience is required. In brief: Semenov has not merely provided an elegant and ingenious solution to a problem which his fellow-Marxists have preferred conveniently to ignore; the solution he offers is full of powerful resonance for the Soviet citizen, pondering his condition.

ENTELECHY[9]

The problem of the roots, nature, and authority of the acquisition by early humanity of our shared species-essence, is not the only one for which Semenov provides a solution which is virtually a model of ideology-construction. There is another problem which has long haunted Marxist theory, namely that of the application or applicability of the canonical five or more stages of human history to the actual empirical material of history. Have all societies really passed through primitive communism, slave society, the Asiatic mode of production (the inclusion of this item is of course itself a major bone of contention), feudalism, capitalism, socialism ...

Semenov has in fact contributed significantly to the debate concerning the existence and historic location of the Asiatic Mode of Production. This problem has evidently troubled him over a long period and his persistent attempts at furthering its solution testify to an intellectual quest without dogmatism, just as his account of the history of the central debate in Western economic anthropology bears witness to his erudition and his capacity to sum up, with great fairness and accuracy, positions which are not his own and with which he disagrees fundamentally. But it is not his contribution to the specific problem of the Asiatic Mode of Production, but rather his handling of the more general problem of the status of social formations and their place in world history, which is of interest here.

Do the canonical stages of Marxist theory, with or without the problematic Asiatic Mode of Production, actually apply to concrete societies? During the first and very partial Thaw in the '60s, an influential and symptomatic book[10] appeared which reviewed the question, and the crucial essay in it observed that the *exceptions* to the law of stages, if that is what it is, appear to be more numerous than the cases of conformity with it. It is in fact exceedingly difficult, or impossible, to locate a society which is known actually to have passed through all the stages of social development which Marxism credits to the inner logic of social development, to the dictate imposed by the growth of the forces of production on the social organization and class structure within which they operate. So?

There is an interesting answer to this problem, and Semenov offers it. Basically, it runs as follows. The law of stages, the applicability of the various stages and the sequence in which they are meant to appear, applies and is meant to apply not to individual societies, but only to *world history as a whole*. Too many expositors (virtually all of them, Semenov seems to imply) have uncritically assumed the wrong interpretation, which would turn the Marxist thesis into something like this—for any society, the development of that society will proceed from primitive communism via Asiatic society and slave society and feudalism to capitalism and then to socialism and communism. The correct interpretation—which of course raises its own problems with which Semenov then deals—runs, by contrast, as follows: these stages apply to mankind as a totality, to the global history of humanity, but not to the individual societies which compose it. What the thesis, when correctly interpreted in this matter, implies for individual societies, remains to be seen.

This interpretation has some considerations in its favor, and some less so. On the positive side, it is obviously the case that the theory had indeed been inspired, not by the contemplation of the fates of individual societies, but by reflections on world history. It emerged at a time when Europeans still tried to confuse their own history with world history as such. As against it, there are various thoughts: if this is the correct view, why has it so frequently been ignored or contradicted within the Marxist tradition itself? Why was the Marxist community so frequently in error, without being corrected by its own intellectual leaders, who should have known better? If Marxism claims to be "scientific", as it does, ought not the same scientific laws to apply in all similar cases, and in any case, how can a *single* unrepeated sequence also be a law? In the case of an unique sequence, how can we distinguish between a necessary connection, exemplifying a lawlike necessity, and a mere contingent succession?

When I first heard this suggestion of Semenov's, I held it to be ingenious, interesting, and endowed with a certain inherent plausibility, but contrary to the real spirit and intention of the founders of Marxism. Since then, I have become much less sure of this last point, and it may well be that Semenov exaggerates the originality of his own interpretation, and that in fact it is more pervasively present in the Marxist tradition than one might suppose. For instance, it appears that a similar view had been put forward by the influential Soviet theoretician Bogdanov. Even more important, it is plausible to attribute such a view to Marx himself, at any rate in his youth. Roman Szporluk's penetrating book on *Communism and Nationalism*[11] argues that precisely such a view underlies *The Communist Manifesto*, which on Szporluk's interpretation is a coded debate with Friedrich List (though the only explicit internal hint seems to be a pun, when the authors of the Manifesto refer to the "*listig*"—cunning—German bourgeoisie). Szporluk's account of Marx's basic argument is this: the German bourgeois can never, never catch up with the British or the French, and List's advice to the Germans on how to do it is absurd, pointless, and doomed to failure.[12] Germany has no hope of ever going through the transition from feudalism to capitalism, which would seem to be a kind of exclusive privilege, an *initium*, of the English and the French. All the Germans can hope to do—and it is really a privilege and an advantage, rather than a deprivation—is to join in a wider, world-historical transition, in which, it would seem, the Brits provide the economy, the French the politics, and the Germans, the most advanced philosophy (exemplified above all by Marx himself). In other words, Marx in his youth intended to bestow on the Germans, without even being solicited to this effect, that historic chance of stage-hopping which, very much later in life, he considered accorded to the Russians, on the insistent bidding of Vera Zasulich. It must of course here be said against the Semenov/Szporluk reading of Marx that the sheer fact that, in his correspondence with Zasulich, he spoke of the possibility of stage-passing as a rare opportunity offered by history to Russia, so that, at any rate later in his life, he himself subscribed to the conventional interpretation of his own position, as a law-like generalization applicable to all societies, rather than a strange law with but a single exemplification, namely human history seen as a whole.

But let us assume now that this interpretation is to be accepted—which of course has the advantage, from the viewpoint of defending Marxism, that individual societies are no longer expected to exemplify all stages, and so their failure to do so no longer constitutes a scandal—what are the problems it faces, and how does Semenov cope with them? If individual societies no longer directly exemplify the slave-owning, feudal, or any other stage of world history, how do they relate to these stages? Or, to put it the other way round, how are these stages, or the social formations which define them, incarnated in the concrete life of mankind?

The answer offered is the following: mankind finds itself in a given stage, or, if you prefer, the social formation defining a given stage is present, when the *leading* society, or cluster of societies, of that particular time, exemplifies the social formation in question. For instance, mankind finds itself in the slave-owning period when the leading society of the time, which happened to be that of the classical Mediterranean world, is based on a slave-owning economy. How does one identify the *leading* society? It is the one which will engender the next higher stage in the sequence. This definition introduces an inescapable teleological element into the scheme, but Semenov does not appear to mind this. Moreover, it also means that one can only identify stages with hindsight, when one already knows where the next and higher stage actually emerged. These objections would not seem to be fatal to the scheme. But what it all means is that historical periodicization, and attribution of a social formation to an age, is *not* done by some counting of societies, let alone of individuals, and deciding that humanity is in a given period when the majority of societies live under a given social system, or when more men live under it than under any other. No: the stage is determined by means of the dynamics and direction of the system. It is the social *leaders*, collectively speaking, who decide. The collectivism is important: Semenov, though very Hegelian in spirit, knows only world-historical nations, but not world-historical individuals. (At an international anthropological conference in the 1970's, the French Marxist Maurice Godelier described Semenov as an Hegelian, somewhat to the latter's embarrassment, given the presence of an entire Soviet delegation. At that time, a Soviet scholar did not care to be called a Hegelian in public. In fact, Semenov knows Hegel well and likes him, and his work is certainly not devoid of the Hegelian spirit—which is not to cast doubt on the sincerity and orthodoxy of his Marxism.)

The pattern of this historical leadership is interesting, in Semenov's scheme. There is a marked tendency, throughout human history, for blockages, dead-ends, impasses, or, to use the expressive Russian word he employs, *tupik*-s. So, for instance, ancient Asian society did not progress, and the breakthrough to the next stage, to slave-owning society, only occurred at the very margin of the old Middle East world, in the Balkan peninsula, where Dorian barbarians, iron-users endowed with an early form of class-structure, came together with a peripheral element of ancient society. The same happened the next time round: slave society did not seem capable of the breakthrough to feudalism, which only occurred at its periphery, in NW Europe, where a marginal part of slave society came into contact with a new wave of barbarians. Although Semenov does not spell it out in so many words, this passing of the torch of progress sideways, the interplay of the old periphery with new entrants, also occurred at the transition from capitalism to socialism, which occurred not, as those who anticipated it had supposed, at the very center of the capitalist world, most ripe for the explosion and the transformation, but, on the contrary, at its edge, in backward Russia. ... On Semenov's philosophy of history, which stresses this tendency of the sidestepping in progress, of the role of the *new* entrants, this ceases to be a difficulty and an embarrassment for Marxism, something which calls for special explanation, and becomes, on the contrary, just what one would expect.

There are of course some oddities or asymmetries in this system. The sideways-passing of the torch of progress does not occur in *all* transitions. It cannot occur right at the start, in the first transition, from primitive communism to ancient society (or whatever the first stage is after primitive communism), for the simple reason that at the time when *all* societies were in the condition of primitive communism, there were not and could be no leaders, so no one was holding the torch and so no one could hand it on. Moreover, that particular transition seems to have happened quite independently in a number of places all over the world, thereby, on Semenov's own account, confirming the scientific accuracy and depth of Marxism. (Perhaps: but in saying so, does he not implicitly revert to the "lawlike", multiple-application interpretation of Marxism, which in his main argument he repudiates?) The sideways-passing also cannot occur in the very last transition, for the opposite reason: although there is, most emphatically, a leader prior to the transition who is holding the torch high, there will no longer be anyone to whom it could be handed, for with the coming of the final stage of communism, there is only one global society left, and there can no longer be either leaders or led.

But by far the most important exception to the sidestep rule of historical advance is of course the transition from feudalism to capitalism. The torch was not handed over to anyone on that occasion. The West Europeans, the French and the English, had been prominent under feudalism, and they became quite specially prominent under capitalism. Societies and cultures remained fairly constant, and so did international leadership and preeminence. It was of course precisely this transition which was at the center of all European sociological preoccupation, including that of the Marxists. It was this particular transition which led to the attribution of primacy to internal, endogenous factors, and to the shift from concern with international rivalry and conflict, to a preoccupation with *classes*, i.e. intra-social categories. This particular transition could hardly have had any other form: it is hard to imagine barbarian conquerors settling in the keep of the feudal baron whom they had conquered, and promptly turning to commerce, finance and finally industry. It was this transition which had, above all else, inspired Marxism, and maybe it was indeed a mistake on the part of the founding fathers to try to assimilate all the other great transitions of history, whatever they be, to this model. Semenov does not really try to do the reverse, but basing his general theory on a supposed shared feature of the other transitions, has to leave this one discreetly aside, as somewhat untypical.

One might say this for the Semenovian interpretation of Marxism: unlike the interpretations prevalent earlier, it is no longer Eurocentric. It has the great merit of relating Marxism to the situation as it crystallized *after* the October Revolution, and above all to the world in which expectation of an imminent proletarian revolution in the developed capitalist world, was replaced by an international competition between rival social systems, and in which the home-land of the revolution had or claimed the leadership of the socialist bloc. Semenovian Marxism avoids Eurocentrism twice over: it pays at least as much attention to the great historic transitions other than that from feudalism to capitalism, which had so obsessed West European thought, and it is preoccupied with the problem of peripheral societies and with the relationship between societies which lead the way to a new social form, and those which follow. None of this was at the center of attention of those who originally formulated Marxism, but, by the second half of the 20th century, it was not something which could easily be ignored. The system incidentally endows ethnic plurality, cultural and political diversity, and backwardness, with a historic function: history still moves endogenously, but only if one thinks of all mankind—when one thinks of individual societies and ethnic collectivities, diversity acquires an essential function, it has a crucial role to play in making historical progress possible. Even backwardness becomes indispensable. In classical Marxism, all crucial developments were endogenous, but this was assumed to mean internal to individual societies. Cultural plurality, the diversity of nations, the existence of backward societies, were so to speak contingent, inessential accidents, which perhaps complicated history but made no difference to its essence.

Now, in the new scheme, all this is changed. Ethnic diversity has its role, the fact that the Revolution occurred in backward Russia is no longer a problem and an embarrassment, but a confirmation of a well-established historical trend, and the notion of a society being the leader and pioneer on the path to a new social formation acquires respectability and authority. This is a form of Marxist theory which can be linked to the international stance of the Soviet Union, as the leader, or putative leader, of the socialist camp, after 1945. Whereas it would have been difficult to seek much inspiration or guidance for the problems arising from this situation in the older formulations of the doctrine, this variant clearly contains suggestiveness, encouragement, the reinforcement of faith in the perception that what is happening is but one further instance of the mechanism which guides history, of the Cunning of Reason in action. ...

So, this version is ingenious, interesting, plausible, reasonably compatible with the founding Texts of the doctrine, and above all, richly suggestive and full of resonances for any thoughtful Soviet citizen, concerned with the condition of his country and willing to relate it to its official faith. All this being so, it would have deserved wider recognition and acclaim than in fact it received. *If* only the Soviet Union had continued successfully to lead one large segment of the international community towards a new social order which in due course secured the recognition of its own economic superiority ... and if the Soviet Union, in the period of stagnation, had been a society in which anyone took an interest in the elaboration of Marxist doctrine, then this particular contribution might have been, if not acclaimed, at least granted sustained attention. But the period of Stagnation was not an age of faith, much less so than the previous age of Terror had been. Those in power had little interest in the theory which was supposed to legitimate their position, and those eager to change the system, either because of its inefficiency or its inhumanity or both, no longer sought clues or guidance within the ideology. The time for the refinement of Marxism had gone.

In the history of beliefs as in the history of other activities, it is not only the victors who are of interest. Much as I admire R.G. Collingwood,[13] I have never been able to bring myself to accept, or even sympathize with, his view that we can only reconstruct the logic of the thought of those who succeed. In history as in a football Cup, the losers outnumber the victors, but their strategies and adjustments are not without interest. Semenov's interpretations of Marxism start out from the perception of problems which are indeed central and crucial for Marxist theory, and he solves those problems with ingenuity and in a manner which makes his answer pregnant with meaning for the *bien-pensant* Soviet citizen of pre-Perestroika days. The fact that this clientele was no longer receptive, and that history moved in a direction such that the faith was eventually beyond all saving, is another matter. This does not really distract from the interest of that ideological enterprise as a display of theoretical skill of a high order.

Ernest Gellner

Cambridge University

PHILOSOPHY AND IDEOLOGY: THE CASE OF POLAND

Introduction

In what follows I shall attempt to delineate the main contours of ideological development in post-war Poland, with particular reference to those leading up to the collapse of Communism. I shall then seek to extrapolate some of these into the future.

The role of individual philosophers in the political process in Poland has been not so much negligible as difficult to trace in detail. Certainly, there was the towering figure of Leszek Kołakowski, originally an orthodox Marxist philosopher (he received his philosophical education entirely in the Poland of the post-war period). Kołakowski received from the Party as his "combat tasks" (carried out vigorously in the early 'fifties) the denigration not only of the Thomist philosophy cultivated at the Catholic University of Lublin but also of Maritain's and Mounier's doctrine of personalism—a doctrine popular among Polish Catholic intellectuals because it promised a sort of compromise with Marxism. After the first Polish "thaw" (in October 1956) Kołakowski began to reflect critically not only on the historical roots of the Marxist doctrine and on the actual practices of the Marxist state, but also and perhaps most importantly on the situation of the philosopher therein (e.g., in his *A Priest and a Jester* of 1959, where he praises the "jester's" attitude of questioning every absolute and every dogma). And though he did indeed pose himself as a jester (or as a libertine *à la* Gassendi), he also took pains to vindicate anew certain elements of Christianity in what he took as the culture of the new enlightened and progressive (and no longer orthodox Marxist) intellectual elite (e.g., in his essay *Jesus Christ—A Prophet and a Reformer* of 1965, and in his study of the "non-confessional Christianity" of some Dutch Protestants of the 17th century). There were others, like Bronisław Baczko, Krzysztof Pomian, or Helena Eilstein, perhaps more "technical philosophers" than Kołakowski, who went a similar route from the (Leninist-)Marxist orthodoxy to "Revisionism". Thus they shared in the attempt to rethink the very foundations of Marxism in the light of its own assumptions and origins (especially the young-Marxian and Hegelian ones) as well as of other traditions, both old and new (Kołakowski is known for his interest not only in unorthodox Christianity, but also in positivism[1]), and who thus incorporated a personal union of philosophy and political activity.[2] There is also the utterly ambiguous figure of Adam Schaff, probably the best known exponent of Polish Marxism in Western Europe, who much longer than the "Revisionists" stayed faithful to the Party orthodoxy, and only in the early

Eighties managed to be expelled from the Party—but who had infuriated Party officials as early as 1965 with his book *Marxism and the Human Individual*, which suggested that even Marxist Socialism could not overcome the alienation of the individual. There were also quite numerous, even if dispersed, members of the so-called "Lvov-Warsaw school" active in Polish universities (some of whom had, however, been suspended from their university posts in the Stalinist period of 1949-1956).

The "Lvov-Warsaw school" was not actually a "school" in the sense of an established corpus of doctrines. Rather it was a living tradition (originated in 1895 in Lvov by a student of Franz Brentano, Kasimir Twardowski, at a time when South-Eastern Poland was under Austrian administration). It was a tradition of doing philosophy "from below", by means of careful, meticulous, logical and semantical analyses (but also by means of analyses of empirical data).[3] In contradistinction to the logical positivism of the Vienna Circle (to which it is sometimes compared), the Lvov-Warsaw school did not harbour any reductionist commitments, (nor any world-outlook or political commitments). It could therefore inspire a wide scope of philosophical enquiry, from logic (Stanisław Leśniewski, Jan Łukasiewicz, Alfred Tarski and Czesław Lejewski are here perhaps the best-known figures), through the foundations of praxiology (Tadeusz Kotarbiński's *The Treatise on Good Work*, 1955), to such elusive topics as the nature of beatitude (handled with enviable clarity and precision by another philosopher loosely connected with the Lvov-Warsaw tradition: Władysław Tatarkiewicz). Due to the critical spirit and reluctance to embrace any sort of philosophical grandiosity of the Lvov-Warsaw tradition, its heirs were able to exert an important sobering influence on young minds otherwise in danger of being seduced by the Marxist-Leninist ideology availing itself of the venerable ideals of justice, peace and free individual development pervertedly adapted from other, older European traditions.

Mention must be made also of the role of Poland's Roman Catholic Church in the context of the overthrow of Communism in that country, and of the fact, sometimes forgotten, that courses in (Thomist) philosophy—with its strains of civil disobedience and natural rights—constituted an important part of the education of Polish priests.

There were also a few isolated figures, like the philosopher Henryk Elzenberg, who, though himself neither a Catholic nor a member of the Lvov-Warsaw school, dealt with remarkable clarity and consistency with socio-ethical problems raised by the advent of the great ideologies of the present century, stressing the moral relevance of thought, in a way similar to that of T. G. Masaryk and J. Patočka of whom Jan Pavlík has so much to say in his contribution to this volume. Elzenberg thereby inspired some of the most significant members of the democratic opposition, as for instance the outstanding activist historian and publicist Adam Michnik.

Last but not least, there was the Catholic University of Lublin—at that time the only university between Berlin and Seoul on which Communists did *not* attempt to impose their doctrine—where, not unexpectedly, not only personalistic ethics and Neo-Thomism (of a Gilsonian orientation), but also the Lvov-Warsaw school was represented, and where Marxist doctrines were analyzed for polemical purposes, but in a fair and thorough fashion.

All of this must have played a role in the processes which resulted in Poland's renouncing the "dictatorship of the proletariat" in politics and the principle of state-ownership in economics. Yet the majority of educated Poles were for all that not *aware* of philosophy's practical importance in the socio-ethical and economic sphere—in the way that they were conscious of the role played by poets (such as Czesław Miłosz), novelists and film-makers.

There were, indeed, factors positively counterproductive to their understanding the role and the powers of philosophy. All university graduates, for instance, went through a compulsory course of philosophy, intended—an intention not always realized in practice—as part of Communist indoctrination. As a result, the very word "philosophy", like "ideology", was reduced almost to a term of abuse. Indeed the social status of all university scholars and scientists is very low in Poland today, a fact due in part to their salaries, which can barely compete with the wages of unskilled manual workers. But the philosopher, especially, enjoys the reputation of an intellectual humbug, often with politically suspicious affiliations. The word "philosophy" is otherwise taken as a general term for loose, literary considerations concerning the meaning of life, of society and of history.

On the other hand, we may be interested in the vicissitudes which various politically relevant ideas have undergone in a country like Poland—the first to throw off totalitarian, Communist rule. For it is undeniable that such "objective" factors as the collapse of the Communist economic system, Reagan's toughness, or the advent of Gorbachev, do not explain all of what has happened in Eastern Europe since 1989, as is proved by the examples of Rumania, Serbia or Albania, not to mention some of the Soviet republics, where different forms of Communism have still (*anno* 1991) survived. At any rate, it seems clear that unless the subjects of a given political system begin to *think*—and to think in a certain manner—then no external-political factors, no matter how favourable, can bring about a radical change. Thus it is interesting to investigate what this manner of thinking was.

Politically relevant ideas which pertain not just to some particular details of the political system but rather give a general outline of it or of other relevant dimensions of the nation's life, are sometimes called "ideology" in Poland.[4]

This, admittedly non-standard sense of "ideology" is all but indispensable in Poland, though it is also misleading to a Western observer, who tends to see in "ideology" either a deceitful representation of some particular interests as general ones, or a collectivist utopia, a sort of scenario which tells everyone what he shall do in the "harmonious unity of the nation". This tendency manifested by Western observers is reasonable in the sense that (as I have argued at length elsewhere[5]), what best accounts for our multifarious and sometimes nearly inconsistent intuitions about ideology is a view of ideology as consisting in a program of social action ("action" in the broad sense, including omissions) proposed allegedly for the sake and in the interest of some large social group. (This is the neutral concept of ideology which we have just referred to.) Such a program is in addition such that, if it were put into practice, it would serve some (possibly very shortsighted) interests of a smaller group within the larger one, *without there being any justification for this in the program itself*.[6] I have also given reasons[7] why any and every program of social action can be suspected of being ideology in the above sense, so that it is no mere equivocation to substitute the pejorative concept of ideology just spelled out for the neutral one, which we had in mind earlier. Yet the distinction between the neutral and the pejorative senses can be made, and it is useful. For, as should be borne in mind, since at least her first partition in 1772, Poland has been in a state of constant destruction and reconstruction, and sometimes (as now, after the Communist era) this reconstruction has to begin almost from scratch. That means that even the most elementary questions concerning the structure of power and authority have to be decided upon *ex abrupto;* minor changes against an established background of stable political institutions will not do, simply because the relevant institutions were and are absent. Certainly there *is* a temptation to construct a national or nationalistic utopia as an answer to those questions. But what Poles face now (as so many times before) is rather the very *choice* between utopianism and a sober vision of a pluralistic democracy where power is distributed in accordance with purely procedural criteria and stability is at best a matter of an always unsteady consensus. The sorts of considerations one brings forward in the making of this basic choice, now, are referred to as "ideology". Such considerations will typically be fundamental and "earnest", with many philosophical or even theological ingredients, but they need in no way be fundamentalist or otherwise biased in favor of utopianism.

The Ideology of Civic Virtue

It appears, now, that Poland and other countries of the former Soviet block are particularly in need of an "ideology" in this specific sense.

Fifty years of totalitarian rule have left them in a state of ruin not only with regard to their economies or their infrastructure, but in other, spiritual, respects too. Western business consultants visiting these countries often complain that their bureaucracies are lazy and inefficient, their workers and servicemen lazy and demoralized, their businessmen lazy and overly obsessed with easy lucre. And while all of this might be discounted as a result of measuring Eastern European realities against Western standards, even a (sociologically informed) Pole sometimes gets the impression that his country is made up entirely of struggles in a Hobbesian war of each against all, the all only painfully learning to get along with one another in a civil society. This may be unavoidable after what Poland has been through; but perhaps a better institutional and legal framework could make that learning easier.

Poles sometimes complain among themselves that in their newly freed country no kind of honest toil really pays—no more than it did under Communist rule—and that honesty is the worst of all possible bases on which to live one's life. Sometimes it seems as though our people were masters of zero-sum games in which only the shrewdest cheaters get their shares, while the general pool shrinks to the dramatic detriment of the not so shrewd. But people are forced to play zero-sum games and to choose suboptimal strategies in them wherever a general lack of confidence or a positive distrust prevail;[8] these can give rise to destructive "class" conflicts, along whichever lines these classes are divided. Under the Communist rule, we used to have an "official" antagonism between the working class, the peasants and the "working intelligentsia" (white collar workers and all non-self-employed university graduates) on the one hand, and the somewhat mythical "propertied classes", or whatever had been left of them (craftsmen and shopkeepers, for the most part) on the other. In fact, however, the natural diversity of interests of workers, farmers and intelligentsia made it easy for the propaganda to play off these three groups against one another; not unexpectedly, it was the intelligentsia which was most often exposed as the villain of the three. Today, we do not have any rigidly ideological, doctrinaire propagandistic centre in Poland, yet the suspicion persists that some "they"—the "Leftists", the Jews, the nationalists, businessmen, clergymen, journalists, or simply the "mob", are out to foist their ideas on "us" and to grab power. No society is able to flourish in an atmosphere such as this.

An important fact in this connection is that Poland is not a new nation which only now seeks self-identity and a vision of social order to replace some obscure and ominous tribalistic fervur. On the contrary, during her 1000-year history Poland has had many ideologies—in the sense here proposed—and some of these have allowed her to survive the totalitarian period of the latest fifty years. On the other hand, Poland has also had other traditions which were decidedly fatal. Thus it is generally assumed, whether rightly or wrongly, that it was what we call *prywata* on the side of the aristocracy—an excessive concern for one's own interests, coupled with the complete absence of concern for public affairs—which allowed 18th century Poland, a democratic country with weak executive powers, to suffer the fact of becoming partitioned by neighbouring absolutistic monarchies and to its subsequent political demise in 1795.[9]

Life in a country partitioned between Russia, Prussia and Austria was for obvious reasons not overly favourable to the development of practical conceptions of a social order. For supporting the states which had annexed parts of his country was the least of the concerns of a Polish patriot. The rule by terror of the Germans during the Nazi occupation, similarly, was not a school of civic virtues, though the self-organization of the society in the form of an underground "state", including the existence of an underground army, was a proof that this part of Europe is not inhabited by an amorphous tribe—contrary to what German propaganda had maintained.

Another very important fact to be noted here is that, while pre-war Poland had its mixture of all the common types of political ideologies then represented in Europe, the bearers and above all the producers of these ideologies were, as members of the Polish intelligentsia, decimated, indeed almost exterminated, first of all by the Nazis and then later by the Soviets and subsequently by Stalinists of a more native breed. Obviously, if the ideas involved in a vision of social order are to be somewhat more sophisticated than the blind support of an all referred to as "us" and the equally blind denigration of all of "them"—along whichever lines these "us" and "them" are divided—then people of culture and education are indispensable.

Yet in Poland the percentage of such people in, say, 1950 was desperately low as compared to the pre-war state of affairs. The post-war education of the working class and the peasants, often claimed by the Communists as one of their undeniable achievements, was in fact not so great a success, given that even today Poland has a considerably lower ratio of university graduates or of those holding university entrance qualifications than do most Western nations. (That Poland boasts so many good philosophers and logicians can be explained by the fact that an academic career was one of the very few honest careers open to intellectually talented persons who would otherwise have chosen politics, business, or law—until recently, that is, for universities have already noted a considerable decrease of interest in philosophy or other "unpractical" studies.) All in all, Poles are a largely plebeian nation, with the self-appointed "intellectual elites" being looked at suspiciously by the electorate; and the debacle of the "ideological system"—the very word "ideology" connotes the orthodox ideology of Soviet Marxism—adds to the plebeian's distrust of all ideas.

The End of Communism in Poland

Fortunately, however, not all producers and bearers of ideas concerning social order were either dead or emigrated after 22 June 1944, when the Communists, backed, or rather imposed, by the Soviets then "liberating" Poland, usurped power in the country.

It may appear as something of a tautology that among those who were allowed to voice their ideas in public almost all were committed to socialism of one form or another. This fact is on closer reflection rather less obvious, however, since the filtering system of censorship and open terror could not operate as effectively during the first years as it did later. The reason was first of all that the Communist regime had to keep up the appearances of complying with the Yalta and Potsdam agreements concerning free elections. It allowed, therefore, some restricted free space for other parties, providing that socialist tenets were not too radically criticized. On the other hand, although in the later decades the word "socialism" came to designate the Communist system only, during the first post-war years it supported a greater variety of meanings, much as it does in the West. Moreover, the strong socialist traditions of pre-war Poland, the country's rather poor economic record during that period, with vast areas of poverty and glaring inequalities, and the memories of the Great Depression of 1929 and after—all of these were motives for regarding a nationalized economy, free health care and education, as the most attractive of all possible alternatives. Important in this context also, and not entirely without justification, was the belief that the aberrations of the Nazi and Bolshevik-Stalinist totalitarianisms had been causally linked to certain imperfections of the then capitalist systems. It was thus quite natural for the Socialist Party—one of the few which was licensed to compete with the Communists in the first elections—to seize upon ideas like those mentioned above. And even the Farmers' Party, though understandably opposed to any form of that Soviet-style collectivization which was to begin in 1948 and be given up in 1956, endorsed the agrarian reform which had been carried out in 1946 by the new authorities.

Even some Catholic intellectuals were tempted to think that, for all that Communism's "superstructure"—to use its own terms—was hostile, the "basis", which it had just revolutionized in the name of the people, did indeed contain some sort of response to truly human needs as they conceived them. They looked back to the social encyclicals of the recent Popes, and further back still to the "Christian Socialism" of Abbé Lamennais and others, but primarily they looked up to the writings of the French Catholic personalist Jacques Maritain, and of Emmanuel Mounier (with his passionate and at the same time slightly dreamerish criticism of the capitalist society), for hints at a compromise with Marxism.

There were, finally, those, and they were not so scarce, who seriously believed in the advent of a "just society". They were to be found especially among the lower classes, where a perspective of breaking away from the deprivations of their life seemed to have opened up, whether in the form of free and accelerated education or in the participation in a reconstruction and industrialization of the country—both on a new "socialistic" basis seemingly favourable to the common man. How illusory this perspective was would become clear in only a few years.

Many new enthusiasts of the Communist system were to be found also among the intellectual elite, not least (as Czesław Miłosz suggests in his *The Captive Mind*) due to the irresistible charm of the hypothesis of "historical necessities".

In all cases, the awareness of the geopolitical situation of Poland may have been a motive for rationalizing what was in any case inevitable.

Immediately after the war there was also a limited number of other political orientations, such as that of the Christian Democrats. After the fraudulent elections of 1947, however, with the subsequent suppression of independent ideologists in all licensed parties and the forced unification of the Socialist Party with the Workers' (i.e., Communist) Party, all independent thought began to gravitate to either of these two poles: the remnants of the socialist ideology, and the Catholic social doctrine. The latter, however, did not have a political representative in Parliament, and could be publicized only on the pages of a few periodicals, all of which were closed down in 1953 after they had refused to publish an apologetic obituary of Stalin.

The sorts of socialism acceptable to pre-war socialists on the one hand and to Catholics on the other were of course different. Yet both of them were worlds apart from the socialism which, having declared itself a preparatory stage on the way to Communism, was set forth after the 1947 elections as an aim to be reached by the new "people's democracy". The chasm grew deeper as the authorities went on arresting, torturing and executing soldiers and functionaries of the underground Polish state that had been built up in the German occupation period regardless of their political views, at the same time plaguing the Church with countless restrictions, culminating in the arresting of the Polish Primate, a man of great authority in the nation. Naturally the Party state was also untiring in combatting whatever the catastrophe of the war had left in the way of private industry, trade, and indeed farming, which, however, stubbornly refused to yield to collectivization. Party rule meant also the suspension of nearly all civil liberties and the control of the whole public sphere. The development of political ideas did not, under these circumstances, flow continuously. Rather, it went on in paroxysms of public discontent and disobedience, which had to be strong and massive enough for the authorities to be forced to react other than with simple repressions.[10]

Communism was thereby bent and twisted out of shape. The young zealots in the Party and in its subordinate youth organizations, many of whom came from the pre-war underclasses and initially had some sort of belief in, and gratitude for, the new regime, soon discovered that cynicism and careerism, rather than dedication to Marxist tenets, was the name of the game. The broad masses of society learned to perceive Communist rule as tolerable by comparison with that of the Germans and the Soviets, and they were still moved by enthusiasm for the reconstruction of the country. After a few years, however, they started longing for more consumer goods by way of reward for their efforts. Such goods remained however in very short supply, as the State, now the owner of all industries of any size, redirected vast portions of its income to investments, thereby implementing a program of Soviet-style forced industrialization. This was obviously a reason for discontent. But another reason—apart from the ever-present political terror—was the general climate in the public sphere, heavy with the official hatred for "imperialists"—including such examples as Josif Broz Tito—for internal "class enemies", and for the "Western style of life" (which meant, among other things, consumer goods). Still another reason was the not officially sanctioned yet ever-present contempt for the common man: for his "bourgeois virtues", such as honesty and thrift in private affairs, for his "backward" religious beliefs, and for his very individuality, as something contrasting with the collective power of the Party. Those who had already been workers before the war promptly discovered that they were given worse treatment in factories belonging nominally to them than they had in the bad old days of capitalist exploitation.

The death of Stalin in 1953 did not change things immediately. The ruling elites were uncertain about the development in Moscow and they were nervous for this reason. It began to be clear that the time of rule by terror was over; how, then, to keep society under control? The "Inner Party"—to use the Orwellian phrase—was soon split into factions over this question, and this brought about a certain relaxation of the atmosphere—the first symptoms of a "thaw", one result of which was that a number of semi-independent political periodicals could start to be issued. One Party faction hit upon the idea of using the anti-Semitism still alive in some sectors of society, coupled with the fact that persons of Jewish descent were over-represented in the Party apparatus and in the political police, to disclaim any responsibility for the crimes of Stalinism, in the hope of thereby winning legitimacy for their Party's hold on society. But this did not work: most effective ideologically were those Communist intellectuals who interpreted Stalinism as a deviation from "genuine Marxism", as a period of "errors and deformations". These were called "revisionists", and Kołakowski was one of the brightest minds among them. In strictly ideological questions they adhered to something like the Yugoslav model, with self-management of factories as its shibboleth.

As uncertainty among the rulers continued to grow, ever broader groups in society began to feel increasingly more self-assertive, with the result that things which had been impossible earlier now appeared feasible. For instance, the unilateral disbanding of the obligatory cooperatives by the farmers concerned.

When in June 1956 it came to strikes in the large industrial city of Poznań, the authorities did crack down with outrageous brutality. But these repressions, which compromised the Party leadership in the eyes of public opinion, only accelerated the process of political change.

A new Party leadership took over the reigns of power in October 1956 after a complicated series of events, in which not only public manifestations triggered off by the blatant unfairness of the court proceedings against most of the June activists but also intrigues within the Party apparatus and the presence of Soviet troops played a role. The new leadership, which was headed by Władysław Gomułka, a remarkable politician who was well reputed for his unwillingness to adopt Soviet patterns in a mechanical way and for his austerity, sincerity and straightforwardness—Gomułka had indeed been placed temporarily under arrest by the former Party leadership—announced a new "Polish Road to Socialism". This at least partlyreflectedthe general acceptance of Socialism in the broadest sense of the word among the wider society. And given the importance which Poles—neighbors of Russia and Germany—attach to the conformity of their institutions to native cultural patterns, it can be no surprise that the slogan of a *Polish Road* caught on. Even the Catholic Primate, newly released from confinement, encouraged the people to support Gomułka. The new Parliament, elected soon afterwards, was indeed more representative in that it included also a small group of Catholic deputies.

The revival did not, however, last for long. Very soon afterwards Gomułka began gradually to move towards the austerity Socialism of old, though naturally without Stalinist rhetorical embellishments. Culture and art enjoyed greater freedom of expression, and in many of its products ironically critical undertones with reference to the Polish situation were unmistakable. Yet the general attitude of the politically informed in society was, or seemed to be, one of indifference. The task of ruling was left to "them", i.e., to the Party and its apparatus. For this reason, although the pressure of totalitarianism was incomparably smaller than it had been before October '56, the discomfort of political and ideological alienation grew more and more intense. More importantly, Gomułka seemed to be trying slowly to restore the orthodox Stalinist models—such as the collectivization of farms and the total state control over the educational system—by small legal steps.

A materialist historian would perhaps say that Gomułka could have proceeded further along this road had he but achieved some sort of economic success; thus he could have made up for a decline in freedom with an increase in available jam. But this did not happen: economic stabilization was achieved, but on a rather miserly level, while the muzzling of independent thought and of freedom of religion was effected with remarkable diligence and intensity.

It was in the early Sixties that the revisionists and Catholic intellectuals began to recognize their common cause and to unite in certain symbolic actions against the regime, for instance against the excesses of censorship. On a wider plane it was becoming clear that both wings of the opposition were—their differences notwithstanding—much nearer to each other than to the regime on such questions as the self-determination of the society in cultural and educational matters or the ownership of the means of production. As to the latter, while it was accepted that, e.g., coal-mines or steelworks should be public property, this was distinguished from *state*-ownership. (Understandably, the general trend was towards finding a third way between individualism—which was rather difficult to practice in a totalitarian state—and the absolute reliance on the state.)

The decisive step in the direction of an alliance between the socialist and the Catholic wing was taken in 1968, when a small group of independent Catholic deputies in Parliament denounced the government for its repressive actions against those students and intellectuals who had protested (in March of that year) against the gagging of non-Communist culture. These deputies stood closer to the Revisionists than to Catholicism. The repressions had, incidentally, an overtly anti-Semitic character (more than five thousand people of Jewish origin, mostly entirely assimilated, left Poland as a result), something which neither the Catholic deputies nor the Primate of Poland failed to denounce.

Already at that time it became generally accepted that no form of socialism—with or without "errors and deformations"—was suited to the people of Poland. Still, the regime managed to retain its power, and it was only two years later that an untimely drastic price increase—or rather the outburst of popular protest occasioned by this increase in December 1970—brought it down.

The new leadership promised a farewell to the austerities of the Gomułka era, and for a couple of years they did indeed fulfil this promise thanks to Western credits, by which Poland is still encumbered in the form of foreign debts. On the one hand these Western credits allowed more consumer goods in Polish stores, including the symbolic Coca-Cola, which had earlier been held out as an epitome of "Capitalist depravity". After the ascetic Gomułka period, this was certainly a breath of fresh air. An air of shoddy consumerism spread itself across the country and lured especially the young. Most of the more experienced citizens, however, were aware that the new lifestyle propagated by the state media was wildly inappropriate given the country's economic situation, and they adjusted themselves to the new circumstances either with cynicism or with resignation.

On the other hand, the common man found himself exposed more than ever to arrogance and outright contempt on the part of those in power. In science, education and culture only servility and flattery paid off, and nearly all institutions were reformed in a neo-Stalinist fashion with the adjective "Socialist" (i.e., "Communist" in the Western vocabulary) tagged to their new names. The process culminated in a reform of the constitution, whereby the country's dependence on the Soviet Union was established as a matter of law. At the same time, Poland participated in the Helsinki European Conference and signed its Final Act; the new anti-democratic measures had therefore to be put forward as steps towards "liberalization", adding a new dimension of hypocrisy to already poisoned relations between the authorities and the people. Circumstances like these, however, elicited further cooperation between the Catholic and socialist intellectuals (the latter becoming less "socialist" and more "liberal" in the American sense of the word). This cooperation was not only tactical; the intellectuals concerned did not fail to note the basic similarities of content between such encyclicals as, e.g., *Populorum Progressio*, and the United Nations' Bill of the Rights of Man.

As in the case of Gomułka, the costs of these "improvements" soon began to be felt, as the new leadership went on sinking more and more of the national product into heavy industry, most of which was useless from an economic point of view. The difference was that if Gomułka stressed "tomorrow" when promising the jam, the new rulers tended to drop this adverb.

When in 1976 it came to new outbursts of unrest, occasioned by another increase in prices, the authorities did not hesitate to crack down with ruthless brutality and arrested and tortured many hundreds of workers. This time the intellectuals reacted promptly in publicizing the case in the West, with the result that even Enrico Berlinguer considered himself obliged to chastise his Polish comrades. What was more, some intellectuals, both socialist and Catholic, went to the aid of the repressed workers in material and practical ways, and these activities, as well as bringing socialists and Catholics together, represented an important crossing of the line that had hitherto separated workers and intellectuals. They were accompanied by a rapid growth in publication of periodicals and books in *samizdat* form. Unofficial organizations were formed which aimed at stimulating ideological thinking against the cynical nihilism of state propaganda, organizations which did their best to keep their existence *not* secret. The underlying idea of these activities was that they were not part of a secret, "underground" world, not, in other words, a counterpart of the "underground state" which had grown up during the period of Nazi occupation—let alone a conspiracy against the state. Rather they were part of a non-state-controlled

self-organization of society, a "parallel polis" in the terminology of Czech dissident philosophers such as Jan Patočka and Václav Bělohradský. Needless to
say, the practice of maintaining in existence illegal but yet not secret organizations brought with it considerable costs for some of the participants: arrests and
temporary detentions, humiliating examinations by the police and confiscations
of such "instruments of subversion" as typewriters, books, and manuscripts;
these were especially painful to philosophers, who cannot work without typewriters, books and manuscripts. Yet the authorities stopped short of taking any
sweeping, radical measures against these new forms of societal life.

This self-organization went so far as to reach the point of setting up independent and illegal trade unions, which later—known as "*Solidarność*"—
became legalized after the upheaval of August 1980.

Solidarity

It is difficult to say anything sufficiently general and at the same time unrestrict-
edly valid about the "ideology", i.e., the political and social vision, of
Solidarność. It was on the one hand a trade union, so it had to put first the
defence of workers' rights. This meant also, however, given that the employer
was in every case the state, the defence of human rights in general and of the
dignity of the individual. Basic socialist and libertarian concerns were therefore
united in the *Solidarność* social philosophy, and the movement itself represented a final stage of that alliance of socialist and Catholic oppositionists which
had begun to form itself after October 1956. The name "Solidarność" was hardly fortuitous: it expressed the basic idea not only of mutual help and support,
but also of renouncing advantages gained from compliance with the authorities,
or even endangering oneself by active disobedience to the authorities (e.g., in
so-called "solidarity strikes"[11]) for the sake of helping others to achieve their
goals.

Put another way, the social philosophy of *Solidarność* consisted in a deliberate search for and adoption of optimal rather than suboptimal strategies in
social games; or yet another way, it was a way of practicing, perhaps not charity, but brotherhood on a larger scale. This was on the psychological level a
katharsis-like experience for many people who had been taught, against their
inner nature, that the most shortsighted egoism *was* the only effective survival
strategy in the prevailing social conditions. (As I lived some hundred meters
away from the headquarters of *Solidarność* at that time, I well remember how
enthusiastically people brought there, as a response to an appeal by the
Solidarność leadership, clothes, blankets, and whatever they considered necessary for the victims of an earthquake in Italy in autumn 1980.) That the name of
the trade union was a common, though abstract, noun, had the advantage of

enabling writers to propose general considerations on solidarity, with evident application to the movement known under the same name, yet avoiding looking like a party ideology (in the pejorative sense), and at the same time reminding the movement of what it should be (in the writers' opinion). Józef Tischner, an interesting and eloquent Cracow philosopher, an apt translator of Heidegger known for his interest in Husserl's phenomenology as well as in Hegel, brought out in 1981 a book entitled *The Ethics of Solidarity*. The book had clear moralizing intentions for "*Solidarność*" and Tischner was indeed recognized as the semiofficial philosopher of the movement. It had an outspokenly Christian basis (Tischner himself is a Catholic priest); yet it shunned the word "*Solidarność*" as a proper name, (and the same is true of vast parts of the Pope's difficult, philosophical sermons from his 1987 visit to Poland. (The relevance of this visit and its sermons for the subsequent developments in Poland still awaits investigation.)

Hostile to the very word "socialism" though it was, the social vision of "*Solidarność*" did nonetheless contain important socialistic elements. For instance, one of its pivots was the idea of self-rule or self-government, both on the level of the single factory (reflecting basically the Yugoslav idea of "self-management") and at the level of the region or the country as a whole (signifying the desire to keep Polish dependence on the Kremlin within limits). What exactly would have developed out of all of this must however remain a mystery since *Solidarność* was not predestined to survive for more than sixteen months.

What happened as far as ideological developments are concerned after the declaration of martial law in December 1981 is still difficult to summarize in the same way as we did with regard to the former periods of recent Polish history. It is certainly true to say that the organizational structure of *Solidarność*, not to mention other organizations, many of which were illegal even between August and December of that year, was if not completely smashed still thrown into considerable disarray. The attempts to rebuild it in the underground were only a partial success, as too few people believed that a fresh start was possible. Many lost interest in political projects of any sort, sinking into apathy or simply concentrating on their profession and family. Others turned away from the conception of self-government towards other, more firmly established traditions, such as liberalism, conservative or otherwise, Christian democracy, or even socialism of a more traditional sort. As a result, the highly artificial unity of the *Solidarność* ideology was split into many distinct, if not openly opposed, orientations. The divisions could be overcome for the purpose of ousting the Communists from power in June 1989, but soon afterwards they reappeared, with the result that today those who still identify themselves with the social vision of *Solidarność* are just one small sect among many others.

This certainly more adequately reflects the variety of opinions actually held in Poland concerning the question how the country should be reconstructed. On the other hand, however, it caused a great deal of cynicism as to the possibilities of a consensus on that question. And while a return of Communism is now certainly no longer a danger, a growing number of Poles believes that Poland will remain a country belonging not to the whole nation, but rather once more to some "them" distinguished on political grounds, whether they be Liberals, Christian Democrats, Social Democrats. or what one will. What is still worse, the ideals of justice, hard work, decency and social peace which the Communists abused rhetorically for their own purposes, are increasingly perceived as belonging entirely to the Communist era and therefore as not worth cultivating at all. People who out of honesty refused to join the Communist Party and suffered unpleasant consequences for their professional careers are now, whenever they protest that even the agents in a market economy should be (and, in a sound economy, generally are) honest, themselves proclaimed to be Communists at heart. This adds to the basic uncertainty which many Poles experience, and to the increasing and rather sad impression that for some categories of people—including philosophers—Poland will not become a livable country in the foreseeable future.

We are witnessing a real end of ideology in Poland—ideology not only in the usual pejorative sense of a utopian, totalitarian scenario, but also in the sense of any conception of how the country should be run, how people should get along with one another, and how the mechanisms of authority and power shall be structured. During the 45 years of Communist rule an overwhelming majority of the Polish nation abhorred and rejected Communist ideology at least in their hearts, but they were all but helpless against its propaganda and its police. It was mainly, though not exclusively, people of liberal-socialist convictions and people of Christian inspiration who overcame their misgivings and unified their efforts for the sake of articulating the national, and the simply human, interests of Poles and of defending them practically. When they at last succeeded, it turned out that we do not any longer know what these interests are.

Wojciech Żełaniec

Internationale Akademie für Philosophie
Liechtenstein

MARXISM AND THE PROFESSIONALIZATION OF PHILOSOPHY

There is much more to say on Polish post-war philosophy than is contained in Dr. Żełaniec's paper. It is particularly interesting to look at the Polish philosophical scene after 1945 in order to answer the following question: what is it which is to explain the fact that Marxism was practically dead in Poland before Communism itself had failed. As one spectacular sign that Marxism had became very weak in Poland one can take a decision of the Polish Ministry of Higher Education in the early '80s to the effect that a general course in Marxist philosophy should no longer be obligatory for students at university. What is remarkable is that this decision was enacted at a time when martial law was in full force.

Certainly, to grasp the reasons for the collapse of Marxist philosophy in Poland it is not sufficient to mention individual philosophical dissidents, like Kołakowski, or "ambiguous figures", like Schaff, alongside a general picture of the Polish philosophical tradition. Let me try to say what more is needed.[1]

In order to understand Polish philosophy after 1945, one must take into consideration its shape in the interwar period. This was a remarkably good time for philosophy in Poland. Philosophy was truly pluralistic, in spite of a dominance of the Lvov-Warsaw School. Two other streams, namely Catholic philosophy and phenomenology should also be mentioned. Marxism as a philosophy or ideology was rather a secondary current in Poland at that time. It attracted some people, mainly sociologists and some who were actively involved in the communist or socialist movements.

The years 1945-1949 can be considered to a considerable extent as a prolongation of what had become important in the interwar Polish philosophical thought. The same institutions (the universities, the Polish Academy of Arts and Sciences — PAU, the Polish Philosophical Society) organized philosophical life, and the same periodicals—*Przegląd Filozoficzny* (Philosophical Review), *Ruch Filozoficzny* (*Philosophical Movement*) and *Kwartalnik Filozoficzny* (*Philosophical Quarterly*)—appeared once more. Above all, the main movements of Polish pre-war philosophy were cultivated as before.

What about Marxism at that time? The first department of Marxist philosophy in Poland (with Adam Schaff as its head) was established in Warsaw in 1946. However, the development of Marxism in Poland was very difficult in the immediate post-war years. Most of those who had been sympathetic to Marxism before 1939 had lost their lives in 1939-1945, and only a very few minor philosophers had embraced Marxist principles since then. However, due to an official protection of Marxism by the Polish state (which began especially after

1947 to provide instructions for Communists) the population of Polish Marxists increased; Leszek Kołakowski and Bronisław Baczko appeared among the Marxists at this time.

The liberal policy in Poland ultimately came to an end about 1950. Philosophical studies were liquidated, with the exception of the University of Warsaw and the Catholic University of Lublin (KUL), which had the status of a private university. A new Polish Academy of Science, under Communist control, replaced the PAU. The old philosophical journals disappeared and *Myśl Filozoficzna* (Philosophical Thought), an entirely Marxist periodical organized along the lines of the Soviet *Voprosy Filozofii*, was established. The government declared several scholars, including Ingarden, Tatarkiewicz, Dąmbska and Elzenberg *personae non gratae* and prohibited them from teaching; officially they were deemed to have acquired the status of pensioners. The teaching activities of others, like the Ossowski's for example, were considerably reduced, and some so-called "bourgeois" philosophers, for example Ajdukiewicz, Kotarbiński or Czeżowski, were permitted to teach logic only.

Marxist zealots began a very intensive battle against the bourgeois movements represented in Poland. However, although the strength of Marxism grew to the position of dominance in Poland in 1950-1955, it did not win this battle. Most Polish philosophers of the older generation did not change their earlier views, and many of their students rejected Marxism.

Certainly the period 1950-1955 must be regarded as a very dark time in the history of philosophy in Poland. However, some positive development can also be reported. The school of existential Thomism arose in Lublin. Due to the teaching activities of Ajdukiewicz and Kotarbiński, many logicians and philosophers of science appeared. The Polish Philosophical Society survived and became a forum of philosophy in the academic sense; when the Stalin era ended many papers were able to be published which arose on the occasion of talks delivered at meetings of the Polish Philosophical Society. Thus although philosophy independent of Marxism was limited to a great extent, it by no means disappeared entirely in Poland in the period 1950-1955.

The so-called De-Stalinization brought essential changes. Formerly retired philosophers triumphantly came back to universities and other scientific institutions. Regular philosophical studies were reinstated at first in Cracow and Wrocław, and then also in other universities. *Ruch Filozoficzny* once more appeared and the Soviet-style *Myśl Filozoficzna* was replaced by the new journal *Studia Filozoficzne* (Philosophical Studies). Certainly the latter more or less protected Marxism; but it was open also for different ideas, and more important still was the fact that almost all its editors consistently imposed high professional standards in their treatment of the papers submitted for publication. Thus Polish philosophy became once more pluralistic, with phenomenology being singled out as an especially important movement. Although the Lvov-Warsaw School came to an end with the death of its last representatives, students of the Lvov-Warsaw philosophers continued the tradition of logical research in Poland. And Catholic philosophy flourished, too.

But especially interesting things happened also to Marxism in Poland. Polish Marxists proposed a program of "open Marxism", by which they meant: open to problems and even to solutions taken from "bourgeois" philosophy. This movement split itself into two schools, namely "humanistic" and "naturalistic". The former, influenced by existentialism in its various forms, concentrated its activities on philosophical anthropology; the latter, influenced by the Lvov-Warsaw School and by logical empiricism, was mainly involved in the philosophy of science. Thus there was created a general intellectual climate which facilitated the formation of two schools in Polish Marxism, namely the Warsaw school of the history of ideas (Baczko, Kołakowski, Walicki) and the Poznan methodological school. Other movements welcomed this "open" Marxism. As results of this new situation we can note the growth of mutual exchange and discussions and even cooperation as well as a minimalization of inter-philosophical barriers rooted in different general perspectives. Thus, research in particular philosophical fields gradually became at least as important as belonging to definite movements. This process can be termed the "professionalization" of Polish philosophy, and I think that it is precisely this professionalization which is to a great extent responsible for the relatively early death of Marxist philosophy in Poland.

By no means do I want to suggest that Poland in 1956-1989 was a philosophical heaven. This period was full of dramatic events in the sphere of politics. These took place in 1968, 1970, 1976 and 1980-1981. Political and philosophical hardliners (at least some of them) tried on such occasions to bring about the victory of Marxism by administrative means. However, their successes were rather limited and temporary. Even when, in 1968, several revisionist Marxists (mainly Jews) lost their posts at universities, official Marxist propaganda demonstrated an explicit sympathy to bourgeois philosophy. Even if we regard this as a strategic move, the fact in itself is quite interesting. The "degeneration" of Marxism in Poland was not halted by various forms of administrative protection, financial support, possibilities of publishing, quicker promotion, and so on. And even though such protection was granted up to 1989, Marxism was still so to speak "demoralized" in relation to its colleagues in the same professional philosophical environment. When the Fifth Polish Philosophical Congress took place in Cracow in 1987, it became clear that Marxism was just one of many philosophical streams in Poland. Hardliners simply rejected invitations to participate in the Congress. Some of them were ashamed to come, others were offended that such a horrible event (i.e., a general philosophical congress) could take place at all; but both parties had no power to mount an effective counterattack. Remember that "Solidarity" was still illegal at that time.

To explain fully the process of professionalization of Polish philosophy, one would have to take various factors into account. Some of the peculiarities of Poland under Communism, for example the role of the Catholic Church or the only partial collectivization of agriculture, have been clearly noted by Żełaniec in his paper above. However, I think that a very important role in this process was played also by the continuous presence of independent and pluralistic forms of philosophical life in Poland. Perhaps this is an important lesson which can be drawn from the Polish experience: pluralism in philosophy creates a massive barrier against totalitarianism. Remarkable also is that a philosopher may play a political role not only as someone involved in so-called political philosophy— or politics—but also by a serious execution of his professional duties.

Jan Woleński

Institute of Philosophy
Jagiellonian University
Cracow, Poland

PHILOSOPHY, "PARALLEL POLIS" AND REVOLUTION: THE CASE OF CZECHOSLOVAKIA

Introductory remarks

In an article concerning the Soviet putsch in August 1991, Václav Bělohradský wrote that "the Communist state has arisen from the spirit of Western philosophy".[1] According to Bělohradský, Communism is a natural outcome of metaphysics, which he defines as the striving to found human life not on mere *doxa* but on *episteme*—on knowledge of the truth. The Communist party (the state) is then the main instrument for submitting mere opinion to objective knowledge, an instrument which does not depend on individual human persuasions. All those traditions and customs which are not confirmed by the dialectical method are mere anachronisms and have therefore to be liquidated. Post-Communism, then, comes to mean for Bělohradský a reestablishing of the prevalence of mere opinions over objective knowledge. Thus, the era of post-Communism is also a post-philosophical era, since the idea of philosophy as a search for the truth has been exhausted.

Democracy, according to Bělohradský, means that all knowledge, every attitude, every principle is reduced to mere opinion, and that the prevailing of one opinion over another results from the fact that those who assert this opinion are able to use the art of rhetoric in a more effective way than are their opponents. The great democracies of England and America are, accordingly, nothing but forms of institutionalization of rhetoric, of argumentation and persuasive behaviour. The legitimacy of democratic power is based on the fact that its representatives have persuaded us that their viewpoint is advantageous to us.

This Heideggerian rejection of Western metaphysics results, however, in a dangerous revival of the subjectivistic tradition of the Sophists. It amounts to nothing less than a rejection of all the principal prerequisites of Western culture and civilization. Thus Bělohradský's thesis leads to the consequence that logic is merely an instrument of the art of persuasion, an instrument which stands on the same level as personal authority, charisma and other instruments of persuasive behaviour; scientific or theoretical discussion or argument is on this view not possible at all.

However, Bělohradský's thesis is—like all *sophismata*—in itself contradictory. If we follow his arguments, we must arrive at the conclusion that his thesis expresses no truth but only his own, personal opinion. His thesis can in addition be criticized from a factual point of view. European metaphysics as a whole is not the ideological foundation of the Communist state; this role is played only by one specific part of European metaphysics—by German idealism, and especially of course its Marxist-Leninist tributary. Another part of European metaphysics, represented by the line Descartes—Locke—Hume—Smith—Mill, etc., has, I want to argue, provided the ontological and epistemological foundation precisely for modern liberal democracy and for the market economy.

The connection between this latter strand of Western metaphysics and the establishing of the modern tradition of democracy is very deep: the abstract principle of human rights had to be acknowledged as a truth if it was to be put into concrete existence in democratic revolutions and reforms. The striving for and the belief in truth is an unavoidable prerequisite of human activity and particularly of that sort of political or even military activity that is directed at the establishing, preserving or reestablishing of democracy. Surely, all political forms presuppose belief in truth on the part of those who fight for them. Hence it follows that the philosophical (and not only the rhetorical) legitimation of democracy is the very root and pillar of democratic consciousness. The thinking of great democrats is deeply rooted in metaphysics (and indeed also in religion)—we can quote in this connection Locke, and the theorists of natural law, but also Masaryk's well-known definition of democracy as "the political materialization of charity".[3]

The real solution of the problem of the interrelation between *episteme* and *doxa* can start from Hayek's conception of the self-limitation of reason:[4] our reason can evidently (through *episteme*) know the boundaries between the sphere of its own justifiable application and the sphere in which it is necessary to leave matters to the functioning of a spontaneous order or to the free play of different political opinions or of individual economic evaluations. In line with Hayek, philosophical reason can be applied only to the legitimization of the basic conditions of the functioning of spontaneous order. But then it must to this extent be applied, and applied with diligency: philosophical reason must defend the objective validity of the basic principles of democracy and of the free market order.

The Austrian Philosophical Tradition: A Preliminary Characterization

Our conception of the relation between democracy and philosophy implies that the inner decay and revolutionary destruction of totalitarianism which arose as a consequence of the realization in practice of Marxist-Leninist philosophy did not proceed automatically in the manner of a spontaneous order and nor, *a fortiori*, will spontaneous order suffice for the political re-establishing of a democratic society. Human activities which result in such political changes must necessarily be led by philosophical ideas and theories. Naturally, these philosophies must be radically different from those of Marxism. This thesis seems to be valid especially in the case of the Czechoslovak "velvet" revolution, which was not a result of unbearable poverty and all-pervasive cruel oppression as was, e.g., the revolution in Rumania.

The philosophical legitimization of the moral, cultural and political rejection of Communist totalitarianism in Czechoslovakia can be understood, in fact, as a continuation of an earlier confrontation between what, at some risk of over-simplification, we can call the *Austrian* and the *German* philosophical traditions.

The Austrian philosophical tradition, which could be more suitably described as the philosophy of the Danube monarchy,[4] is represented by the intellectual development which includes Bolzano and Brentano, Brentano's pupils (Masaryk, the early Husserl, Meinong, Ehrenfels, Marty, Stumpf, Twardowski, etc.) and the early Wittgenstein. This Austrian philosophical tradition stimulated also the remarkable development of Austrian economics from Menger to von Böhm-Bawerk, von Mises and von Hayek.[6]

One aspect of the Austrian philosophical tradition consists especially in its radical criticism of philosophy as this developed in the other German-speaking statelets and principalities. More precisely, it means opposition to German classical philosophy and to those philosophical trends which arose therefrom. This applies initially to the transcendental subjectivism of Kant; in later developments, the critical attitude is more conspicuously directed against the totalitarian spirit of those of Kant's followers who transformed his conception of transcendental subjectivity into various conceptions of super-personal (collective) subjectivity.

However, it has to be said that the anti-totalitarian orientation of the Austrian philosophical tradition is not primarily in the field of political ideas. The Austrian tradition can be seen rather (and again at the risk of some simplification) as the search for ontological fundamentals able to function as a philosophical justification of the liberal and individualistic world view and of the associated approach to democracy. This becomes apparent especially in Brentano's synthesis of Cartesianism and Aristotelianism, which serves in turn as one philosophical starting-point of Masaryk's philosophy of democracy as well as of the liberal approach of the Austrian economists.

The first confrontation between Austrian thinking and Marxism in the field of political and social ideas is documented in Masaryk's famous work on the "Social Question" published in Prague in 1898. Later, this theoretical confrontation came into practical existence in the military fight of the Czechoslovak Legions against Bolshevism in 1918-1920.

The German Philosophical Tradition from Kant to Lukács

What are the causes of the substantially antithetical character of the Austrian and German philosophical traditions as here conceived?

Philosophical traditions serve to provide a more or less conscious ontological and epistemological legitimization of the moral and political goals and tasks which are set by different societies or cultures in different periods of development; the antithetical character of the relations between the Austrian and German philosophers is determined by the fact that their goals and tasks arc radically contradictory.

For concerned Prussians and the other non-Austrian Germans, morally and mentally traumatized by the consequences of the Peace of Westphalia as well as by the humiliating treaty with the Russian Empire, which converted the Prussia of Frederick the Great into a subordinate instrument of Tsarist politics,[6] the establishing and preserving of the centralized state as a unifying totality came to appear as the highest moral and political ideal. The Kantian transcendental subject serves, it is true, only to guarantee the universal validity of objective (scientific) knowledge and of the categorical imperative. In Hegel, however, we find an objectivization of transcendental structures into a totalitarian state entity, so that transcendental philosophy comes to serve a political function. Later, in Marx and Lukács, transcendental subjectivity loses its universal dimension: it is transformed into a (bourgeois or proletarian) collective class consciousness historically conditioned by economic relations.

Both Hegel's theory of the state and the philosophical project of Communist totalitarian society are characterized by the application to history of the Aristotelian idea of *telos*. This consists in the transformation of the unreflected totality of the Hegelian "moral substance" (or of the unreflected totality of the proletarian class) into the politically reflected totality of the state. (According to Marx, the Communist state should be a materialization of philosophical and political class consciousness.) Free individual human activity is from this point of view incorporated into the processes of a dawning self-reflection and self-materialization of the historical *telos* and thus serves merely as an instrument of more deep-seated teleologically founded historical laws. Individual morality is reduced thereby to the status of an epiphenomenon. According to Hegel, individual moral actions are an inferior, rationally unreflected mode of self-realization of a rational, super-personal social reason—a Smithian "unseen hand". Adopting Rousseau's and Kant's idea of autonomy, Hegel asserts that only the state as a form of the fully conscious self-structuring of human society is the real sphere of freedom. Thus, Hegel's theory of the state is an ontological legitimation of the priority of positive law to natural law, and thus also an ontological legitimation of the priority of Machiavellian rational politics in relation to morality. The final consequence of Hegelian degradation of morality is the materialism of Feuerbach, Marx, Engels, Nietzsche, Lenin and Lukács.

In Marx, morality is only a part of class consciousness; in fact it is merely a "superstructural" phenomenon reflecting the economic situation of a certain class. In Lukács' completed formulation of Marxist philosophy, proletarian class consciousness, characterized through its overcoming of "bourgeois" morality and philosophy, strives for the abolition of its own particularity, i.e., for a broadening into universality via what comes down in the end to revolutionary terror and concentration camps. It would be absurd to accuse, e.g., Kant of having brought about this outcome. Yet still, it cannot be denied that Kant's absolute subordination of empirical individuals to the universal transcendental subject as their essence directly implies the "unbearable lightness of being" of individual human beings, and yields a very suitable starting point for the making of holocausts of all kinds.

Hegel's subordination of what he calls "unreflected objective mind" (morality, economics and technology) to the self-reflecting objective mind which is politics deeply influenced all of German thought and culture until the present day. All human activities in which consciousness is not aware of itself as the hidden source of seemingly external objectivity are seen as something secondary and as lacking in full value. The priority of self-reflecting over unreflected consciousness was transformed by later German thinkers into the dichotomy between *Kultur* and *Zivilisation*.[8] According to Thomas Mann, for instance, in his *Betrachtungen eines Unpolitischen*, this dichotomy expresses the substantial difference between Germany and liberal Western societies such as England and France. The *Zivilisation* of the West is abstract, businesslike, materialistic, torn from the inner sphere. *Kultur*, in contrast, a product of the life-world, is rooted in the spirit of the *Volk*; *Zivilisation* is a sphere of objectivistic non-authenticity, of calculation and universal convertibility; *Kultur* is spiritual, authentic life. In German thought the dichotomy between *Kultur* and *Zivilisation* makes itself felt also in the dichotomies of *Gemeinschaft* vs. *Gesellschaft*, *Verstehen* vs. *Erklären*, *Organismus* vs. *Mechanismus*, *Person* vs. *Individuum*, *Dialektik* vs. *Positivismus,* and so on. German national identity, then, was to be based on the endeavor to overcome these dichotomies dialectically, in the form of an organic state totality whose historical task is that of extracting *Lebensraum* from the mechanistic, individualistic and egoistic West. World War I, in accordance with this conception, was interpreted as the war of German *Kultur* against Western *Zivilisation*.

The later Husserl's doctrine of the life-world, too, can be seen against this background. According to this doctrine, the sphere of idealized objects of scientific knowledge was at a certain point in history torn away from the sphere of immediately evident personal experiences via the idealizing activity of our thinking. In Husserl, this historical process is described by the term "sedimentation".[8] Having been torn away from their living sources, the idealized objects of scientific knowledge are incorrectly regarded as forming a purely objective and impersonal basis of subjective experience. In this way, modern man comes to be subordinated to his own product. The fact that the idealized objects of modern scientific knowledge include natural laws implies that people, regarding these laws as a basis of their subjective experiences, come to regard their experience of freedom as a mere "subjective" appearance. Starting from the premise that European culture is based precisely upon the idea of a free and rational structuring of human life (i.e., upon the idea of rational autonomy), Husserl arrives at the conclusion that the misunderstanding of modern science is the main cause of the crisis of modern European man. According to Husserl, the task of transcendental phenomenology consists in finding the original sense of various forms of idealized objects of scientific knowledge through their re-animation in immediate experience; this reanimation unveils the derivative character of the objective sphere in relation to the life-world in a way which would make possible the restoration of European culture on a basis of evident "phenomenological" knowledge.

In the early Heidegger, the motive of Western *Zivilisation* is expressed in terms of the notions of "everydayness" and of "*das Man*", the motive of *Kultur* in terms of "authenticity". Heideggerian authentic *Existenz* can be regarded as transcendence in itself, as absolute transcendence devoid of all positive contents. In criticizing the inauthentic forms of individual existence found in Western civilization, Heidegger radically rejects the Aristotelian foundations of the German philosophical tradition. A human being cannot find its identity in any identification with some social or historical *telos*, but only (as it were) in face-to-face confrontation with the nothingness of its own death. In Heidegger's conception, the only and supreme value consists in the pure structurizing of self without any influence of *das Man*, in the authenticity of the choice of one's own individual life. Human existence in the authentic sense is nothing but an empty structure, a formal *a priori*, which can be filled by any arbitrary contents. It follows that the Heideggerian notion of the authenticity of the self is ethically neutral—existing moral norms, customs and values are merely forms by which the absolutely free (self-structuring) existence is reduced to the objectivity of *das Man*. In Heidegger, the voice of conscience is an incentive to reach one's pure (formal and empty) self-identity.[9] The priority of pure transcendence over all kinds of positive morality, inspired especially by Nietzsche's conception of the superman "beyond good and evil", is then fully in accordance with the spirit of the German philosophical tradition as here conceived. Another expression of this tradition can be seen in Heidegger's rejection of modern science and espe-

cially technology, which he presents as the most desolating form of objectivization of pure transcendence. Heidegger's negative view of science and technology is inspired not only by Ernst Jünger,[10] but also by mystical and irrationalistic
creeds spread during the Nazi era (Hörbiger's theory of the eternal ice, etc.[12]).

The affinity of Heidegger's conception of authenticity with Hegel's conception of political self-structuring as well as with Nietzsche's idea of the bio-
psychic self-structuring of man enabled Marcuse, on the other hand, to connect
the Heideggerian notion of authenticity with Marx's conception of man's self-
production in economic relations, a conception expressed in explicit form in
Marx's early manuscripts first published in Germany in 1932. Later, Marcuse's
Heidegger-Marxism was welded on to Freud's psychoanalysis on the basis of
the affinity of Marx's and Lukács' conceptions of social false consciousness
with Freud's ideas on individual false consciousness. In Marcuse, Fromm, etc.,
this connection of Heidegger-Marxism with Freudianism became an instrument
of the radical criticism of the foundations of Western civilization. A social and
political materialization of this criticism was the left-wing student movement in
the 1960s as well as the sexual revolution which was philosophically legit-
imized as the expression of "authenticity" in the human-biological sphere.

The Austrian Philosophical Tradition: From Bolzano to Popper

As opposed to German idealism, the Austrian philosophical tradition arose
against the background of an established centralistic state. The moral philosophy of Bernard Bolzano (1781-1848) was formed at the beginning of the absolutism of the Metternich era, a time devoid of all remnants of the earlier
Josephinian Enlightenment. However, this was a time also when the moral ideals of the French Revolution were still exerting an impact on the thinking of the
Austrians. (The political circumstances which preceded Brentano's philosophical activity were analogous—the democratic revolution in 1848-49 and the subsequent era of reaction.)

Under such conditions, the main moral and political aim of progressive and
concerned thinkers in Austria was that of reforming the rigid and undemocratic
Habsburg central state and establishing a political and social order which could
guarantee relative autonomy for the different ethnic and social components of
Austrian society. The different forms of Habsburg centralism (both
Metternich's and Bach's absolutism as well as the relatively moderate centralism of the post-Bach period) can from this perspective be seen as having endan-
gered the very basis of the Austrian state by strengthening Czech, Hungarian
and other nationalisms. Modern Czech nationalism, especially, arose as a reaction against the introduction of German as official language in the Czech lands
during the centralistic rule of Joseph II. This is why the birthplace of the liberal-

ly-oriented Austrian philosophical tradition is Bohemia: Bolzano's philosophical activity coincides with the rise and development of that phenomenon which
is known as the Czech National Revival.[13]

The second source of the anti-authoritarian and anti-totalitarian orientation
of Austrian philosophy can be found in the negative stand of Bolzano,
Brentano, Masaryk, etc., in relation to the authority of the Catholic Church, a
relation manifested in Bolzano's conflicts with his superiors, in Brentano's
withdrawal from the priesthood, and in Masaryk's conversion to Protestantism.

The affinity to both British and French thinking, which finds its expression
in the influence of Descartes and Mill on Brentano and of Hume and Comte on
Masaryk, is another important feature of the Austrian philosophical tradition.
Although the historical and political background of the liberal and anti-metaphysical orientation of modern British philosophy is to a certain degree different
from the Austrian philosophical tradition inspired mainly by the national problems of the Austrian monarchy, still there is the common denominator of an
anti-totalitarian and anti-metaphysical orientation, and in this light it is significant that the two traditions are brought together in the work of Hayek and
Popper.

As opposed to Hegel's *étatism*, Austrian philosophers claim that all political structures (the existing as well as the planned—cf. Masaryk's criticism of
Marxism) can and should be subjected to moral criticism. The fact that Bolzano
places morality higher than politics results not only from his critical attitude to
the Austrian state and to the Catholic church but also from his critical attitude to
French revolutionary terror and the Napoleonic wars. From Bolzano's point of
view, these events demonstrated that the materialization of moral ideals through
political and military power is simply not possible. According to Bolzano,
social evil (illustrated for example by the inequality in status of the various different nations in Austria) cannot be abolished politically, but only through a
moral regeneration of the people.[13]

Bolzano's moral utopianism, as well as his criticism of German idealism, is
closely connected with his doctrine of logical Platonism and his conception of
the "proposition in itself". Platonism excludes in its very essence the possibility
of identifying ideas (essences) with any existing reality; thus Platonism is
always a better instrument of moral criticism of really existing society than
Aristotelianism. It is necessary in this connection to mention the analogy
between Bolzano's rejection of Kant's and Hegel's Aristotelianism on the one
side and Wyclif's and Huss' rejection of the Aristotelian philosophy of St.
Thomas on the other. Like Bolzano, Wyclif and Huss adopted Platonism in
order to legitimize philosophically their moral criticism of the Really Existing
Catholic Church.

Bolzano's criticism of German idealism can be characterized as a revival of the famous polemic between Socrates and Plato on the one side and the Sophists on the other. From Bolzano's point of view, Kant's transcendental subjectivism is nothing but a modern version of Protagoras' "man is the measure of all things". In Kant's sophisticated version of the relativism of the Sophists, truth is reduced to the adequacy of the thoughts of the empirical (individual) subject to the structures of *a priori* syntheses of that transcendental subjectivity which is common to all humans (and only to humans). It follows that truth is something which depends on mankind as a whole. This is only a consequence of that central principle of German idealism according to which the being of all that exists (including truth) is teleologically founded in the absolute act of self-reflexion.

The anti-totalitarian character of the Austrian philosophical tradition becomes especially explicit if we compare the Aristotelianism of Franz Brentano (1838-1917), the second founding father of Austrian philosophy, with the Aristotelianism of Hegel and Marx. As opposed to those German thinkers who applied Aristotelian teleology to the development of human society as a whole, Brentano applied Aristotle's ideas to the individual psyche.[14] The synthesis of Aristotelianism with Cartesianism enabled Brentano to produce a variety of individualistic philosophizing in a way which can be seen to have initiated a new era in European thinking.

In Brentano's ethics, morality is not based upon the conscious self-limitation of will as it is in Kant's conception of the categorical imperative. Brentano insists, rather, that there exist acts of correct evaluation (in Brentano's terms "intentional acts of correct loving and hating") which are in many respects analogous to correct judgements.[16] The intentional acts of correct evaluation are such that the immediate reflection upon them is accompanied by an unintentional feeling of pleasure. This feeling of pleasure, being an immanent part of the intentional act of correct evaluation, cannot be consciously influenced by our will. The same is valid also for the unintentional feeling of displeasure which accompanies our incorrect evaluations. Thus, in Brentano, morality is founded in the very nature of individual psychic life (in conscience).

The ethical views of Brentano are more realistic than are those of Bolzano, who verges on moral utopianism. Brentano embraced the utilitarian "principle of summation", but he conceived this principle as deriving from an evident, *a priori* characteristic of correct acts of preferring (i.e., of those acts of preferring which are accompanied by an unintentional feeling of pleasure). We are, he held, able to choose the supreme moral value in every act of preferring, precisely by choosing the highest sum of goods selected from all attainable sums. Correct love, for Brentano, includes our duty to realize the supreme moral value in our practical life. Brentano then stresses that the duty of realizing the supreme moral value should function as a natural sanction of all positive law-making, and in this he worked out deep philosophical foundations of the priority of natural over positive law.

The anti-*étatist* tone typical of Austrian philosophy, too, can be found in Brentano's ethics: he claims that normally the most effective way to further the supreme (attainable) moral value (in Brentano's terms "the overall practical good") is by caring for oneself, and, in concentric circles, for one's own family, city, region, state and so on. In addition to this, Brentano claims that the happiness of the whole of mankind should evidently be preferred to the welfare of the state.

Václav Bělohradský: Really Existing Communism as a System of Impersonal Power

The most important and influential attempts at philosophical interpretation of the system of general mutual coercion and political ritual can be found in the works of Václav Havel and Václav Bělohradský.[16]

The philosophical point of departure of Bělohradský's analysis is Husserl's (and Patočka's) theory of the life-world. According to Bělohradský, both the Nazi and Communist totalitarian systems are results of that process of depersonalization and objectivization of the state, law and politics which started in the Renaissance as a social counterpart of the process of objectivization of nature in modern science. In that process, state power, law and politics are continually broken away from their moral and religious ground; Bělohradský identifies this ground with the life-world, which is in his eyes the sphere of personal, immediate and evident moral and religious experiences. Being torn away from the life-world and being destitute of transcendence, politics becomes a rational science; the modern political and legal system becomes the incorporation of pure, impersonal, objective and technological rationality. Consequently, personal responsibility, conscience and religious experience are reduced to mere "subjective" opinions or appearances. They are thus not qualified to criticize the purely rational and objective politics of the state. Thus modern objective politics, functioning out of the reach of personal conscience, becomes "innocent" in its impersonality. According to Bělohradský, the most monstrous manifestations of impersonal, "innocent" state power are Nazi concentration camps and the Soviet Gulag.[17]

It must be said that Bělohradský's attempt to apply the conception of the life-world to the theory of the modern state is not very successful. It is of course correct that that form of state power which is a materialization of the ideology which reduces morality to a secondary (e.g., superstructural) phenomenon can be at variance with the moral experience of the life-world. Instead of the morality and religiosity of the life-world, however, such ideologies assert the objective validity of such values as "nation" and "economic equality", values which are able to be experienced personally and even morally, too. If the state ideology which asserts such values is a living ideology (as it was in the case of the Nazi state), then the state power based on this ideology will not appear as impersonal. There were totalitarian régimes (e.g., Mussolini's, Hitler's and Stalin's dictatorships) in which people did identify themselves with the person of the charismatic dictator. The motto "*L'état, c'est moi*", expressing the identification of the state with a person, was pronounced already by the absolutist monarch Louis XIV.

Certainly the state machinery *can* appear as something impersonal, but this, I would suggest, will happen only if it is a materialization of an *extinct* false consciousness, i.e., only if the state ideology is so obviously senseless that it has become impossible to identify with it personally. And such extinction is rare: the "technological" (Machiavellian and Cartesian) rationality of the typical modern state can never be torn away completely from the sphere of immediate moral experience.

This is not to deny that the relation of "technological" reason to morality is more problematic than is the immediate unity of rationality and morality in the Platonic-Aristotelian type of rationality. In the era of "technological" reason, the unity of rationality and morality must be mediated through the constructions of philosophical reason: all great modern philosophical systems are expressions of a striving to achieve this unity. The philosophical unification of modern rationality and morality is the basis of all modern ideologies which, in turn, aim at providing a foundation for an existing (or planned) rational state organization in the sphere of perennial values. In this way, the ideological or philosophical legitimization of "technologically" rational social orders gives sense to the social life of modern man.

In his criticism of "impersonal power", Bělohradský starts not only from Husserl's conception of the life-world but also from the theory of "the end of ideologies" of Daniel Bell.[18] In a completely de-ideologized state, the state power would in truth turn naturally into an "impersonal power". Unfortunately however the theory of "the end of ideologies", having started from the incorrect premise of the convergence of the capitalist and Communist systems, is as we now know wholly inadequate to reality.

Václav Havel: Really Existing Communism as a "Post-Totalitarian" System

Havel prefers direct insight to abstract philosophical theories and he analyzes the system of mutual coercion far more accurately than does Bělohradský. Havel makes us aware of the function of extinct ideology in preserving Communist society. According to Havel, ideology is a fundamental system of communication which integrates the whole structure of Communist power; ideology is the "cement" of this structure as well as the instrument of its inner discipline. In order to stress the difference between the "classical" military dictatorship (in which the role of ideology is negligible) and Communist society, Havel characterizes this society by the (not altogether apt) term "post-totalitarian" system. The role of ideology in this system, he argues, makes people subordinated to the "dictate of rituals", rituals which preclude the exercise of free will in all spheres of social activity. Not even leading politicians can exercise their individual will. They, too, act only in accordance with the ideology; they are reduced to mere functions in the "self-movement" of the system. Political power in the "post-totalitarian" system thus becomes anonymous. Living under the dictate of omnipresent political and ideological rituals, all people are both subjects and objects of political control, i.e., both victims and pillars of the post-totalitarian system. Havel sees the post-totalitarian system as a combination of dictatorship and the consumer society. He argues that the fact that people accept the system of mutual political control arises from their being addicted to a certain style of living resting on the availability of (limited supplies of) consumer goods. No particular social group can be regarded as responsible for the form of such a society, for everybody who lives in the post-totalitarian system is more or less responsible for its preservation and reproduction.[19]

These ideas of Havel, first accepted by the representatives of Czechoslovak dissent and later by the masses of the people, became a very important part of the "ideology" of anti-totalitarian revolution in 1989 and they contributed to its nonviolent character. Havel's diagnosis was in this respect fully adequate to the situation in Czechoslovakia: if dissenters and revolutionaries would have threatened Communists with bloody revenge, then the Communists would have defended themselves by all the means at their disposal and this could only have led to a catastrophe.

The Philosophy of Dissent: Jan Patocka[20]

After the Communist revolution in 1948, the prevailing majority of Czechoslovak philosophers accepted Marxist ideology and rejected Masarykian (Western) democracy. Thus Czechoslovak philosophy and culture found itself under the influence of the German philosophical tradition, of Hegel, Feuerbach, and so on. According to Bělohradský, Patočka's introduction of Husserl's and Heidegger's ideas to Czechoslovak philosophy can be regarded as just one further stage of its "Germanization". Bělohradský adds only that Patočka did not accept the German "deification of the state".[21]

However, Patočka's relation to the German philosophical tradition is not so simple as Bělohradský would have it. Bělohradský ignores the fact that in Patočka the conceptual schemes of German philosophy obtained a substantially new, ethical sense, and as a depreciation of the morality of substantial portions of the German philosophical tradition, Patočka's philosophy cannot be unequivocally interpreted as a mere continuation of this tradition.

It was the endeavour to develop ethical versions of Heidegger's idea of human authenticity and of Husserl's theory of the life-world which determined the whole development of Patočka's thinking. The first attempt in relation to Heidegger can be found in Patočka's lectures on Socrates, as well as in his study "Eternity and Historicity", written in the 1950s.[22] Patočka criticizes that sort of metaphysical "eternalism" which prescribes perennial moral goals for man and thus frees him from the necessity to fight for his morality (and thus for his freedom). He criticizes also the emptiness and arbitrariness of the Heideggerian and Sartrian notions of "authentic existence" and introduces instead the conception of the "historical essence of man" in which metaphysical "eternalism" and the negative historicism of the existentialists would be overcome in a higher synthesis. According to Patočka, the perennial and yet historical essence of man consists to that extent in a perennial negativity, in a perennial absence of all that is given positively; this perennial negativity calls on man to self-realization, to make of his life an intrinsically moral task.[23]

Patočka says that it was Socrates who first identified human existence with this task of moral self-realization. However, Patočka begrudges the idea that one might give to this moral task some positive character: moral action for him consists in being not identified with any given instinct, routine, predilection or fancy. This ethical conception of Patočka (which could be called "negative ethics") is based upon a conviction that all evil is rooted in certain given, inertial or "natural" aspects of human life.[24] The good therefore consists in a perpetual negation of all that is given. We can see here that Patočka's "negative ethics" did not really overcome the emptiness of the Heideggerian conception of human authenticity.

Later, Patočka's endeavour to establish the ethical dimensions of human authenticity is expressed in his idea of a unification of what he calls "vertical" and "horizontal" transcendence.[25] Vertical transcendence is defined as man's negative relation towards all given aspects of his existence, something which enables him to go beyond himself through the making of always new goals. Vertical transcendence is thus the way in which man frees himself from *das Man* and gains his authenticity. Horizontal transcendence, on the other hand, consists in a certain active relation towards the world and things, which also enables man to go beyond his limited individual self. In opposition to Heidegger, Patočka says that the orientation towards the world is not identical with being addicted to that which is, i.e., with the attempt to escape from the torture of being aware of one's own mortality by being absorbed in the everyday world of what is given. He stresses that man's striving for authenticity must necessarily be realized through his relation to the world and things. Under the influence of Hegel, he argues that man's going outward from himself is simultaneously a way of returning to his authentic self. Thus horizontal transcendence can be exactly defined as that relation of man to the world and things which provides a determinate way of realizing his striving for authenticity (i.e., of vertical transcendence).[26]

We can see that Patočka's concepts of "vertical" and "horizontal" transcendence express only two inseparable aspects of man's authentic living in the world. In introducing the concept of "horizontal" transcendence, Patočka is trying to avoid the emptiness of the Heideggerian conception of authenticity which excludes the possibility of authentic moral action. Heidegger, according to Patočka, misunderstands the real character of transcendence, and thus he reduces it to its emptied, "vertical" aspect.

Seeing that every practical relation to the world occurs under concrete historical circumstances, Patočka arrives at the conclusion that "horizontal" transcendence connects man's moral striving for "pure" authenticity not only with the sphere of practice but also with history. This conclusion enables him to develop his idea of the historical essence of man. According to Patočka, it is just the unity of "vertical" and "horizontal" transcendence, i.e., the unity of the lasting negative relation of man to all that is and of the changing relation of man to the changing world, which constitutes the lasting and yet historical essence of man.

Care of the Soul

Patočka's ethical treatment of the idea of human authenticity culminates in his conception of the "care of the soul"; which is based on his interpretation of Socrates and Plato, but also on his ethical and political reinterpretation of Husserl's theory of the life-world. Patočka distinguishes three basic dimensions of the life-world:

—the "movement of acceptance" (this movement, manifesting itself especially in love, enables people to accept each other and constitutes the sphere of family relations);

—the "movement of self-sacrifice" (this movement finds its expression in man's eschewing of his immediate animal pleasure; it leads to the constitution of the sphere of work and economy, in which man becomes responsible for his own life);

—the "movement of truth" (which constitutes the sphere of authentic politics and philosophy).[27]

According to Patočka, the most important dimension of the life-world as the sphere of authentic human existence is just that movement of truth which constitutes man's being *zoon politikon*, his being a citizen of the *polis*. Influenced by Hegel's famous interpretation of the myth of Antigone and by Heraclitus' no less famous sentence *"polemos pater panton,"* Patočka argues that the world of authentic politics was born in ancient Greece around 600 B.C. as a consequence of a social struggle which shook the whole of society out of its absorption in the immanent world of family, work and economy and thus ended the traditional, inherited, "natural" and prehistorical submission to the world of everydayness.

Struggle (*polemos*) does not only separate people; it also unifies them as interrelated opposites. Thus on being shaken by the destruction of the values of the world of everydayness, people came to acquire feelings of solidarity which enabled them to establish a *polis* as the authentic sphere of political life.[28] In authentic politics, people do not accept the forms of their social life as something ready and unchangeable; on the contrary, this life is understood as something which can and should be transformed. Man's free production of his own social life in authentic politics (i.e., in political autonomy) is possible only under the condition that he sees this life as a whole and as it really is. In transforming his life, however, man cannot rely upon traditional and mythological interpretations and paradigms, because shaking the immanence of everydayness is identical with bringing about the extinction of mythology (which is something like the ideology of prehistorical everydayness). Man, destitute of the support of myths and traditions, acquires the feelings of uncertainty and wonder (*thauma*); these feelings, connected with man's striving for new foundations of the sense of his life as a whole, result in the arising of philosophy. This, as opposed to mythical reverie, aims at a rational knowledge of the truth. In philosophy, such basic features of authentic politics as autonomy and man's relation to his life as a whole assume an explicit and developed form. (This is why Patočka subordinates authentic political life to what he calls the "movement of truth".)

A philosophical striving to achieve rational knowledge of the truth, being a negative relation to all given and inherited traditions, myths and prejudices, becomes a basic form of man's transcendence. This character of philosophy finds its expression in the fact that philosophy, developing itself in the form of active dialogue, is a sphere of permanently changing interpretations of the sense of human life. The changes in the philosophical interpretation of the sense of human life result in real changes in all spheres of human activity and especially in the sphere of rational politics, for all these spheres are structured with respect to an accepted interpretation of the sense of human life. In this way, the movement of truth in philosophy becomes the motive force of the history of mankind.[29]

Thus the arising of politics and philosophy coincides with the arising of history; the act of struggle, leading to the constitution of both politics and philosophy, founds the historical essence of man.

Through the original "solidarity of the shaken" the citizens of the *polis* begin to compete in an effort to be more beneficial to the public welfare. The fact that rational philosophy is the starting point of political order implies that, in the *polis*, morality manifests itself in people's aiming at the public good and is thus unified with rationality and politics. According to Patočka, the rational structuring of the *polis* in authentic politics is the basic feature of European culture; this character of European culture is especially apparent in the fact that philosophy and rational politics as "new" forms of moral and rational transcendence of the sphere of everydayness displaced orgiastic exaltations as the only prehistorical form of transcendence.

The birth of history in a sphere of authentic politics is identical with the birth of the historical essence of man as the unity of "vertical" and "horizontal" transcendence. In his "Heretical Essays", Patočka gives "vertical" transcendence the new name 'care of the soul' with a view to stressing the moral contents of human authenticity as well as the connection to the ethical philosophy of Socrates. "Horizontal" transcendence, in turn, is identified with authentic politics amalgamated with morality, i.e., with the "care of the *polis*". And now the care of the soul, performed especially in philosophy, cannot be separated from the care of the *polis*. Authentic life, then, consists in a sacrifice of self for the public good.

Patočka's ethical conception of the life-world (which includes, now, also authentic politics as the expression of the care of the soul) can be regarded also as a philosophical basis of natural law in confrontation with positive law.

From the standpoint of Patočka's ethical conception of the life-world, the Communist system of general mutual coercion, in which absurd pseudo-political rituals are substituted for authentic politics, is nothing but the alienation of the authentic historical essence of man. This alienation, being expressed in the fact that the mythology of inertial everydayness displaced the existential and political "movement of truth", is identical with the return to a prehistorical style of life. (Following Patočka, Havel argues that the non-historicity of living in the Communist system leads to the absence of dramatic situations in human life and to the banality of life under Communist rule.[30]) The only way of reviving the authentic historical essence of man is by bringing about a repetition of that original act of transcendence in which history and authentic politics were constituted. This means that, given that the making of authentic politics is impossible, the only solution is the renewal of the "movement of truth" on the basis of what Patočka called the "solidarity of the shaken".

Writing his "Heretical Essays" in the early 1970s (i.e., in the era of "normalization" when it seemed that no anti-totalitarian movement could be successful), Patočka considered that the only stimulus which could shake the people and break them out of their "prehistorical" everydayness is the eternal threat of global military conflict.[31] According to Patočka, the solidarity of the shaken is able to say "no!" to the conditions which render global military conflict possible. (This means especially that they are able to say "no!" to the aggressive ideology and politics of Communist totalitarianism.) However, Patočka remains loyal to his conception of "negative morality": the solidarity of the shaken should not trace out any positive program; like Socrates' *daimonion*, the voice of the shaken should utter only warnings and interdictions.

Patočka's negative programme is nevertheless in full accordance with the idea of the defence of human rights, which implies saying "no!" to the omnipresent interventions of totalitarian state power.[32] The defence of human rights is a defence of man's freedom from state power. Regarding the programme of the defence of human rights as a practical consequence of the idea of "care of the soul" via "care of the *polis*", Patočka comes close to Sartre, according to whom the only authentic aim of authentic human activity is defending and extending the sphere of freedom.

Naturally, under the rule of the Communists, "care of the *polis*" leads necessarily to persecution and suffering. But, according to Patočka, "life is worth living only if there exist things which are worth dying for". Like Socrates, Patočka materialized his philosophy in his own life and death. Patočka's death, being a consequence of ruthless police interrogation, revived the Socratic ideal of authentic philosophy which requires a unity of knowing truth and living in truth. In addition, the Communist state power disturbed the dignity of Patočka's burial in a monstrous way, thereby revealing the extent to which it was at odds with even the most sacred norms of human life.

Taking into account the fact that Masaryk, under the influence of Bolzano, Havlícek and Brentano, was the first who understood that the struggle for the authenticity of the nation through the fight against mendacious myths is primarily a moral task, we must conclude that Patočka's ethical treatment of both the theory of the life-world and the Heideggerian conception of human authenticity can be interpreted as a return of the idea of human authenticity to its original Austrian roots. Aiming at a philosophical legitimization of resistance against the totalitarian system, Patočka (like Sartre before him) had necessarily to get at the original ethical ("Austrian") background of the idea of human authenticity. It could be objected that, in regarding politics as the "right" sphere of human transcendence, Patočka is a follower of Hegel. But we should not forget that

Patočka (in line with Masaryk) identifies authentic politics with the manifestation of goodness. The Socratic and Platonic motives in Patočka's philosophy are also significant marks of his affinity to the spirit of the Austrian philosophical tradition. Patočka's programme of moral criticism of totalitarian power, connected with his abnegation of all participation in "alienated" pseudo-politics, is deeply rooted in Bolzano's, Havlícek's and Masaryk's theory and practice of "unpolitical politics". Thus it was just the fundamental motives of the Bolzanian-Brentanian-Masarykian tradition in which Patočka's philosophy culminated and which enabled it to become the instrument of anti-totalitarian criticism. It can be said that, in the long run, Patočka's philosophy enriched the Austrian philosophical tradition with those elements of German philosophy which were compatible with the anti-metaphysical style of central European thinking.

The Philosophical Meaning of Havel's Plays

In treating Havel's philosophy, we must first of all mention the philosophical dimensions of his plays. In his famous dramas "Garden Party" and "Memorandum", Havel presents the mechanisms of functioning of the extinct Communist false consciousness. His criticism concerns especially the Communist bureaucracy and its main instrument—a "newspeak" devoid of all authentic sense. In Havel, the absurdity of such rigorously consistent, logically structured ideological systems as the dogmatic Stalinist version of Marxism-Leninism, systems which are divorced from reality and yet really function, is presented in the form of absurd drama. Later, in "Audience", Havel shows the means by which the totalitarian system preserves and reproduces itself through the concerns and interests of everyday life, in which a deification of the stars of pop music and film displaces authentic transcendence.

Havel's philosophy of dissent, expressed in his essay "The Power of the Powerless", arose under the influence of Patočka's ideas. Havel differs from Patočka however in a number of important aspects. Being more realistic than Patočka (and thus more closely connected to the heritage of Havlícek and Masaryk), Havel supplements Patočka's philosophical scheme of the "movement of truth" with an analysis of the concrete mechanisms of the functioning of totalitarian power and of dissent under the rule of the Communist system. Havel's analyses of the functioning of totalitarian power can be seen as the philosophical counterpart of his plays.

In "The Power of the Powerless" Havel observes especially the "anti-existential" dimensions of Communist ideology.[33] As a complex, coherent, logically structured and therefore understandable system (comparable with a secularized religion), the Communist ideology comprehends within itself a set of ready replies to all possible questions. Upon accepting this ideology, man delivers himself of all existential and metaphysical uncertainties and anxieties; his world becomes clear, lucid and full of sense. The price, however, is a loss of his personal conscience, responsibility and reason. Consequently, the acceptance of Communist ideology is a form of the "Fall". This analysis, however, which ought to have explained the causes of mass acceptance of Marxist ideology, omits the utopian dimensions of Marxist false consciousness as well as its affinity to the "bad" nature of man.

Nevertheless Havel shows that the majority of people in "post-totalitarian" societies do not believe in ideological schemes as these had been transformed into absurd rituals. According to Havel, people who allow themselves to become addicted to the life of average everydayness and who submit themselves to the system of mutual coercion are living a lie.[34] But, Havel stresses, "living a lie" can never annihilate its opposite which is "living in truth". As opposed to Heidegger (and also to Patočka), Havel asserts that the striving for truth, for human dignity, and for human rights, is a necessary attribute of the human essence. He argues, in other words, that man can be alienated only if there is something which he is alienated from.[35]

Thus in Havel the idea of human authenticity is delivered from its existentialist emptiness. It is not man's being aware of his mortality which leads him to truth and authenticity. Rather, the Heideggerian negative unveiling of truth is replaced with a positive striving for truth and human dignity. This positive "authentic intention" of human life (which is nothing but the "good" nature of man) can be suppressed, but it can never be totally destroyed. Beneath the decent surface of "living a lie" is the hidden sphere of "living in truth". (It is evident that from the standpoint of orthodox existentialism, Havel's optimistic conception of man must be dismissed as metaphysical.)

According to Havel, the indestructibility of the striving for truth is confirmed by the fact that Communist ideology can function only under the pretence of its being true and rooted in the "human order". The system of "living a lie" functions only on the basis of the assumption that its sphere is universal and omnipresent; it is not able to bear the co-existence of living in truth. Every departure from living a lie denies it as a principle and endangers it as a whole. If somebody is living in truth (i.e., is identical with his essence) and thereby disturbs the complex and omnipresent tissue of ideological lies, the rules of the game are broken and the game is unveiled as such, i.e., as a *mere* game.

Consequently, the idea of "living in truth" has not only an existential dimension (consisting in man's returning to himself) and a noetical dimension (which enables him to discover the true character of reality); it also has a clear political dimension, in virtue of the fact that mere truth functions as a political power.[36] Naturally, purely theoretical or contemplative truth cannot function in such a way; only the practical (public) manifestation of a recognized truth (e.g., in the form of refusing to participate in the absurd ritual of Communist "elections") can disturb the tissue of lies.

Believing in the impossibility of a total destruction of what is good in man, Havel is persuaded that there exist certain limits to the alienation of humanity. If totalitarian power exceeds these limits, than man's alienation becomes unbearable, in a way which necessarily leads to the overthrow of the system responsible. Truth and love must thus necessarily win over lies and hatred. The fact that Havel never ceased to believe in the good in man implies that his thinking, notwithstanding the fact that it was influenced by existentialism, is deeply rooted in Czech humanism, one constitutive part of the Austrian philosophical tradition. Havel is, as already pointed out, a follower of Masaryk, who made the old Hussite motto "the truth prevails" the motto of the Czechoslovak presidents and who, under the influence of Brentano's ethics, stated that the feeling of humanity and charity is an innate and inherent attribute of man. As in the case of Patočka, the most important part of Havel's philosophy results directly from the heritage of the Austrian philosophical tradition. Havel's conception of the "power of the powerless" is (just like Patočka's programme for the defence of human rights) a continuation of Bolzano's, Havlícek's and Masaryk's conception of "unpolitical politics" or "small work".[37]

The Philosophy of Living Sub Specie Aeterni

In "Letters to Olga" which deal with many philosophical problems, Havel's affinity to the Austrian philosophical tradition is expressed in the clearest way. The letters were written in a Communist prison. Thus they serve as a proof of the great spiritual power of their author as well as a manifestation of the original function of philosophy as an ontological legitimization of moral attitudes and feelings; in performing this function, philosophy supports man's moral resolve.

In "Letters to Olga", Havel's philosophical reflexions concern especially the ethical interpretation of both the idea of human authenticity and the Heideggerian conception of being. Following Emanuel Lévinas, Havel argues that human authenticity and even the identity of the individual self can be based only upon responsibility.[38] According to Havel, man finds himself in responsibility sooner than his ability to choose and decide arises. Being responsible means nothing other than: standing as guarantee for oneself in time; being responsible, man is resolved existentially to confirm and plead for all his past, present and future attitudes. In Havel, the universal character of responsibility consists in man's being-in-the-world; man can never avoid the presence of the world which is "imbued" with being as its absolute horizon.[39] Havel therefore attempts to connect the ethical foundations of human authenticity with the conception of being of the late Heidegger. This attempt results again in an ethical interpretation of this conception: being, as the absolute horizon, is identical with the moral order. Being is not only the "reason" of all that is, but also "the voice" and "call".[40]

According to Havel, the individualized self arises from the "before-self" which is directly connected with the fullness of all-embracing being.[41] The original rootedness of the "before-self" in being implies its appurtenance to all that is, and this original unity of the "before-self" and being finds its expression in the fact that the "responsibility for all things" is an essential intention of the "before-self". Being the background from which the mature and individualized self arises, the "before-self" enables the self to hear the voice of being. The before-self is, then, nothing other than man's conscience, in which infinite and perpetual being speaks to man and drives him to be responsible for all things. Moreover, in speaking to man, being as an infinitely great "heart" of all that is, assumes a personal face.[42]

Havel concludes that living in this world in a bearable manner is possible only under the condition that humanity in its here and now relates to the infinite, to the absolute and to eternity.[43] Havel's interest in Heidegger's conception of being results from the fact that this conception implies the rejection of the idea of the universal achievability of all goods and projects and thus the preserving of the mystery (and non-calculability) of the world. Havel is inspired by the fact that the inexhaustibility of being sets insuperable bounds to the "fatal conceit" of "constructivist rationality". It was this idea, above all, which led him to transform Heidegger's conception of being into a philosophical basis for the criticism of the Communist system, a system which is based precisely upon the idea that all goods can be achieved through the political materialization of philosophical reason.[44]

In the frame of this criticism, which includes also certain ecological motives, the Communist system is understood as a consequence of the inadmissible reduction of being to "substance" in Marxist metaphysics. (Although Havel's criticism is similar to Hayek's rejection of constructivist rationality, its being connected with the Heideggerian criticism of Western civilization makes Havel unable to accept Hayek's positive idea of "spontaneous order").

The rejection of the idea of universal (Faustian) achievability was one of the main aims of Masaryk's criticism of Romantic Titanism and in his ethical treatment of the Heideggerian conception of being, Havel in fact finds himself close to Masaryk's attempt at a philosophical solution to the crisis of modern man. In Havel, being, interpreted as the source of moral transcendence, and consequently as the basis of human authenticity, plays the same role as God (or Jesus) in Masaryk's philosophy. For, man can escape the objectless void which would result from the total unification of subject and object only under the condition that there is being (or God) which (or who) transcends all possible forms of the unity of subject and object. Being imprisoned and yet free spiritually, Havel revealed that 'living in truth' is identical with living *sub specie aeterni.*

"Parallel Polis" and the "Velvet" Revolution

The conception of "parallel *polis*" arose as a philosophical reflexion of existing forms of anti-Communist dissent in the countries of the Soviet bloc; it includes also an attempt at defining the tactics and the positive strategic aims of the anti-totalitarian movement.

According to Havel, the term "dissenter" is very problematic because its meaning in Latin is "apostate".[45] Havel stresses that dissenters do not apostatize or lapse from anything; on the contrary: they are returning to themselves. At the most, they have lapsed from "living a lie". Havel thus argues that being a dissenter is not a specific profession which would consist in professional malcontent and which could be chosen like other professions. Dissent is an existential attitude which does not comprehend the intention of being a dissenter. Moreover, this existential attitude is proper not only to well-known "dissenters" in the conventional sense of the word, but also to thousands of anonymous others. Thus dissent is not the business of an isolated group of publicly active and well-known people (especially intellectuals); rather, it arises from a sphere called the "independent life of society".[46] According to Havel, "living in truth" takes on this "independent life" if it exceeds the bounds of "mere" individual revolt and becomes purposeful and structured work which is materialized in manifest activities. The sphere of the "independent life of society" is very extensive. It comprehends independent self-education, free cultural production and its distribution through the mediation of *samizdat*, free citizens' engaging in independent social organizations, etc. Havel stresses that dissent is not possible without some background in the "independent life of society" and is in fact only the most visible and most clearly articulated and (seemingly) the most political manifestation of this "independent life".

Concerning the tactics of dissent, Havel asserts that it must be based upon the principle of legality.[47] The dissenters' programme of "unpolitical politics", consisting in the defence of human and citizens' rights against interventions of state power (i.e., in exerting public moral pressure on the totalitarian power in order to drive it to keeping the obligations it had assumed in Helsinki) implied that the dissenters themselves had to respect all existing norms of "Socialist law" with total consistency. Following Solzhenitsyn, according to whom "living in truth" is the only possible form of resistance against Communist totalitarian power, Havel argues that in "post-totalitarian" society no conspiracies or terrorist actions can be successful. In a totalitarian system which disposes of perfect mechanisms of both direct and indirect supervision of the whole of society, illegal resistance of all kinds is not only hopeless from the political point of view but also impossible technologically.

It can be said that Havel's stressing the principle of legality is inspired not only by Solzhenitsyn's ideas but also by the Realistic heritage of Havlícek and Masaryk, and the dissenters' programme of defence of human rights was also in accordance with Brentano's idea of the "highest attainable good".

In addition, Havel grounds his justification of the principle of legality in his analysis of the function of law in "post-totalitarian" society. According to Havel, the main function of the Communist legal system consists in its being an "alibi", i.e., in its giving seeming legitimization to the "vulgar" exercise of totalitarian power. Simultaneously, it functions as a necessary instrument of inner ritual communication of totalitarian power. But notwithstanding the fact that everybody knows the buck-passing character of the totalitarian legal system, the invoking of the law makes deep sense because it reveals the ritual and mendacious character of the system itself. Moreover, the invoking of the law drives all who take shelter behind the "alibi" of the legal system to the hardening of this alibi and to the striving to make it more credible. Naturally, Havel knows that the results of the invoking of "Socialist lawfulness" are very restricted; but being inspired by Masaryk's idea of small work, he asserts that these restricted results (consisting in the fact that the lives of a few persecuted citizens became more bearable) are more important than abstract solutions on the level of principles.

Developing the ideas of the Czech philosopher Václav Benda, who is the author of the term "parallel *polis*", Havel argues that, since totalitarian power divests all those who are "living in truth" of all possibilities of self-assertion and of participation in existing social structures, this leads to the transfer of the social dimensions of human activity into the sphere of the "independent life of society"—which means that this sphere itself assumes the character of a social structure[48]—it becomes a parallel society. Havel states that the structuring of the sphere of the "independent life of society" manifested itself first in the "second culture", the theoretician and practitioner of which was rock musician and poet Ivan Martin Jirous. Later, the "second culture" comprehended also other forms of independent art as well as humanities and philosophy. The social structuring of independent cultural activities resulted in the arising of elementary organizational forms of the "second culture" such as *samizdat* editions and journals, apartment theatres, apartment universities, private concerts and exhibitions, etc.

Reflecting the development of this parallel culture, Benda assumed that parallel social structures will also develop in other spheres of human activity; thus he forecast the arising of parallel education (private universities), parallel information networks, parallel trade unions, parallel contacts with foreign countries, a parallel economy, etc. All these parallel structures in their interrelations will become a basis for the forming of a "parallel *polis*", which will of course comprehend also all authentic political life.

According to Havel, this "parallel *polis*" should not be regarded as a form of taking refuge in an isolated ghetto; on the contrary, it should become the most suitable basis for deepening the responsibility of the whole society. Moreover, Havel argues that the "parallel *polis*", based as it is upon an existential revolution, is not only the starting point of the abolition of the totalitarian system; it is also the only possible way out of the crisis of modern civilization.

Accepting Heidegger's criticism of Western technological civilization, Havel asserts that the self-movement of the totalitarian system is only an extreme version of the global self-movement of the "planetary" power of technology. This self-movement finds its expression in the fact that man ceases to be master of his own situation. In agreement with Heidegger, Havel is persuaded that Western (pluralistic) democracy is not able to face the self-movement of technological, industrial and consumer society. He assumes that the freedom of asserting authentic human intentions in Western democracy only covers up the crisis of modern man, which results in man's inability to reveal his own situation of crisis. This implies that people in democratic societies are more absorbed by the crisis than people who live under totalitarian régimes. Thus Havel casts radical doubt upon the belief that traditional pluralistic democracy as a "well-tried" political form could guarantee man's dignity and his capacity to manage his own affairs. Havel appreciates also Solzhenitsyn's criticism of Western civilization which concerns especially the supposedly illusory character of democratic civil liberties.

According to Havel, the only solution to the general ("technological") crisis of modern man consists in an existential revolution which will lead to a moral re-constitution of society, i.e., to the radical revival of the "human order". This existential revolution presupposes a new experience of being as well as a new understanding of man's higher responsibility for other men and for his community. Havel believes that the mode of political materialization of this existential revolution could be based on the experience of "parallel *polis*"; thus the moral revival of society should be realized through social structures which are unified by a commonly shared experience in the full sense, instead of by commonly shared ambitions directed "outwards". Such structures should be open, dynamic and small; they should arise from below as a consequence of social self-organization.

Havel stresses that traditional (formalized) political parties must be replaced by new organizations and movements which, being enthusiastic about achieving their goals and unified by the common involvement of their participants in the given situation, would arise *ad hoc* and then fall away after these goals had been achieved. This conception of communities unified by common experience is applied also to economic life in a way which leads to the project of an economic self-government which would arise from people's responsibility for the results of their common work.

The existential and moral revolution against the "post-totalitarian" system should thus lead to the arising of a completely new social order which, being based on "living in truth", would displace not only parliamentary democracy but also the market order. According to Havel, this new social order is characterized as a "post-democratic" system.[49] Havel's analyses imply that only the unbearable fact of living under a totalitarian tissue of lies can drive man to a radical turn to his own essence. "Living in truth" under the rule of a totalitarian system which is an extreme outcome of the crisis of modern man enables man to reject not only the false consciousness of Communist ideology but also the empty and illusory liberties of pluralistic democracy. Havel assumes that a "parallel *polis*", being a social expression of "living in truth", will arise in all political systems which deprive man of his personal responsibility.

Havel's optimistic conception of the human essence implies that the replacing of the existing order of the world with a "post-democratic" system will be asserted not politically or through instruments of power; rather, the "post-democratic" system will arise from the free decisions of a people who will cease to accept life under systems which are not adequate to the authentic human essence. (Havel always stressed that dissenters do not want to *lead* other people politically: those who are "living in truth" should at most inspire others, whose choice is then left for their own free consideration.)

Havel's conception of a "post-democratic" society can in this respect be regarded as a direct continuation of Bolzano's moral utopianism. In Havel, the Bolzanian philosophical heritage is enriched with the ideas of Masaryk, Husserl, Heidegger, the early Marx, Sartre and Patočka. Being under the influence of Heidegger's criticism of Western civilization, Havel leaves Masaryk's realistic idea of the moral revival of the existing form of democracy and replaces it with the project of a "post-democratic" society. Appreciating Heidegger's statement "Only some God is able to save us", Havel is also close to the Czech philosopher Rio Preisner who asserts that the only way out of that modern nihilism which manifests itself both in totalitarianism and liberal democracy is a return to true Christianity.[50]

The "Velvet" Revolution and Philosophy

Notwithstanding the utopian character of Havel's programme, the origin and course of the "velvet" revolution in Czechoslovakia seem to verify the conception of "unpolitical politics". The expelling of reform Communists (especially intellectuals) from the Czechoslovak Communist Party after 1968 precluded a reform from above in the style of Soviet "perestroika" or of the Kádárian "quiet" reform in Hungary.[51] After Gorbachov's rise to power, the Czechoslovak Communist bosses made only a pretense of embracing "perestroika"; having personally been involved in that neo-Stalinist politics of "normalization" which suppressed the reform movement in the Czechoslovak Communist Party, they could not accept Gorbachov's reform ideas, for these were similar to the programme of the very Czechoslovak reform Communists which they themselves had earlier suppressed. After the relatively recent purge in the Communist Party, no Czechoslovak "Gorbachov" was possible. It should be stated that Havel's optimistic conception of the human essence implies the necessity of such a person as Gorbachov arising in society; but in Czechoslovakia, a new "Gorbachov" (or a new "Dubček") could have come only after the change of generations in the Communist Party. Nevertheless, people's awareness of the fact that Soviet power did not support the politics of the Czechoslovak neo-Stalinists was the most important factor in the activation of the anti-totalitarian movement.

Taking into account the fact that the existing non-Communist parties in Czechoslovakia, being a specific form of the "alibi" of totalitarian power, were fully subordinated to the politics of the Communist Party itself, we must arrive at the conclusion that the abolition of the Czechoslovak Communist régime was not something that was able to be brought about in the frame of the official forms of political life. This means that the only form of change of the social system in Czechoslovakia was a radical abolition of the political system as a whole through mass revolutionary action. For if the top of the system of mutual coercion is immune to the striving for "living in truth", then this system can be destroyed only under the condition that great masses of people all at once cease to perform the roles which the system prescribes.

But under the rule of totalitarian power, masses can become prepared for revolutionary action only through "unpolitical politics", i.e., only through an inner moral revolution. However, the fact that a moral revolution occurs in the heart of man implies that the co-ordination of public manifestations of moral revolution is very problematic. Before the revolution, the main form of the spontaneous timing of joint actions were anniversaries (The anniversary of the heroic deed of Jan Palach, especially, functioned as a stimulation to joint public manifestation of the inner moral resolve of isolated individuals.)

The majority of people participating in pro-democratic demonstrations were young people who had not personally experienced the trauma of Soviet occupation in 1968, i.e., people who "did not know that it is impossible to make revolution".[52] But, in consequence of the relative economic welfare in

Czechoslovakia, the number of protesters was never higher than 10,000. (It is known that a demostration of about 100,000 people cannot be suppressed effectively by the police.) Nevertheless, the brutality of violent suppression of demonstrations in October 1988 and January 1989 evoked deep disgust for totalitarian power among the greater part of the Czechoslovak citizenry. The suffering of demonstrators beaten by the police—who were not only members of the "parallel *polis*" but also ordinary people manifesting their right to "live in truth"—was therefore not useless; it publicly revealed the "vulgar" character of totalitarian power.

Now we must quote the prophetic words of Josef Safařík, an excellent Czech philosopher whose work "Seven Letters to Melin" deeply influenced the thinking of Havel: "If moral example and mutual moral influence among people are not sufficient, there is no other way of shaking and awakening the human heart than tragedies, catastrophes and apocalyptic fury."[53] The extremely brutal suppression of the students' demonstration on 17 November 1989 (comparable with the Nazi terror against Czech students in November 1939) as well as the news of the assassination of a student by policemen were just such a manifestation of the apocalyptic fury of the totalitarian régime and were enough to awaken the moral consciousness of the majority of Czechoslovak citizens and drive them to participating in mass demonstrations all over Czechoslovakia.

This evidently suicidal character of the last gasp of totalitarian power led to the arising of a hypothesis according to which the beating of the students on 17th November and the spreading of the (untrue) rumour about the assassination of one of them was organized by the bosses of State Security who, acting in agreement with the Soviet KGB, aimed at using the people's revolt to install new, pro-reform Communist leaders. In accordance with another interpretation, the massacre of the students resulted from a secret conspiracy of prominent dissenters and Communist leaders; this conspiracy was to have guaranteed the Communists' being let off unpunished as well as the preserving of their economic power. This interpretation would imply that "authentic" politics, being in need of an organizational dimension, compensated for this by a colossal act of manipulation. Having recognized Havel's philosophical conception of the human essence according to which the good in man must necessarily win, however, we can state that Havel's participation in any such conspiracy is at the most doubtful; the advantage of that speeding up of the revolution which Havel held to be necessary could not have compensated for the betrayal of all the basic principles of his life.

In the course of the "velvet" revolution, the anti-totalitarian movement was structured in line with Havel's project of "post-democratic" politics. The "Civic Forum" as well as the Slovak movement "Public Against Violence" were originally groups of people who were unified by their "entering" into a revolutionary situation and who shared the experience of authentic human existence. The original "Civic Forum" was an association of people of different political views who were brought together through their common interest in the abolition of the totalitarian system.

The "velvet" revolution, having arisen as an expression of total moral disgust[54] with totalitarian power and its representatives, was a revolt of moral consciousness. Using Aristotle's term, we could say that the function of Havel's, Patočka's and Masaryk's philosophy in the "velvet" revolution consisted in its giving the form to the matter of a moral consciousness in revolt. Thus it was precisely the heritage of Czech humanism (and of the Austrian philosophical tradition associated therewith) which determined and shaped the humane or "velvet" character of the Czechoslovak anti-totalitarian revolution. The main slogans of the "velvet" revolution (e.g., the slogan "We are not like them!" which expressed the attitude of the revolutionary masses to the methods of Communist pseudo-politics) arose against the background of the philosophy of dissent. Concerning Havel's moral utopianism, its great historical significance can be seen in the fact that the strategic goals of moral utopianism were able to be accepted and embraced by the prevailing majority of Czechoslovak citizens (including honest ordinary Communists). For the "velvet" revolution was able to assume its mass character only under the condition that the main aim of revolutionary activity was defined as a re-establishing of fundamental *moral* values. In Czechoslovakia, where Socialist ideas were deeply rooted in the thinking and attitudes of the masses, a direct orientation of unrestrained revolutionary activity to the re-establishing of the capitalist system was simply not possible.

The fact that philosophers like Patočka, Hejdánek, Benda, R. Palous, M. Palous, Kosik, etc. played a very important role in Czechoslovak dissent, as well as the fact that some of them participated directly in the revolution, led to the revival of people's confidence in philosophy and other kinds of intellectual activity. The majority of people in Czechoslovakia had hitherto known philosophy only in the form of that dogmatic Marxist philosophy which had resulted in a depreciation of philosophy as such. It can be said that Czechoslovak intellectuals (philosophers, writers, artists, actors, etc.), being the most important part of the anti-totalitarian movement, atoned for the historical treason of older generations of Czechoslovak intellectuals who were not able to resist the influence of Communist and Socialist ideas. However, it was not only the activity of intellectuals which introduced philosophical ideas into mass consciousness; some remnants of the ideals of Czech humanism had been able to survive in deep levels of the national consciousness also independently.

The Decay of "Unpolitical Politics" and the Tasks of Philosophy

After the "velvet" revolution, the real development of the economic and political situation destroyed the dissenters' dream of the moral revival of mankind through "unpolitical politics".

For the transition from the system of planned economy to a free market system through the general privatization of nationalized property is necessarily accompanied by a revival of some of the putatively immoral features of early capitalism. The necessity of rekindling certain elements of the early-capitalist era rests on the fact that the system of collective ownership and of totalitarian politics involved a return to pre-historical forms of economic and social life. Thus the "cultivated" form of capitalism could not be realized as a "step back" from the Communist position, but only in the form of a compressed repetition of the entire history of civilized mankind.

Like the first capitalists in England, the first Czechoslovak capitalists were mostly people who had grown rich in a non-capitalist way. Thus they were especially the former Communist bosses (who used their political power to effect an unlawful appriopriation of state property); they were state officials who had access to important economic information; or they were pilferers, swindlers, underhand money-changers and thieves. But the "dirty money" of those people as well as their ruthlessness, their rapacity and their "entrepreneurial spirit" were and are in fact necessary for the rapid establishing of a free market system. People who, working honestly for wages, have no chance of coming into the possession of capital, can immediately see that the new economic system favours immorality instead of honest work. The substitution of the immorality of early capitalism for totalitarian immorality is reflected in feelings of despair and in moral resignation and scepticism. An expression of the hopelessness of post-Communist society is the well-known *bon mot* "God is dead, Marx too, and still I do not feel any better", which concerns especially the feelings of intellectuals previously oriented to Socialist ideals. Artists, also, affected by the disgusting commercialization of cultural production which results from the new restrictive financial politics suffer from the banality and spiritless character of a time when endeavour to attain the average Western standard of welfare has turned into an almost hysterical drama. The substantially banal character of post-Communist times arises from the fact that the great and dramatic effort to re-establish the free market system is only a repetition of history.

In the early capitalist period, the system of power of the absolutistic monarchy as well as the strict norms of religious (Protestant) ethics, moderated the wild rush for money to some degree. In the post-Communist era, in contrast, the wild egoism of homo oeconomicus, being not moderated by any "higher" metaphysical and religious values, is directly reflected in the sphere of political struggle. Under such conditions, "unpolitical politics", aiming only at public welfare and representing no particular economic and political interests, become impossible. For in the system of multi-party democracy every single party has to relate its project of public welfare with the particular interests of some group or class; otherwise it cannot win elections. The general projects of public welfare of the different political parties are so similar that the voters prefer that party which clearly expresses his group or class interests or enables him to be in personal contact with political representatives. In a pluralistic democracy, no political body representing only the "pure" interests of the *volonté générale* is possible.

Moreover, when the dissenters became the establishment, people started to lose their confidence in the sincerity of dissenters' conduct. This implied that the philosophical ideas of dissent, being on the same level with other current political phrases, were discredited, too. If it is generally known that every political party connects its project of public welfare with particular interests, then the program of "unpolitical politicians" accompanied with a strictly moral philosophy, appears as an especially disgusting hypocrisy. (Now, only Havel, having decided to remain superior to party politics, asserts the principles of moral revolution.)

In addition, the loose organizational structure of such movements as the "Civic Forum" or "Public against Violence" precluded their being successful in competition with other "classically" organized political parties. Eventually, the Civic Forum, being a group of people unified only by their negative attitude to the Communist régime, had necessarily to divide into two "classical" political parties because of the fact that its members were of different views as to the positive political and economic tasks.

That conception of "unpolitical politics" which arose in the situation of an absence of political freedom and which was successful in the fight against a totalitarian régime, loses its hold in a free democratic society since it cannot take the form of a particular political program. Naturally, Masaryk's (and also Havel's) specific program of "unpolitical politics", of destroying all kinds of false myths and ideological lies in order to educate the whole society, can be realized in the post-Communist era, too. However, it can be realized only under the condition that those who criticize generally accepted lies do not speak out in the name of any political party, and indeed Masaryk's own Realistic Party was able to be successful in elections only via some alliance with a "classical" party; after the establishing of a functioning system of pluralistic democracy in 1918 the Realistic Party, consisting of people of different political views, melted away.

The failure of Havel's program of "unpolitical politics" is a consequence of the extreme optimism of both Havel's and Patočka's philosophy of man. Patočka and Havel, stressing the good in man and identifying man's essence with pure existential and moral transcendence in a way which "dilutes" all given and inherited characters of man, depreciated the real potency of such attributes of human existence as the will to power and to ownership. Living in a dissenter's ghetto, they did not observe that their conception is not adequate to "ordinary" man, who is typically able to transcend the "bad" dimensions of his existence only in the "limit" situations, i.e., in situations in which his will to power and to the accumulation of possessions enters into an extreme conflict with the highest moral values.

Consequently, real democratic politics cannot be identified with Patočka's "authentic politics", a philosophical idealization of the ancient Greek polis. The very fact that the divorce of politics from morality (*moeurs*) was realized in history is a proof of the impossibility of the reduction of politics to a public manifestation of the "good" nature of man.

No political system can be based upon purely moral qualities of man. (It was often argued that the Communist system would function if people were ideally good.) The idea of a political system must take into account both the good and bad sides of human nature.

It is precisely the political system of liberal (pluralistic) democracy, the "unseen hand" of which is able to transform the egoistic *libido dominationis* into public welfare. The character of this system implies that if political representatives want to win the next elections, they must necessarily work for public welfare. Being free in his decisions, the democratic politician is coerced to working for the public welfare only through his inner political aspirations, i.e., only by his desire to preserve his position. By transforming individual economic egoisms into the satisfaction of the needs of the whole society, the "unseen hand" of the market economy performs *mutatis mutandis* the same functions as the system of liberal democracy in the sphere of politics.

Man can become free (i.e., free from external authoritative coercion to the performance of prescribed activities) only if the materialization of his inner egoistic aims are conditional on working for the public welfare and with maximal efficiency. This amalgamation of egoism with service to the public welfare is identical with a substantial limitation of the evil in man and is based upon generally accepted conditions such as the rule of law, a plurality of political parties, the system of private property, competition etc. Being based upon these conditions, the systems of interiorized mutual coercion function automatically, i.e., as a "spontaneous order". The automatic character of the functioning of these systems does not imply their impersonality: as a means of structuring human activities they function and reproduce themselves through personal interests and

preferences. Their assumed "impersonality" consists in the fact that their functioning does not depend on the (uncertain) moral qualities of man; on the contrary, it depends on (much less uncertain) egoistic motives. It is just the
independence on the good side of man's nature which is the main advantage of
these systems.

In liberal democracy and the free market system, the non-democratic direct
moral and ideological (mythological and religious) foundation of all human
political and economic activities is replaced with the moral and philosophical
foundation of the conditions of the functioning of these systems which manifests itself in people's personal responsibility for preserving and reproducing
these conditions.

The democratic political system can function only if the basic conditions of
its functioning are regarded as morally legitimate. But after the divorce of politics from morality, the moral legitimacy of the political system is not given
immediately; it must be fought for and guaranteed through philosophy or even
ideology. The historical experiences of Nazism and Communism prove that
when doubt is cast upon the basic conditions of the democratic and free market
systems, then this results in a catastrophe. Thus the philosophical legitimization
of the basic conditions of the functioning of the democratic political system is a
necessary condition of its reproduction. Consequently, philosophy should reveal
the ontological grounds of the connection between the highest moral values and
the basic conditions of the functioning of liberal democracy and the free market
economy, a philosophical task which should be discharged permanently,
because the ever-changing character of human reality tends permanently to cast
doubt upon the "classical" forms of philosophical legitimization. In addition,
the fact that democracy and the free market economy are not absolute goods,
but only a minimalized evil, implies that various criticisms of democracy as
well as various forms of utopian projects tend also to make themselves permanently felt.

As in the era of early capitalism, so also in post-Communist societies, people need a philosophical legitimization of the new social order they are building
up. They need especially to be reassured that the system of market economy and
liberal democracy is able to turn the unbiased egoism of the new capitalists to
the ends of public welfare. People need to know that the "unseen hand" functioning behind wild economic and political egoism will guarantee not only
material welfare but also the dawning and continuous renewal of a "civilized"
capitalism which will be destitute of immoral features of early capitalism. Thus
they need to hear the voice of such great defenders of the free market system
and liberal democracy as Locke, Smith, Mill, Popper and von Hayek. In connection with the revival of religiosity and with the attacks against liberalism of
Catholic politicians such as the former Slovak Prime Minister Jan Čarnogursky,

it is important to propagate also the ideas of those, like Michael Nowak, who interpret liberalism as a political doctrine fully compatible with the Catholic world-view.

It could be contested that in discharging this task philosophy would become a substitute for a Marxist (utopian) *Prinzip Hoffnung*. As opposed to Marxism, however, whose realization resulted in millions of murdered and tortured human beings as well as in extreme poverty, the validity of the principles of the free market system and of pluralistic democracy has been verified in the historical experience of mankind.

Havel's moral utopianism sought to replace pluralistic democracy as an "impersonal" system of interiorized mutual coercion with a non-systematic foundation of social life in the moral responsibility of a morally revived people. The failure of this position does not imply that philosophy should resign from its main task of providing a rational foundation of moral values and attitudes. On the contrary, in the period of transition to a free market economy, philosophy should squarely face the feelings of despair, disappointment, hopelessness and moral resignation which arise from the experience of the renewal of early capitalism. Philosophy should give new rational certainties to the shaken sphere of the "higher" values; showing man the ways of connecting his "here and now" with the highest moral values. Thus it should help him in transcending the banal sphere of everyday concerns and interests and drive him to living *sub specie aeterni*.

If the philosophical heritage of such representatives of the Austrian philosophical tradition as Bolzano, Brentano, Havlícek, and Masaryk played the decisive part in the clarification and legitimization of different ways of resistance and fight against the materialized form of Marxist-Leninist false consciousness, then the return to the original sources of the Austrian mode of thinking should be the most important task of philosophical research in all the countries of the former Danube monarchy. This return to the sources ought to clarify the philosophical foundations of the cultural identity of the Central European region and become the basis of a more intensive communication among philosophers from Austria, Hungary, the Czech Republic, Poland, Slovenia, Croatia, etc.

Especially Czech philosophy should disencumber itself from the influence of (North-) German philosophy, an influence which is still very strong. The dependence of many Czech and Slovak intellectuals on the German style of thinking is reflected in their fascination with post-modernism, which is nothing but a continuation of Heidegger's attack on Western civilization in different guise. Post-modernism became an intellectual fashion especially among artists, architects, ecologists, and journalists. It is symptomatic of the character of the Czechoslovak intelligentsia that it is mainly non-leftist politicians and economists (e.g., Kroupa, Bratinka, Jezek, Klaus) who are interested in the study of the work of von Hayek, Popper, etc. Hayek's work, which argues in favour of the fundamental values of Western civilization, has thus become a theoretical basis of Czechoslovak political conservatism. Instead of being the business of academic philosophers, the return to the Austrian philosophical tradition thus arises directly from the needs of political and economic life.

From a general point of view, it is very probable that a new, deeper knowledge and evaluation of the basic values of Western civilization will arise precisely in the post-Communist countries in which these values are not taken for granted as they are in Western countries. But a new appreciation of these values as well as of their philosophical legitimization can be realized only through progress in philosophy itself, and it can be assumed that the contemporary social and economic crisis in post-Communist countries will stimulate new positive initiatives in philosophy. But philosophy can discharge no task, it can legitimize neither democracy nor anything else, without performing a new, positive legitimization of its own right to discover truth. Philosophy must defend its own existence against the attacks of such liquidators of philosophy as Heidegger, Derrida and Bělohradský who, being obsessed with their desire to become the "last philosophers" in history, try to liquidate the basic principle of the philosophical discipline. Thus the fact that Heidegger's arguments against metaphysics are extremely fascinating means that the most urgent "inner" task of philosophy is nothing other than that of providing arguments in favour of the idea of truth and a defence of this idea against post-modernistic neo-Sophists.

The self-liquidation of philosophy as projected in Heidegger, Derrida, Bělohradský, etc., would clear the way for orgiastic exaltations, for a mythology of everydayness, for Oriental mysticism, for spiritism, psychotronics, astrology and charlatanism of all kinds. Moreover, the functioning of the democratic system is deeply connected with its philosophical legitimization. The replacing of philosophy with Sophistic rhetoric would lead to the transformation of democracy into a sphere of pure manipulation; moreover, it would lead also to the absolute rule of the majority or to the dictatorship of charismatic leaders. Thus, the self-liquidation of philosophy would essentially endanger Western civilization based as it is on the idea of rationally recognizable truth, and it would clear the way for a pre-historical (orgiastic and mythological) way of existing.

Philosophy has its own quite special responsibility for the destiny of mankind, and their awareness of this responsibility should drive philosophers to reject irresponsible and dangerous freaks of post-modernistic neo-Sophistry as well as to defend the right of philosophy to discover truth.

Ján Pavlík

Katedra filosofie, Vysoká skola Ekonomická
The Czech Republic

VISIONS FROM THE ASHES: PHILOSOPHICAL LIFE IN BULGARIA FROM 1945 TO 1992

The present essay, a joint undertaking of an American and a Bulgarian philosopher, is intended to serve several functions. In view of the political changes in Eastern Europe for which 1989 constitutes the watershed year, it seeks to illuminate the life of philosophy and of philosophers in Bulgaria before, during, and since the overthrow of the dictator, Todor Zhivkov, on November 9 and 10 of that year, as well as, at least incidentally, some of philosophy's connections with the national politics. It will be seen that those connections were and are quite extensive. In the course of documenting these matters, it raises questions about the nature of philosophy, including "political philosophy" whenever that notion comes to be understood, as it was and by many still is, as a set of ideas, whether about democracy or about the nature of matter or of cognition, that are placed at the service of, and subordinated to, a government or political party — be it Communist, post-Communist, or anti-Communist. On the assumption that such subordination is highly undesirable, this article holds out the hope, without entering very much into details, that a new intellectual synthesis with roots in the country's past could emerge "from the ashes" of the turbulent and in many respects depressing philosophical atmosphere of the period upon which, for obvious historical reasons, we are concentrating. In so doing, the article treats Bulgaria as what Sartre calls a "singular universal": the story to be told is uniquely Bulgaria's own, and yet it incarnates past and present realities and future possibilities that have numerous common counterparts elsewhere.

A final, central function of this article that is rather unique and pioneering stems from the fact that so very little about Bulgarian philosophy, and in particular so little of an even quasi-comprehensive nature, has ever appeared in Western publications; this has been verified by extensive searches. If there is something a bit problematic about referring to "Bulgarian philosophy" in the same way as one might refer, for example, to "French philosophy" or to "German philosophy", one can at least speak without hesitation of a "philosophical life" in Bulgaria, and this is our subject for the period in question, a subject which we shall document in detail for the historical and philosophical record. Of the handful of articles, generally not very impressive, that have previously appeared on the subject in the West,[1] undoubtedly the most important is that by the former dissident Assen Ignatov, for some years editor-in-chief of the journal, *Studies in Soviet Thought*, and contributor to "Die Deutsche Welle". Apart from the fact that this study deals with a very limited portion of the philosophical life of Bulgaria (it mostly stops with the 1950s and 1960s), one is already forewarned by its title, "Philosophy of the Rearguard", so redolent of the old-fashioned polemical type of thinking with all its ideological baggage. To judge from this article, the chief characteristic of Bulgarian intellectual life is its lack of "intellectual sophistication", and it is this "comparative intellectual primitiveness" that contributed to the dissemination and triumph of Soviet philosophy after the establishment of the Communist regime.[2]

If that were the case, what is one to think of the French, famous for their refined taste, among whom Marxism became dominant for a considerable period after World War II and even the so-called "orthodox" version of it enjoyed a certain vogue?[3] And if in fact, as Ignatov claims, Bulgaria had continued for so many years in an atmosphere in which other traditions had been completely forgotten, in which any deviations from Marxism-Leninism were insignificant, and in which the extent of de-Stalinization was extremely limited, then how can one account for the rebellion of the "younger generation" from 1987 on and the active role of Bulgarian philosophers in the overthrow of the Zhivkov regime? How explain the fact that the core of the opposition was formed in the Todor Pavlov Institute of Philosophy, abolished by order of the country's Politburo in 1988 and reopened one month later under the new name of "Institute of Philosophical Sciences", after the rebels had been dismissed? If there were nothing but Marxists of either the "dogmatic" or "revisionist" stripe in Bulgaria, then how are we to explain the fact that the last Congress of the Bulgarian Philosophy Society, which quite by chance coincided with the days of Zhivkov's overthrow in 1989, voted to exclude the adjective "Marxist" from its by-laws? The new winds of perestroika undoubtedly played a fairly significant role in these events, but to understand the development of Bulgarian philosophical life, which has resulted in enormous changes in recent years, we must rely on something better than prefabricated ideological schemas.

To begin with, Ignatov points to an alleged "absence of the mystical, of the erotic, of fantasy in the folklore and in general in the national worldview" of Bulgarians;[3] but this assertion is completely false. It is true that the five centuries spent under Turkish domination impoverished the cultural tradition of the Bulgarian nation, a tradition that is traceable to already flourishing Ninth Century origins and that experienced its golden age under the Second Bulgarian Empire (1185-1396), when diverse literary, religious, philosophical, artistic, etc., schools, which strongly influenced the art and the heresies of Medieval Europe, grew and prospered.[4] But the mere fact that this country survived intact, preserving its language and its alphabet (which it had at one time passed on to other Slavic peoples) despite persecutions and brutal tortures, is in itself significant. What ensued must therefore be understood, not as a lack of tradition, but as the aftermath of the first fatal break (1396) in a very distinguished cultural tradition.

From a philosophical point of view, the effect of this break centuries later was that almost all the great names of Bulgarian philosophical life after the achievement of independence and throughout the period from 1878-1945 undertook their studies either in the West (particularly in Germany, France, and Switzerland) or in Russia. This explains why most of the Bulgarians' philosophical culture prior to 1945 had been imported from countries more advanced in this area. Thus, before (or at least at the same time as) the so-called dissemination of Marxism-Leninism, Bulgaria experienced a burgeoning of positivism, pragmatism, *Lebensphilosophie*, Bergsonianism, neo-Kantianism, neo-Hegelian philosophy, empiriocriticism, mind-body dualism, Freudianism, immanentist philosophy, and so forth. This is not to say that there were only imitators of foreign movements during the period in question. Among original Bulgarian thinkers, probably the most characteristic and noteworthy were those strongly oriented towards mysticism. One need only mention the eight volumes of Peter Beron's *Panepisteme*, published in Paris (1861-1870), the school of Master Peter Deunov, who has followers today in Germany and France,[6] or the encyclopedic work of the theosophist and mystic philosopher, writer, painter, and art historian, Nicolas Raynov.[7]

It is only against this background that one can begin to understand the second fatal break (1944/45), the beginning of the period upon which we shall be focusing here, which resulted in the beheading of these numerous currents and the enthronement of a single doctrine, sovereign explanation of everything: the Stalinist version of Marxism, which was of course at the same time a beheading of the thought of Marx.[8] In this period following the "second break", which lasted until 1989, we can distinguish roughly three stages in Bulgarian philosophical life: (1) militant dogmatism, 1945-56; (2) the struggle between dogmatists and their opponents, 1956-87; and (3) the crumbling of Marxism, 1987-89. Correspondingly, we can identify several types of philosophers: the old "bourgeois professors", victims of repression; the dogmatists (generally Party functionaries, charged with the duty of popularizing Marxism); the anti-dogmatists ("revisionists", dissidents); the "faceless" (compilers, philosophical clerical workers so to speak); and the "marginals" (people who took refuge in less ideologically charged areas of philosophy such as logic, aesthetics, ethics, and the history of philosophy, in which they could work on something besides "diamat" and "histomat"). What were the most widely discussed topics of this entire period, and, in the last analysis, what may await this strange philosophical life after its third break in 1989?

Under the Sickle

To be exact, it should be noted that the liberation of Bulgaria from the fascist regime and the beginning of what is generally known as the "Communist era" of its history took place on September 9, 1944.[9] But we have chosen 1945 as the first year of our study for several reasons. First, it was in 1945 that the Philosophical Review (*Filosofski Pregled*), directed by Professor Dimitar Michaltschev, was replaced by *Philosophical Thought* (*Filosofska Misul*), under the editorship of Todor Pavlov. Secondly, it was in November of that same year that Georgi Dimitrov returned from the Soviet Union and his Bulgarian Workers' Party (Communists) won its decisive victory in the legislative elections. From that time on, the direction of philosophical life was to be determined by political events and changing strategies, to which it either submitted under coercion or acted as an obsequious servant. Philosophy and politics, in the guise of "the Party line", were to march forward together.

In the introductory note to the first volume of *Filosofska Misul*, which emphasizes "the dominant role of practice", the tasks of this new journal are laconically indicated:

> Its primary task will be, not just to provide a popularization of the worldview and scientific method of Marxism-Leninism, but also to make an effort at creatively applying it among us. … The problems, needs, and achievements of our politics, economics, culture, science, arts, and linguistic development, particularly the problems connected with September 9 and the nation's war, problems concerning the nature, form, organization, and meaning of democracy … require the most searching, universal, and theoretically concrete explanation possible …. Which means that *Filosofska Misul* will be neither a journal of academic meditation, nor a forum for an unprincipled cult of pure practice.[10]

We thus see from the very beginning the fundamental pretentions of the new reigning doctrine: universal explanation (a sort of master key), scientific certitude, creative efforts at grappling with concrete problems, and the predominance of "practice" as both the basis and the goal of the enterprise. This last-mentioned characteristic was to serve as the justification for introducing the "party principle", which in turn was to become the only principle and the only practice.

In 1945, it is true, it was still not quite at that point, since the editor-in-chief, Todor Pavlov, a fairly well educated person known above all for his book, *Reflection Theory*,[11] was not a thoroughgoing Stalinist. But the fact that philosophy was now being conceived of as a vehicle for legitimizing a certain set of political and social practices, and as nothing beyond that but worthless abstraction, can be seen from the articles following the introductory note to the first volume. There are a few dealing with genuinely philosophical issues (e.g.,

"Matter and Spirit", "The Appearance of Marxist Philosophy", "The Role of Personality and of the Popular Masses in History"), but they are dwarfed in number by those that deal above all with socio-political and economic problems, such as democracy, the nationalities question in Yugoslavia (by Milovan Djilas), the subject-matter and method of political economy, etc.

The tone is set in the very first regular article, after the introductory note, entitled "The Scientific Concept of Democracy and Certain Questions of Our Time"; it is unsigned but was probably written by Pavlov himself. It analyzes the origin and meaning of "democracy", which is taken as the central concept of the new ideology, as well as various forms of this ideology and the socio-political situation in Bulgaria since September 1944. In Greek, the article avers, "democracy" means "power of the people", but we must examine the meanings of both "power" and "people", which have varied greatly over time and must always be understood in their historical concreteness. Greek slaves, for example, had no rights and were not part of the *demos*, but the latter nevertheless played a very positive role in opposing the authoritarian power of the aristocracy. Just so, even though bourgeois democracy has not overcome economic dominance/subordination relationships and exploitation, it was a great step forward by comparison with feudalism. The simple, basic point of the article is to contend that circumstances have changed to the point at which the era of "bourgeois democracy" is at an end, from which it follows that the allegedly "antidemocratic" USSR is the only protector of democracy worldwide, that the Bulgarian National Front is completely popular, i.e., democratic, in nature, and that National Front democracy is the only possible state form for Bulgaria. Finally, it is emphasized that the Popular Front is not a socialist or Soviet institution but a coalition, since private property still survives and the parliamentary system is not based on socialist principles.[12]

However, events that followed led quickly to the establishment of just such a socialist-based system and to the ideologizing of philosophical life to a far greater extent than this article or indeed the entire initial issue of *Filosofska Misul* had implied. In 1946, there was an overwhelming popular vote against continuing the Cobourg monarchy and in favor of a People's Republic; in the same year G. Dimitrov issued a decree "Concerning the Role and Tasks of the Journal *Filosofska Misul*". In 1947 a law nationalizing industrial enterprises was passed. During 1947-48, the parliamentary opposition was eliminated, and gradually there came to be only two remaining parties,[13] which adopted as their common platform the building of "the socialist edifice" with the help of the treaty of cooperation and mutual aid signed with the Soviet Union. Meanwhile, the new constitution and by-laws of the Bulgarian Academy of Sciences (BAS) affirmed the Academy's subordination to the Council of Ministers (rather than, as previously, to the King). This subordination led to a so-called "reorganization", under the guise of which "bourgeois" academics and researchers who were unwilling to accept the new "progressive" scientific presuppositions were retired or, later, executed as "agents of imperialism". The autonomy of the University, of the Academy, and in short of all cultural institutions, which in any case had never been total, gave way to the direct control of the government and the Party, with which even the publishing houses and the press in general were forced to comply.

It may be useful for us to consider in some detail the tasks assigned to *Filosofska Misul*—in other words, to Bulgarian philosophical life in general— by Dimitrov in his directive. Beginning with the basic principle that "practice without theory is blind and theory without practice is impotent", Dimitrov describes the central task as one of bridge-building between progressive philosophy and the people, particularly the intellectuals, or in other words of getting philosophy out of the Ivory Tower and introducing it into daily life. Then five more specific tasks are listed:

1) to denounce fascist ideology (its racism and especially its theory of the *Übermensch*);

2) to unmask the falsification of history, meaning to develop a scientific Marxist-Leninist criterion for explaining the great events and periods of Bulgarian history, particularly its recent history;

3) to help the popular intelligentsia "form a healthy, scientific, Marxist conception of the world and assimilate the essence of Marxism in its new form, Leninism, the *Marxist dialectical method*, not only as the best means of correct explanation of the past and the future, but also *as the directive for action* in the solution of the great, complex tasks of the moment"[14]

4) to fight against retrograde idealist currents that are the ideological weapons of reaction against popular democracy, to denounce concretely and in a reasoned way every attempt to pervert living, militant Marxism, to deal with new problems on the ideological front from a Marxist viewpoint, to elaborate on the new methodological issues in the sciences, especially those having to do with the economic, social, and cultural structure;

5) to generate increased interest in philosophy and the sciences for the education and self-education of youth.

The most important condition for realizing these tasks, according to Dimitrov, is that the journal adopt a popular style of writing, accessible to "average readers". And so:

> For this it is necessary that the authors ... get completely free from the normal custom of bourgeois philosophers, who usually, adopting the haughty attitude of learned men, write in a language deliberately made inaccessible to the ordinary reader, reserving their 'works' for 'specialists', i.e., for the intellectual aristocracy of an elite.[15]

The sentiment expressed here, following the stylized but generally rather bland enumeration of "tasks", was devastating in its implications. What was being said was that the journal and all Bulgarian philosophers, if they wished to remain such, had to accept not only Marxism-Leninism, with its "Party principle" endorsing pitiless struggle against "bourgeois" thought currents, but also to write in an "accessible" fashion. What this latter really meant was to imitate the *vulgar* style of Stalin, as well illustrated in his famous (at the time) *Brief Course on "The History of the United Communist Party (Bolsheviks)"*.

This directive was implemented immediately, as one can observe in the pages of *Filosofska Misul*. Beginning with the first volume of 1947, the following notice appeared on the inside front cover: "In the course of its third year the editorial staff will do everything in its power to bring about a thoroughgoing improvement of *Filosofska Misul* in the spirit of the directives of Comrade G. Dimitrov ..." And this volume then opened with an article by Pavlov himself, "Path and Perspectives of Scientific Bulgarian Thought", purporting to illustrate this point and giving concrete instructions for the euphemistically named "reorganization" of the Academy that we mentioned earlier.

Pavlov begins by remarking that science is becoming more and more unified, that the achievements of science worldwide should be utilized, and that the real worth of Bulgarian scientific development needs to be underscored. In this respect he singles out the positive contribution of the Literary Braille Society (which was later to be integrated within the BAS), certain accomplishments of which had received worldwide recognition. But then he immediately identifies certain of its allegedly negative characteristics (abstract and "scholarly" activity, lack of planning and of connectedness with social developments), and insists on the need to "make use of the experience of Soviet science." He then concludes by making use of this "experience" in order to impose and implement some principles of reorganization that are thenceforth to be considered as determinative for philosophical life in particular. These are:

1) The unity of theory and practice, which means the principle of commitment to class struggle;

2) The principle of collectivism and planning, meaning the imposition of general programs or themes to define the research fields of Academy workers as well as programs for education and instruction in colleges and teachers' training schools, where Marxism-Leninism is to be introduced gradually as a mandatory subject;

3) The principle of democratization of science, which means that its only mission is to "serve the people";

4) The principle of popularization, which will force the BAS to redesign its research for mass consumption and to develop a style of accessibility, i.e., vulgarization;

5) The principle of pan-Sovietism, the excuse given for which is the need for researchers to attend not only to the global problems of humanity but also, following the Soviet example, to the problem of the origin and development of the Slavic peoples (who, according to the Stalinists, obviously originated in Russia);

6) Dialectical materialism as basic principle, i.e., as the basis of all research.[16]

In order to implement these principles, the Party faithful are to "assist" in the intellectual reorganization of bourgeois academics, researchers, and professors and especially in the building of "new cadres".

Thenceforth philosophy was to be the most dedicated servant of politics and of partisan passions. The majority of philosophers were to agree joyfully to be Party ideologues and to compete with one another to furnish the best proofs of their fidelity. Once again the tone was set by *Filosofska Misul*, which, on the occasion of G. Dimitrov's sixty-fifth birthday in 1947, published a saccharine letter from the editorial board that began with the affectionate salutation, "Dear Master ...", together with an article on "Georgi Dimitrov and Marxist-Leninist Philosophy" by Assen Kisselintschev, the most subservient of the dogmatists. This set a precedent: like Dimitrov, all the future Secretaries General of the Party, serving simultaneously as Prime Ministers (V. Kolarov, the best educated of the group, V. Tschervenkov, and finally T. Zhivkov), were to be declared philosophers, and their views on overall development (economic, political, ideological, and cultural) were to serve as the guiding thread of philosophical activity until the 1980s.

Those who did not wish or were unable to "reorganize" themselves within the new order had either to retire without being able to publish anything, or nearly anything, further, or else to be subjected, as were Academy members D.

Michaltschev and N. Raynov, to scathingly critical "public discussions." So it was not enough for T. Pavlov, no doubt upset by Michaltschev's *Philosophy as Science* (Sofia, 1946), a third of which consisted of a critique of the reflection theory so strongly defended by Pavlov, to write a second book of 282 pages (*Balance Sheet on a Reactionary Idealist Philosophy*, published in 1953 by the BAS itself), against this most famous representative of "bourgeois philosophy". In addition, Pavlov felt compelled to organize a discussion that was in effect a trial concerning Michaltschev's work, *Traditional Logic and its Materialist Argumentation*,[17] in which this Bulgarian expert on the work of the German philosopher of immanentism, Johannes Rehmke, had tried without success to bring his own thought into conformity as much as possible with historical materialism. In this "discussion", which took place in March 1953, Michaltschev remained completely alone, abandoned by his disciples, assistants, and friends, and was attacked by two Academy members (Pavlov and S. Ganovski) and seven professors. In the last analysis, the "arguments" offered in favor of condemning him merely repeated the cliché, "reactionary idealist philosophy", enunciated by Pavlov. Nevertheless, the course of the "discussion" is instructive and revelatory of the intellectual atmosphere.

Virtually all the participants began by attacking the starting-point of Rehmke's philosophy, the data that are "given to the subject", as being comparable to Berkeley's *esse est percipi* and hence an instance of unspeakable "subjective idealism". Michaltschev was criticized for "pretending" to believe in objective reality, for having dared to attack materialism. He was said to have held a false "creationism" inasmuch as he accepted the coming-to-be of something out of nothing, namely, non-spatial consciousness from spatial matter. The Russian researcher, Lepechinskaja, had demonstrated, according to these "rigorous" critics of immanentism, that dead matter evolves in the direction of living cells.[18] If, on the other hand, like Michaltschev we set matter and consciousness in opposition to one another, then how can we explain the knowledge of objective reality, how establish the criterion of truth? If a criterion such as that of "nonproblematic evidence" proposed by the Rehmkeans were accepted, then we could not distinguish truths from falsehoods, which often also appear as evident. The initial idealist error had led Michaltschev, according to these critics, to separate thought from language, hence also from the logic of grammar. His fundamental claim against traditional logic, namely, that it is impossible to know *things* since consciousness contains only ideal *images*, and hence that we only know our own *ideas* and not qualities or relations in objective reality, is based on a confusion between thought and language. According to Michaltschev, the laws of identity, of excluded middle, of sufficient reason, etc., are laws of language and not of thought, i.e., of propositions and not of judgments. But the law of identity is not, the critics countered, simply the absolute equivalence "A=A", as idealism would have it; rather, it indicates that the relations and sequences of logical thought can be deduced only through referring our ideas to a single, even if diverse and variable, material object. It is not true, as Michaltschev claims, that what is rational about the law of identity stems from the need always to designate the same notions by the same terms. For example, one can designate the same man as at once "the most distinguished of bourgeois philosophers", "Rehmke's most faithful disciple", and "the implacable enemy of reflection theory".[19]

No doubt some of the arguments against the immanentist theory of Rehmke-Michaltschev were valid. But the way in which the trial was organized, the tone and style of the comments, the outrageous labels such as "servant of the reactionary class", "imperialist agent", etc., in themselves bore witness to the general lack of tolerance and respect for the person, to the lack of any freedom to think differently from "the majority". It is said that after several hours of these attacks Michaltschev spoke only a single sentence in his own defense: "At my intellectual burial here, there has been no one to say a good word for me."[20]

The greatest tragedy, however, is that this "burial" swallowed up not just a philosophy or a doctrine, but all that had still remained of intelligence and professionalism in this philosophical life, henceforth to be surrounded by *rhinoceroses*. Thus, once having swept out all pluralism of philosophical schools, philosophers shut themselves up within their Tower of Monolithic Truth, from which they proceeded to attack enemy schools: pragmatism (A. Kisselintschev, leading critic), physical idealism (A. Polikarov, G. Bratoev, and S. Gerdzhikov), logical positivism and analytic philosophy (A. Bankov, D. Spassov, and K.Delev-Darkovski), legal positivism (V. Zachariev, P. Gindev), Bergsonism (A. Bankov, G. Grozev), neo-Thomism and existentialism (N. Iribadzhakov), etc. Translation work, formerly quite active, was now confined to the "classics of Marxism", including Stalin, whose writings were the objects of frequent commentaries and whose ideas were increasingly adopted.

It is worth noting that the first "anti-Stalinist" article, "Against the Fetishization of Objective Social Necessity," was written by a woman, Elena Panova, who, while pretending to attack her colleagues, A. Popov and T. Valov, and to support E. Mateev, in fact refuted Stalin's thesis that social laws function independently of human beings and argued that they are not reducible to an objective necessity operating through people's conscious actions.[21] *For that time*, this article was rather daring, as was the article by her husband, Dobrine Spassov, "On the Character of Elementary Logical Laws", which was published along with the editorial comment that "In the article there are questionable positions."[21] The purposes of this article were (1) to resolve the apparent conflict between dialectical logic, which reflects objective laws of movement and change, and elementary (formal) logic, which the Stalinists said represented only a state of rest or inactivity; (2) to show that the laws of formal logic do in fact represent thought as a basic knowledge process, a statement denied by certain Soviet philosophers; and (3) to discover their objective content, in order to distinguish among them and to identify the various forms of logical thinking. This rather long article purports to show that, in the last analysis, formal logic should not be rejected, since it is a necessary component of dialectical logic. The laws of formal logic reflect the qualitative determination of objects—their *differentia specifica*—which distinguishes them from other objects and marks what is permanent in them across quantitative changes. It would therefore be an error to oppose the "A=A" of formal logic to the dialectical law, "Both A and not-A", because in order for A to change A must first exist. "In fact the first formula is false", Spassov stresses, "only *when we are referring to the continually changing particularities of the object. If, on the other hand, we see it as the qualitatively determined bearer of these particularities*, as reflected in the corresponding thought process, then its usefulness is perfectly obvious."[22]

Even though Panova and Spassov began their philosophical careers as participants, albeit the youngest and most intelligent, in the Michaltschev debacle, their two articles constitute the only feeble rays of light in the dark night of Bulgarian philosophical life in the period from 1946 to 1956. The later evolution of their positions, as well as the appearance of more moderate and marginal thinkers, will gradually contribute to the movement of de-Stalinization that ostensibly began with the famous "April plenum".

Failure and Dignity of the "Older Generation"

During the final two years of his regime, Todor Zhivkov used to boast that, long before Gorbachev's changes, glasnost and perestroika had been instituted in Bulgaria—as far back, in fact, as 1956 with the "April plenum" reforms. This "historic" plenary session of the Central Committee of the Bulgarian Communist Party is notable above all for its condemnation of the "personality cult" of General Secretary and Prime Minister Valko Tschervenkov. Following the lead of the Twentieth Congress of the Soviet Communist Party, which had condemned the Stalin cult, it made Tschervenkov the scapegoat in order to put power into the hands of a more suitable lackey. Once in power, Zhivkov condemned his predecessor in order to make himself "the Architect" of a *new conception* which was elaborated upon in several dozen volumes written by a team of philosophers, economists, sociologists, etc. This global conception claimed to restore Leninist principles and norms, to reassert the lost link between ideology and practice, to combat dogmatism, schematization, and the doctrinaire spirit, and to promote the creative initiative of artists and scientific researchers. Like a top, the "line" of *Filosofska Misul* spun around immediately. The oppressors became the oppressed and the dogmatists proclaimed themselves free thinkers, at the same time persecuting real thinkers for being "anti-Marxist" or deviating from "the April line".

It is impossible to describe the whole atmosphere of intrigues, tattling, and denunciations which became the favoured literary genre of the time. However, given its pretensions of returning to authentic Marxism-Leninism, "the April line" allowed for the possibility of a noticeable process of differentiation within philosophical life. Thus, alongside the dogmatists (T. Pavlov, S. Ganovski, A. Kisselintschev, G. Girginov, T. Stoicev, A. Katov, S. Popov, et al.) and the innumerable "faceless" individuals, there now appeared the first anti-dogmatists (D. Spassov, E. Panova, K. Delev-Darkovski, A. Gavrilov, N. Merdzhanov, L. Levy, P.-E. Mitev), marginal thinkers (Kantcho Kanev, I. Passy, R. Radev, S. Petrov, G. Bratoev, S. Levy, G. Dontschev, B. Tschendov), a group half-way between the anti-dogmatists and the marginals (N. Michova, S. Avranova, K. Neschev, D. Avramov, E. Nikolov), and finally some dissidents (S. Boianov, Z. Zhelev, A. Ignatov, G. Schischkov). These differences (which are in any case not absolute, since certain writers who were anti-dogmatic on one particular question were often dogmatic on another and vice versa) led inevitably to a war among blocs which was observable especially in the public debates on philosophical issues. The most significant of these, which lasted several years or in some cases a couple of decades, concerned (a) the object and status of historical materialism, beginning in 1957; (b) the ideas of Lysenko, beginning in 1958; (c) the critique of bourgeois philosophy, 1961-63; (d) the reflection theory of cognition, beginning in 1961; and (e) the definition of matter, 1956-64.

(a) Historical Materialism

In December 1957 a public discussion was held in Sofia on the object and status of historical materialism; it generated a mountain of articles and monographs on the subject. The discussion brought out three principal alternative theses, which were developed and argued in different ways depending on the participants:

1) Historical materialism is philosophical in nature, a relatively independent part of comprehensive Marxist philosophy, and at the same time it is scientific sociology.

2) Historical materialism is philosophical in nature, but there must at the same time be a separate Marxist sociology, to be treated as a self-contained scientific discipline.

3) Historical materialism is not philosophical in nature, because it is an exact science.

The first of these theses was at that time the standard one, formulated in the USSR and defended by Soviet philosophers and "sociologists" (who by this definition had no autonomous discipline) until the 1980s. It had been rejected for the first time by T. Pavlov himself in the 1945 edition of his *Reflection Theory*. Pavlov's argument was that, together with historical materialism as a philosophical science, there exists another science, general and precise, which examines structures and structural relations within society—namely, sociology.[24] It was the second thesis, then, that provided the starting-point of the discussion in Bulgaria, primarily because it was given a fresh formulation in Zhivko Oschavkov's 1957 work, *Historical Materialism and Sociology*. Oschavkov's main point was that the object of historical materialism follows logically from that of dialectical materialism, in the sense that dialectical materialism studies the "being–consciousness" relationship and historical materialism the "social being–social consciousness" one, both sharing the dialectical method, whereas the object of sociology is the general laws of social development and not the aforementioned relationships. Criticizing in particular the Soviet philosopher Kamari, Oschavkov defined sociology as having "as its object the structure and specific characteristics of society, the precise general laws of its overall development, and the correlations among all parts of social life; [it is] a specific method of knowledge and of change within the overall life of society."[25] This position was shared for the most part by the philosophers S. Michailov, N. Stefanov, K. Vassilev, and others.[26] It was attacked, in the discussion that followed, by P. Gindev, I. Tassev, B. Mountian, and K. Delev, among others, and in a series of articles by A. Popov, N. Nikolov, and D. Spassov. According to Gindev, historical materialism is at the same time Marxist sociology, because its object is *the most general laws*, understood always in relationship to the connection between social being and social consciousness. Tassev, Mountian, and Delev, on the other hand, maintained that historical materialism is not a philosophical science at all, but rather an exact science analogous to biology, since it consists in the *application* of the principles of dialectical materialism to the analysis of social life. In opposition to both this third thesis and the second one two particularly significant articles were published: "On the Nature and Object of Historical Materialism" (1958), by A. Popov, and "Is There a Difference Between Historical Materialism and Marxist Sociology?" (1961), by N. Nikolov.

According to Popov, in order to understand the real meaning of historical materialism we must understand the real meaning of its object, which includes the relationship between "histomat" and "diamat". This relationship is such that, if diamat, as philosophy, is the most general science of the laws of development of being, thought, and society, it necessarily implies histomat, conceived as the science of the most general laws, forms, and active forces of social development. In other words, the relationship of diamat to histomat is essentially that of whole to part. This also means that historical materialism is strictly philosophical in nature, not scientific like biology, since it employs philosophical laws and categories that are more abstract than those of the special sciences. At the same time, however, it would be a mistake to deny the relative independence of historical materialism and to identify it, as Oschavkov had done, with the simple logical transference of the categories and laws of diamat to society as its object of investigation, thus in effect reducing histomat to dialectical materialist philosophy. For histomat deals with the *specific appearances* of dialectical laws and categories in the social field. We do not need a special science, called sociology, to study the structural relationships of society, such as questions of infrastructure and superstructure, class struggle, etc., since histomat is that general science, the object of which includes the study of all such questions. Thus histomat is the theory and general method of all the other social sciences.[27]

Nikolov, in his article, criticized Oschavkov's view that historical materialism deals with the general relationship between social being and social consciousness, but not the general laws of social development, which according to Oschavkov are the province of sociology. Nikolov also pointed out that, in contrast with Oschavkov, T. Pavlov had accepted histomat's claim to study the general laws of social development; but this is incompatible with Pavlov's insistence on the need for sociology as a separate science. In the last analysis, Pavlov's position is indefensible, since histomat's key claim that social being determines social consciousness constitutes one of the most general laws of society. The very reason why histomat is philosophical in nature is that it studies, and has to study, *the general laws* of social development. One last contradiction to be noted is the one implied by Oschavkov's identification of sociology with scientific socialism, since the latter deals with the principles of transition from capitalism to socialism, whereas, according to Oschavkov, sociology is supposed to study the general laws of society as a whole.[28]

Perhaps the most articulate criticism of Oschavkov's work is to be found in an article by D. Spassov, "A Failed Attempt at Developing Marxism" (1959). Spassov began by showing that Oschavkov's definition of Marxist-Leninist philosophy[29] places exclusive emphasis on its unity and indivisibility. But to take this position, he said, means going back to Ernst Mach's belief in the basic interdependence of subject and object, which entails denying the existence of nature independent of and prior to society, and affirming that objective and subjective laws are indivisible. (This reference to Mach was especially damaging, in the context, in view of Lenin's lengthy polemic against him in *Materialism and Empiriocriticism*.) Materialists should know, Spassov wrote, that although human society is indeed inseparable from nature, the subjective from the objective, and philosophical method from the external laws with which it deals, the converse is not true. Oschavkov's position is still stranger in view of the fact that he does not accept, as Pavlov did, the claim that dialectics, logic, and epistemology are identical. Oschavkov regards development as being a unified and unifying progression of parts of a single whole, the unity being concealed by their "relative divergence". Thus, instead of speaking of dialectical materialism (construed as the identity of dialectics, logic, and epistemology) and of historical materialism (construed as the concrete application of the dialectical method to social life) as distinct, Oschavkov speaks of the unity of Marxist-Leninist philosophy, which at the same time turns out to be divided into "parts or aspects". How can this be?

Rather like the adherents of resemblance theory (Russell, Price, Ducasse, *et al.*), Spassov continued, who contend that when referring to general properties we have in mind, not what remains the same within differences, but rather the greater or lesser resemblance of the things being compared, so certain Bulgarian philosophers deny that there is anything general that would remain absolutely the same amid differences, that would never change as a result of the particular conditions of their appearances. According to Spassov, whoever claims that what is general is altered by its particular instantiations does not in the final analysis allow for there being anything general in common, and hence espouses nominalism. It is unclear what the object of historical materialism would be from this perspective. Would it study the most general laws of development, or rather their particular appearances? If the former, it would be indistinguishable from diamat; if the latter, it would be indistinguishable from sociology as an exact science. If, finally, one wished to conceive of histomat as a synthesis of diamat and sociology, that would only be possible on the basis of the principle that what is most general, when applied to one or another specific sphere, both changes and at the same time remains the same—i.e., remains the most general and common—, and that principle has already been rejected. Moreover, the differences assigned by Oschavkov to histomat and sociology by virtue of the latter's alleged special concern with issues of *structure* lead to a new confusion. If by "structure" is understood the essential and lasting correlations of entities, and that is supposed to be the special concern of sociology, then it would not be permissible for histomat, even though it has been defined as the science of the most general laws of development, to study general structures and the generality of structures. In conclusion, Spassov praised the book for its positive attempt to distinguish histomat from sociology and to advance beyond the positions of Soviet writers, but he remarked that these pretentions to creativity had not achieved creative results.[30]

Fifteen years later, we think it worth noting, just such creative results, leading to an entirely new way of looking at the relationship between sociology and philosophy from a standpoint inspired by the early Marx, were achieved in P.-E.

Mitev's important book, *From the Social Problem to Discovery of a World Concept* (1984). Here, Mitev proposed a view of "the Marxian synthesis"—to be found for the first time, according to him, in the *1844 Manuscripts*—which expresses an integral, internal unity among philosophy, political economy, and scientific socialism, and the core of which is sociology:

> The union of philosophy with political economy and the doctrine of communism is only *the external aspect* of an internal synthesis within the limits of philosophy itself. Society is treated from an ontological point of view, ontology and epistemology from a sociological point of view; the general theory of historical process is 'elevated' to the level of philosophical abstractions, while ontology and epistemology are 'brought down to earth' to the socio-historical level.[31]

Thus the terms of discourse of Bulgarian philosophical life were gradually to evolve into something very different from those of the fifties and sixties.

(b) Lysenkoism

The second area of discussion opened up as a result of the condemnation of Stalin and Stalinist dogmatism concerning the relevance of the concepts of the Soviet biologist Trofim Lysenko, which ten years earlier had been imposed by force on scientific researchers and philosophers.[32] The first public attack on Lysenkoism, which had been supported in Bulgaria particularly by A. Kisselintschev and T. Pavlov (although the latter ultimately rejected it in part), took place in 1958 during a conference on biochemistry and genetics organized at the Institute of Medicine. This made possible the appearance of Stoian Nikolov's monograph, *The Problem of Life* (1962), which demonstrated the inconsistencies of Lysenkoist theses in the areas of genetics and biology, as well as the study by Grozdan Vekilov, one of the conference participants, entitled *Science and Dogmatism* (1963). Vekilov showed the connection that exists between dogmatism, which he defined as the overinflation of one part of the reality under investigation and the absolutization of relative truths, and the pursuit of political personality cults and administrative intervention in creative activity.[33]

But it was above all in Nikolai Iribadzhakov's book, *Philosophy and Biology*,[34] that Lysenkoism received a thoroughgoing critique. Iribadzhakov ridiculed both Lysenkoism's pretensions to being a creative development of Darwinism and its dismissal of classical genetics and contemporary biology as idealistic. First, Iribadzhakov characterized Lysenko's assertion that Darwin's doctrine was a mechanistic materialism, non-dialectical and in the final analysis idealist, as a vulgar revision of the judgments pronounced on Darwin by Marx, Engels, and Lenin themselves and as exhibiting an ignorance of Darwin's role in the development of dialectical materialism. The problem is not that Darwin had been, as the Lysenkoists claimed, a "flat evolutionist", mechanist and "metaphysician" (in the sense of that word employed by Hegel and Engels), acknowledging only slow (evolutionary) development as opposed to "qualitative (i.e., revolutionary) leaps"; rather, the problem is that Lysenko misunderstands the notion of "evolution". Lysenko relies on a fallacious Stalinist thesis that excludes the possibility of the "non-revolutionary" appearances of new qualities. Indeed, Iribadzhakov asserted, quantitative and qualitative changes should not be distinguished and opposed in the first place. Rather, we should regard so-called "revolutionary" developments as forms of evolution itself. Darwin did not deny "qualitative leaps", but he showed that what is essential in evolution is slow accumulations. In fact, the development of the organic world testifies to the absence of supposed "revolutionary appearances" or sudden formations.

Iribadzhakov also rejected Lysenko's claims that Darwin was skeptical with regard to science and was a theist, showing by numerous citations that Darwin accepted the cognitive status of scientific knowledge and was rather atheistic in his final writings. Against Lysenko's views about the absence of struggle within biological species and the existence of a single law of life for all of them, Iribadzhakov offered several proofs that the struggle for existence is real and that Lysenko's experiments with planting trees in clusters or "nests" in previously unforested regions had had catastrophic outcomes. Lysenko's denial of classical genetics and charges of idealism against those with whom he disagreed were absurd, based as they were on the supposed "criterion" of what is or is not the bearer of heredity. The followers of Lysenko maintained that the Weissmann-Morgan theory was idealistic solely by virtue of the fact that it identified as the bearers of heredity alleged parts of organisms called genes that do not exist! But genes are clearly material and not ideal entities, and in any case, even if they did not exist (which is obviously false, their existence having been long since conclusively demonstrated by experiment), can a person be called an "idealist" simply because of having formulated an hypothesis? So Iribadzhakov concluded that Lysenkoism was a vulgarization and falsification of the basic premises of both Marxist philosophy and Darwinism, as well as a false scientific and philosophical appraisal of both classical genetics and contemporary biology.[35]

(c) Bourgeois Philosophy

But even though in this book (which served to bring him into contact with T. Pavlov and his retinue) Iribadzhakov took a somewhat anti-dogmatic stance—against a rather facile opponent whose ideas were by that time already on the wane within the Soviet bloc—he had, in a previous book entitled *'Modern'*

Criticisms of Marxism (1960), adopted such a militant and extremely narrow critical attitude towards "bourgeois" philosophy as to elevate himself to the position of Bulgarian Ideologue Number One. The latter book precipitated a discussion about the forms and principles of criticism of contemporary "bourgeois" philosophy that was to last for several years and to end with a repressive intervention of the Party on behalf of the new ideologue. Already in 1961, as a consequence of the creation (1959), by the Science and Education Division of the Central Committee of the Party, of the Philosophic Council, which circulated directives against dogmatism (*sic*) and in favour of the reinforcement of Marxist criticism, a philosopher of science named Azaria Polikarov had begun to speak of a new form of criticism of idealist philosophy: "immanent critique", which was supposed to conform to scientific facts on the one hand and to the principles of diamat on the other.[36]

Thinking to capitalize on this suggestion and to take advantage of the occurrence of the important plenary session of the Party in November 1961, Kiril Delev-Darkovski decided to subject Iribadzhakov's own book on "bourgeois" philosophy to a sort of immanent critique. He began his article in *Filosofska Misul* by listing as one of its positive aspects the fact that it dealt with broad issues that had previously been treated either very little or not at all and attempted to present a comprehensive picture of contemporary anti-Marxism. But he immediately went on to point out the work's numerous weaknesses: its poor organization (the fact that, instead of dealing, as the author claimed, with the conflict between Marxism and anti-Marxism it dealt with a few forms of the latter while leaving out the most important ones), the schematic nature of Iribadzhakov's general definition of contemporary bourgeois philosophy, the identification of anti-Marxism with bourgeois philosophy as a whole, etc. Darkovski took special umbrage at the characterization of contemporary Western philosophy as "philosophy of imperialism". He noted that this could be understood in either of two ways: (1) philosophy during the imperialist stage of the historical period of bourgeois supremacy, or (2) philosophy of the imperialist forces. Unfortunately, Iribadzhakov had opted for the second of these interpretations, thus generating a good deal of nonsense. Darkovski stressed the necessity of a nuanced approach, based on concrete historical analysis of the diverse schools of Western philosophy and on the importance of studying the particularities that distinguish them from one another and furnish the possibility of real assessments of them rather than primarily whatever they may all have in common. The excessively general characteristics attributed by Iribadzhakov to all the "bourgeois" philosophies had led him to numerous inaccuracies such as, for example, his assertion that not only existentialism but indeed all the movements of contemporary bourgeois philosophy are marked by "despair and dejection". Likewise, it is totally false to claim that all of contemporary Western philosophy is "reactionary", or that Sartre is an "anti-Marxist", or that neo-Thomism is "more acceptable to natural reason" than existentialism, etc., etc. All these anathemata led Darkovski to conclude that what is said in the name of Marxism needs to be verified and that it is unacceptable to sacrifice the truth to tastes or particular interests.[37]

This sane attack on primitive types of criticism produced, as its consequence, a campaign, orchestrated by the Party organization of the Institute of Philosophy and supported by the Central Committee, against Darkovski, as well as against Ivan Markov. (Several months earlier, the latter had accused P. Gindev of having used the criticism of "bourgeois" philosophies as a means of advancing his own career.[38]) The campaign supposedly ended with a letter addressed to the national Party Central Committee and written by the Party organization of the Institute, in which a complete account was given of its meetings devoted to the question of the criticism of bourgeois philosophy. In it, Darkovski was charged with having misunderstood the problems of criticism, having misconceived the idea of a nuanced approach, having failed to realize that bourgeois philosophy was becoming increasingly reactionary and anti-Marxist, and having been unwilling to acknowledge his errors at the meetings. In addition, the letter criticized Markov for having been tendentious, unfair, and subjective, as well as certain editors (A. Ignatov, I. Kirilov, I. Markov himself, and Borev) for having published articles in defense of the bourgeoisie.[39] In fact, these formulary epithets of "anti-Marxism" and "bourgeois influences" lasted well past the time of Darkovski's death in 1986 and were particularly employed, as we shall see, as weapons against the "younger generation".[40]

(d) The Reflection Theory

A long discussion on this question was generated by the publication, in 1961, of A. Polikarov's book, *Matter and Knowledge*. The historical background of this controversy was Lenin's critique of the British Machian, Karl Pearson, who had held that only our sensations and the relations that we discern among them are real, had admitted (unlike Mach) that "a sound idealism" was an accurate label for his version of positivism, and had thought it illogical to believe that philosophy could produce independent awareness of an external world. Lenin, who in *Materialism and Empiriocriticism* treats Pearson as a more worthy adversary than most, had responded that it would, however, be logical to accept the reality of a property homologous to that of sensation, namely, reflection.[41] It was on the basis of this remark that Todor Pavlov had built his own reflection theory, which defines reflection as an innate property of all matter. According to this theory, when a real object, having been reflected, ceases to exist, the reflection does not immediately and totally dissolve, but remains as a "trace", and under certain circumstances these "reflection-traces" can be reactivated.[42] This holds not only for human consciousness, but also for all spheres of reality—inorganic, biological, unconsciously reflective, semiconsciously reflective, and conscious—each of which has its own specific form of reflection.

In opposition to this theory, Polikarov argued that, in the inorganic sphere of reality, it would be better to speak of "proto-reflection" rather than reflection. This would mean reserving "reflection" exclusively for the sphere of living matter, and then the question whether reflectivity is a "property of all matter" would have meaning only in terms of the genetic origins of the connection between reflection and sensing. In other words, Lenin's hypothesis would be either proved or disproved by the natural sciences and should not be seen as a life or death issue for Marxist theory. Moreover, only a part of inorganic matter, not the whole of it, should be seen as having the property of reflectivity, and reflection should be viewed simultaneously as a process as well as a property.[43]

Aristotel Gavrilov then proposed an alternative to both Pavlov's and Polikarov's theories. He defined reflection as an internal reciprocal activity between subject and object, characterized by the subject's surrounding or refracting the content of the activity and then reacting to it in accordance with its own particular nature. In areas of activity other than the purely mechanical, according to Gavrilov, every relatively complete and finite sequence exhibits four elements: (1) an external action by a body A on a body B; (2) resulting activation of a material (spatial) process within body B; (3) resulting appearance of an essential internal relationship of B to A; (4) external reaction of B to A. The second and third of these elements constitute reflection and allow for the possibility of distinguishing reflection processes from other causal sequences. Causal sequences are either purely mechanical (i.e., due to external spatial motion, such as one finds in very large cosmic and planetary bodies), lacking reflectivity of their own, or something more (i.e., due to physical, chemical, biological, and/or social types of movement), exhibiting some reflectivity. But since Gavrilov goes on to say that there are no cases in nature in which a body is found to exhibit the mechanical form of motion without also exhibiting some other forms as well, he in effect affirms, in contrast to Polikarov, that reflection is a universal phenomenon. Thus the evolutionary chain leading to consciousness is just one aspect of the idea of reflectivity as a universal property of all matter.[44]

A final alternative to the first three reflection theories was that proposed by Bernard Mountian. He distinguished three senses of the notion of "reflection": (1) the property, possessed by material systems, of reflecting; (2) the process of reflection; (3) the result of reflection (image-traces). In a broad sense reflection is any outcome of certain causal activities. But in a strictly philosophical sense it is the capacity of matter to receive information. In other words, it is a universal property of matter to reflect and to be reflected. However, the fact of its being a universal property of all matter does not entail that it is a necessary property for all levels of organization of matter. It is only functional systems, i.e., organisms and society, that are unable to exist without the property of reflecting and that therefore require it. In such systems, the outcome of the functioning of one part is the condition for the functioning of another, which requires a coordination of functions and parts—in other words, an information exchange, or reflection. In the most highly developed and complex organisms, where the need for information is greatest, a preponderant role is played by specialized systems for receiving, preserving, and translating information; for example, severe damage to the human brain results in death, whereas a frog lives for hours after the removal of its brain. Mountian's systems approach seems clearly designed, at least in retrospect, to extricate the entire reflection theory controversy from some of the most questionable implications of Pavlov's original gloss on Lenin.[45]

(e) Matter

Another debate, as acerbic as that over the criticism of "bourgeois" philosophy, broke out over the letter written by Zheliu Zhelev, Ivan Dzhadzhev, and Peter Ouvakov entitled "On the Philosophical Definition of Matter", published in the *Deutsche Zeitschrift für Philosophie* in 1964. Here, they criticized definitions of matter that had already been proposed, in interpretive discussions of Lenin's conception of it, in East Germany, Poland, the USSR, and Bulgaria. These were broken down into four essential varieties: (1) "Objective reality" consists not only of matter, but also of its attributes (space, time, motion). (2) "Objective" reality consists not merely of the basic properties and relations of matter, but of all its properties and relations. (3) Not only are the attributes, properties, and relations of matter "objectively real", but so too is individual consciousness, since it exists independently of other consciousness. (4) Within infinite space, the earth is not the only planet on which matter must have become self-aware, which implies that, according to present-day views, there may well be thousands of planets with conscious beings on them even within our own galaxy; hence, in relation to infinity, consciousness is as eternal as matter, and the statement that "matter exists before or after consciousness" is of only limited validity.

From this starting point the three authors drew the basic conclusion that Lenin's definition of matter as "objective reality" leads to insurmountable contradictions. Thus, for example, the first and second variations listed above lead to an identification of matter with its attributes, properties, and relations. In attempting to overcome this contradiction, M. W. Mostep explains that properties and relations are objective just because they belong to objects. But this is a silly argument, since there can be no non-objective properties, or objects without properties. So no one has been able to respond to the fourth definition (formulated by Polikarov), which shows that consciousness is as objective and eternal as matter and therefore impossible to distinguish in terms of Lenin's own definition.

Following from this conclusion, the thesis of the three authors themselves is that the dialectical definition of matter based on an epistemological opposition between matter and consciousness is impossible in principle, since that opposition is only partial and relative. An absolute, total opposition would entail that each was essentially dependent for its existence on the other, hence that the disappearance of the one would mean the disappearance of the other. Certain well-known pairs of dialectical categories, such as quality/quantity, form/content, cause/effect, and so on are opposites of this type. However, it is clear that such absolute opposition cannot characterize the matter/consciousness pair, since we know that, while consciousness without matter cannot exist, matter without consciousness can. Consciousness is at one and the same time a property of matter and its reflection. Therefore consciousness cannot subsist alone without being opposed to matter, but the contrary is not true, which shows the logical inconsistency of attempting to define matter by means of consciousness. The fact that Lenin could see only this one way of defining matter certainly does not mean that matter's property of being "objective reality" is its most essential property. This property is the most essential one only for philosophical materialism of a Leninist type. But, of course, to be the most essential quality of matter and the most essential quality of philosophical materialism are two entirely different things. Instead of dogmatically regarding Lenin's definition as an eternal truth, we should rather understand it within the context of his struggle against "bourgeois" philosophy and his defense of materialism.[46]

Zhelev's critique—his name came to be the most prominent of the three—already begun in his Doctoral thesis, led to his exclusion from the Bulgarian Communist Party in 1965 and eventually to constant persecutions of him by the official ideologists and by the Zhivkov regime, which saw itself as the intended object of his famous monograph, *Fascism* (Sofia, 1982). This work was banned immediately after its publication and circulated only clandestinely. Once again, just as in the 1960s,[47] persons faithful to the "April line" were to be found pronouncing judgments against the book, which in fact was said to be not very philosophically sophisticated.[48] Unwilling to publish the executioners' reviews, D. Spassov, editor-in-chief of *Filosofska Misul* at the time, resigned and then proceeded in his last published work to date, *Dogmatism and Anti-Dogmatism in Philosophy* (1984), to inveigh against administrative sanctions and untheoretical ways of conducting philosophical debate.[49]

Executioner or Victim: The Case of Aesthetics

In such an atmosphere of unrelenting conflict, there appeared a mountain of ideological books of the dullest sort, as well as some efforts at thinking independently of the dominant political forces, if not in opposition to them. Such efforts were especially fruitful in logic,[50] in the history of philosophy,[51] in ethics,[52] and above all in aesthetics.[53] Thus, independent thinkers such as Isaak Passy and Iskra Tzoneva attempted to define the object of aesthetics outside of Marxist-Leninist limits. By intentionally adopting the tautology, "Aesthetics is the science of the artistic awareness of the world" Passy was basically accepting Schelling's refusal of a clear-cut definition in favour of a delimitation of the aesthetic domain. An analysis of aesthetics, he contended, shows it to be a generic concept which includes four subordinate categories that together constitute the principal concepts of aesthetic science: the Beautiful, the Sublime, the Tragic, and the Comic. The Beautiful is the fundamental one, since the Sublime, the Tragic, and the Comic cannot be defined apart from it. As a philosophical science aesthetics is concerned with the principles and structure of the Beautiful, the Ugly, etc., and not with beautiful or ugly things, which are the objects of applied sciences such as design. Aesthetics asks the question, "What is the beautiful?" and not how to create beautiful things. At the same time aesthetics, in reflecting on art and on artistic creation, must also, as part of its purview, take account of a domain that belongs, strictly speaking, to art itself: the analysis of the image and of imagination, of artistic criteria and mastery (talent, genius), of the form and content of the object of art, of the process of creation, and so forth.

For her part, I. Tzoneva advocated approaching aesthetics through a return to Kant, Schelling, and Hegel, with a view to reviving the old identification of the aesthetic (*das Ästhetische*) with axiology (*das Axiologische*). Axiology is produced by a conscious awareness of objective reality that is both determined but also, at the same time, chosen. The aesthetic as such does not have independent objective existence, although it is an aspect of objective reality. It is not necessary knowledge, although it is an aspect of things that are knowable. The aesthetic is value—the sensory image of an internal and essential human activity.[54] In the early 1980s this was a rather daring position, since the person defending it ran the risk of drawing down on herself all the accusations of idealism. The reason why Tzoneva got away with it was simply that her work was too intelligently written and thus incomprehensible to the office of censorship. Despite the fact that she had been and remained a marginal philosopher within the system, during the later time of repressions carried out against Bulgarian philosophers (1987-89) Tzoneva had the courage publicly to reject these repressive methods. In her 1989 article in *Filosofska Misul*, "In Defense of Philosophical Aesthetics", she turned to an analysis of Bakhtin's thesis concerning the receptivity of the aesthetic as well as Losev's idea of the symbolism of art; in doing so, she was deliberately dealing with two martyrs of "official" Soviet aesthetics, an aesthetic tradition which was, as Tzoneva put it, not only an executioner but also a victim. The analogy with Bulgarian aesthetics was obvious:

> Each day we experience a fear, a burning shame at our inability, become almost a second nature, to say what we think, to defend the individual whom those who are unjust but powerful are persecuting, to sacrifice our comfort, to offer resistance in discussions of ideas or in moral struggles.[55]

This fear, especially on the part of intellectuals, and the injustices of political regimes are symbolized in works of art (e.g., A. Platonov's novels or V. Petrov's poetry) and are felt in the development of Bulgarian aesthetics itself, which has evolved in terms of two principal oppositions: reality/symbol, executioner/victim.

It is in terms of these oppositions that, unfortunately, not just aesthetics, nor even just philosophy, but indeed the entire intellectual, spiritual life of the Eastern Bloc was forced to proceed.

Contradictions within the "Younger Generation"

"Anti-Marxism" or "lack of scientific investigation"—these were, during a thirty-year period, the usual accusations that "the faithful" made against philosophers of the "younger generation" in order to protect themselves from them and keep power. What was needed for advancement in this situation was far from professional qualities, but rather just the opposite: strong patrons with enough influence to launch the new candidate for an assistantship or a research fellowship. These patrons were either professors, faculty deans, or department heads at ideological Institutes, or else "all-powerful" institutions such as the Bulgarian Communist Party, the Union of Communist Youth, or the secret services. Thus the majority of these candidates were promoted in an atmosphere that favored flattery and a spirit of careerism. Books and articles written by young philosophers were generally and above all filled with bows to recognized "authorities"—the Secretary Genera of the Party, official Bulgarian and Soviet ideologues, the thesis director, etc. On the whole this style prevailed, despite certain isolated revolts, up to the moment of perestroika. It was primarily that breath of fresh air which brought about more open discussions and the adoption of positions more critical of the "authorities", who began to be objects of ridicule. Such views became evident during the Second Canadian-Bulgarian Exchange (Varna, August 26-September 1, 1987) and especially at the First Symposium of Young Philosophers (Plovdiv, December 10-13, 1987).

The first of these was dominated by young Bulgarian philosophers — P. Spassova, D. Petrova, I. Raynova, A. Stefanov, H. Smolenov, E. Lazarova, M. Marinov, T. Batouleva, *et al.* — an unusual state of affairs for meetings organized by the Bulgarian Philosophy Society; this was due to the paucity of professors of the older generation who spoke French or English. The effect was to create an atmosphere of open discussion free of ideological overtones. The theme of the conference, "The Place of Philosophy in Culture", was more or less recognized by everyone as having a double importance, to wit, that philosophy is in some sense the highest consciousness of culture, and yet at the same time philosophy is born and develops within a concrete cultural milieu. But the young Bulgarian philosophers stressed the relative character of cultural agents' dependence on their milieu and the importance of individual personality and choice of perspective in philosophical and cultural creation in general. In her paper, perhaps the most perceptive of the conference, entitled "The New Social Movements and the Old Utopias", Dimitrina Petrova singled out the extra-institutional or anti-institutional nature of the new movements as their most characteristic feature. By contrast with the idealism of old-fashioned utopias, the image of the new social movements, actively committed to liberation from the existing social order, features lack of organization and of authoritarian methods of leadership, decentralization, tendencies to change lifestyles and forms of cultural communication, non-politicization, and total cultural opposition to repressive social structures. According to Petrova, philosophers should join such movements if they wish to influence contemporary life. In any case they must avoid playing the role of guardians in Plato's ideal state.

Pravda Spassova sought to define the philosophical boundaries of art and in particular of literature. In her paper, "Philosophy and *Belles Lettres*", she observed that if "philosophy" were to be identified with "*Weltanschauung*", then everyone would be a philosopher and in this sense the works of Tolstoy or of Dostoyevsky would be thoroughly "philosophical". On the other hand, as a science, in other words as a systematic or systematized study, philosophy has no place in art; indeed, such a scientific approach leads to a nullification of the artistic value of literary, theatrical, or cinematographic works, as well as to an adulteration of the serious nature of the work of philosophy. When the boundary line between doing philosophy and doing art breaks down, the results are seldom positive. This can be seen, according to her, in the literary and dramatic writings of Voltaire, Witkiewicz, or Sartre. If, then, art is to play an emotional mediating role between different social and cultural groups, it must be communicable and not make use of empty abstractions.

In her paper, "French Existentialism and Contemporary Culture", I. Raynova attempted to clarify philosophy's cultural task by analyzing the one philosophy, French existentialism, that more than any other has affected all the various principal cultural spheres. Having surveyed the existentialist adaptation of Dostoyevsky and the influence of Sartre, de Beauvoir, and Camus on philosophy, literature, theatre, film, sociology, and psychology in the United States, Japan, Germany, Spain, Italy, and so on, she attempted to explicate the deeper reasons for such influence. It was, she said, the ambiguity of history and of a contemporary culture that was torn between a faith in the future with its distinctively human possibilities, on the one hand, and the presentiment of its eventual loss, on the other. Hence the central role of contemporary philosophy and culture is to recover the lost unity of man and world. Only from this perspective could one understand Dostoyevsky's dictum that the true guarantee for mankind lies, not in isolated individual effort, but in common human unity.

This stress on the unity of the world, philosophies, and cultures was an obvious challenge to the dominant "old style" of thinking oppositionally and of always speaking of "two classes", "two blocs", and "two cultures". A couple of the best-known senior participants in the meetings, Dobrine Spassov and Venant Cauchy, noted its novelty and welcomed it.[56]

Paradoxically and tragically, however, the movement in the direction of "Western" pluralism and democracy, undertaken by the "younger generation",[57] had as its outcome a restoration of the old intolerance and division into groups and eventually a mere reversal of slogans. This tendency could already be perceived at the First Symposium of Young Philosophers, where the latter for the first time openly came out in opposition to the "old-timers" and to the Zhivkov regime. Its general theme, Philosophy and Society, was to have been treated in three subsections: "The Real World as a Philosophical Problem", "History and Self-Consciousness", and "Images of the Future". But in fact the participants spoke of nothing but the restructuring (perestroika) of Bulgarian society, the civil state, and coming political and economic reforms. Above all, the talks expressed disagreement with Zhivkov's rejection of Gorbachev's turn and his recent move to have four professors, who had openly criticized him in front of the general assembly of the University of Sofia, expelled from the Party. Since the subsection on "Images of the Future" had been, significantly enough, cancelled, there remained only one forum at the symposium for dealing with more strictly philosophical issues: the round table on "The Tasks of Philosophy". But there, too, only politics was discussed, with the exception of a single paper of a seriously theoretical nature, by the present coauthor (I. Raynova), "The Temporal and Projective Nature of Philosophy: Phenomenologico-Existential Conceptions of the Future".

From this time on, the tendency to speak only of socio-political problems and of the need to dismantle the system came to dominate all "philosophical" discussions. This atmosphere did, it is true, allow for the gradual discovery of the genuine inclinations of members of the younger generation, who, setting aside enormous individual differences, can today be classified (similarly to members of the "older generation") into romantic democrats (D. Petrova, P. Staikov, K. Stanchev, Krassimir Kanev, D. Kdzuranov), "marginals" (R. Stupov, P. Spassova, I. Raynova, A. Litschev, A. Stefanov, I. Kazarski, R. Teocharova, D. Dejanov, M. Tabakov, *et al.*), disguised Marxists, democrats in bad faith, and, as ever, the "faceless" group whom we refrain from enumerating. But how did these profound divisions come about?

In the 1970s, the "young" had been practically excluded from official activities of the nation's philosophical life; this can be seen in a particularly striking way in the records of the Fifteenth World Congress of Philosophy, the first to be held in a socialist country, which took place in Varna in 1973. In the 1980s, on the other hand,when many deans and other administrators left the scene and the anti-dogmatists were on the rise, the situation suddenly changed. Particularly at the Institute of Philosophy, where there was a large number of young researchers, the opposition between generations became increasingly noticeable. Criticism and dissatisfaction with the incompetence and the repressive adminis- tration of the "old-timers" led to revolts within the organizations of young com- munists and within the professional union, which blocked resolutions passed by the Party. The younger people protested against the monopoly held by the older generation over membership in the Party, against their being prevented from playing a more active role in philosophical life and from having any control over the work of the administrative and scientific councils, etc.

Three events in particular finally brought about the closing of the Todor Pavlov Institute of Philosophy: (1) a "power-struggle" between two groups of "old-timers" over the directorship of the Institute; (2) the ongoing clash between the two generations; (3) the leading role played by the younger members and by the Institute's union organization in creating the Committee for the Ecological Defense of the City of Ruse. This committee, formed to protest the pollution of Ruse by a Rumanian factory in the city of Giurgiu across the Danube River, seized the occasion to declare itself in opposition to Zhivkov, who was not doing enough to resolve the problem because of his unwillingness to damage his good relations with Ceaucescu. The preliminary action committee, based at the Institute and also including some activists from Ruse, organized a meeting at the Film Center in Sofia that drew more than 300 intellectuals, despite the fact that the meeting had been banned by Communist Party organizations. Having shown the film, "Breathe!" about the situation in Ruse, these intellectu- als then officially formed the Committee proper and sought to have it officially registered as an ecological organization. Fearing that this organization would turn into an opposition party, Zhivkov and the Party Politburo gave orders to the court not to register it, and the court obeyed. The press was also ordered to keep silent on the matter and did so, with the exception of the "Sofia News". The members elected to the Organizing Committee were called one by one to testify before the Politburo and were ordered to resign from the Committee. Those who refused to comply were expelled from the Party. This brought about a general opposition to the Zhivkov regime on the part of intellectuals. Zhivkov, furious at this turn of events, undertook a number of repressive measures and commissioned the writing of a famous, now historic, document, *Theses on Perestroika in the Intellectual Sphere*.

Ostensibly, this document assigned great importance to the social role of the intelligentsia; once again, mediocrity was denounced, lip-service was paid to the need to de-bureaucratize, to be open to developments worldwide, and to encourage creative initiative. But the real purpose of the document was to denounce the organizers of the Ruse Committee for having acted out of "anti-Party and anti-government" motives, as well as to condemn the Artists' Union for having defended its president, who had been an organizing member of the committee. With a view to eliminating opposition among intellectuals, meetings of all the principal Party organizations were called at which this document was to be discussed, in the presence of a Politburo member, with particular reference to concrete issues of "creativity" within the given organization. After such a meeting with Party members of the Institute of Philosophy (already under close scrutiny by the secret services), at which the "old-timers" argued and the younger members showed their disgust, Politburo member I. Iotov (principal watchdog on the ideological front) whispered to Zhivkov that the best solution would be to close this Institute and then to reopen it after undertaking a certain "selection" process. Those charged with this task were the full and corresponding members of the Academy (BAS) from the field of philosophy. They were to elect the new Scientific Council of the new Institute of Philosophical Sciences and then, along with this group, to select the researchers and employees of the Institute and arrange its structure. This is one of the principal reasons why these Academicians and corresponding members were so fiercely attacked during the meetings of the Bulgarian Philosophy Society on November 9 and 10, 1989. The Tenth being, as it turned out, the day on which Zhivkov announced his departure from the political stage, the opposition felt its strength vastly increased. It therefore confronted the Council and the Society President, N. Iribadzhakov, head-on, and voted in favour of wording in the bylaws of the new Bulgarian Philosophical Association that expressly identified it as "non-Marxist".

In this way November the Tenth marked the date of freedom regained and, simultaneously, of the third fatal break in Bulgarian intellectual life in general and philosophical life in particular. Having regained their freedom, the "younger generation" became increasingly strong and the tone of arrogance in the new power struggle more pervasive than before. True, this new freedom permitted I. Raynova, coauthor of the present article, finally to establish officially the first philosophical society outside of the main professional association, namely, the *Société Bulgare de Philosophie et de Culture de Langue Française*, which had been banned in May of 1989 by Academy member S. Ganovski.[58] But while this society and others, such as the Hegel and Kant Societies, were being established, most philosophers rushed into political life. Zheliu Zhelev, who had participated only distantly in philosophical life after his polemic concerning the Leninist definition of matter and the subsequent publication of *Fascism*, became, first, leader of the opposition, then party chairman of the Union of Democratic Forces, and finally President of the Republic, from which position he has supported the appointment of philosophers to political jobs. Since then, a large number of philosophers have become Cabinet members, party chairpersons, deputies, and ministers. Thus, very paradoxically, philosophy in Bulgaria changed from being the servant of a Party to being at the mercy of diverse political passions. Very few philosophers have spoken out against this new threat of subordinating or even eliminating philosophy as such.[59] It is quite easy to explain this: since November 10, 1989, the main question has changed from "How to get ahead?" to "How to cover all bets for Number One?"

In large measure, the same background situation also explains the choice of theme for the Sixteenth International School of Varna (formerly also named after Todor Pavlov), held in June 1990: "Marxist Philosophy and the Contemporary World", which should be interpreted as "What is to be done?" It was also significant that, for various political reasons, at least three well-known habitual Bulgarian participants — D. Spassov, N. Iribadzhakov, and S. Ganovski — were not in attendance there, the first being involved in parliamentary elections and the other two being out of the picture. The same political whirlwind had also removed such gifted younger philosophers as D. Petrova, Krassimir Kanev,[60] K. Stantschev, and P. Staikov from involvement in the School and explains why the sessions had less to do with the problem of Marxist philosophy than with socio-political questions concerning the changes in Eastern Europe. Among the comparatively rare philosophy papers were those by E. Panova, who dealt with aspects of Marxist theory of knowledge; by the participants in the sessions on "Marxism and Postmodernism" (W. McBride, I. Raynova, B. Zaschev, D. Rasmussen, D. Vorsonovtzev); and by a few other North American participants, notably T. Rockmore and F. Cunningham. For the most part, the members of the large Soviet delegation were preoccupied with their own domestic socio-politico-economic problems; no one who heard the Soviet speakers at Varna should have been greatly surprised at the overall trend of subsequent events in that country. Most of the American participants, other than those already mentioned, came under the auspices of the Society for the Philosophical Study of Marxism, which had received a general invitation. Some of the latter were veterans of old ideological wars in their own country, in particular those of the McCarthy Era; they tended on the whole to defend more "orthodox" versions of Marxism. This led to a distinct picture of a *"verkehrte Welt"*, since, as a Russian speaker jokingly remarked, it seemed that the only remaining real Marxists were the Americans. In fact, just prior to the beginning of his own presentation at Varna, the American coauthor of the present article was admonished by a Bulgarian participant that the extent of several other Americans' sympathy for Marxism had caused offense, and that he would do well not to imitate them.

In short, Political Correctness of a comparatively new variety had taken root in Bulgaria. If, twenty years earlier, the death of Marx had already been proclaimed in the West, it was now the turn of Bulgarian philosophers to take up the refrain,"Communism is dead," and to identify it as responsible for all evils. This refrain was the central one particularly at the international conference on "Responsibility and Guilt" held in April 1991 in Sofia, at which former professors of Marxism-Leninism sought to declare themselves "guiltless" by deflecting blame on others.

And so, as soon as the charges of "anti-Marxism", "idealism", "anticommunism", and "imperialism" had disappeared from view, charges of "Marxism", "materialism", "communism" (meaning Bolshevism), and "totalitarianism" followed in their wake. A new wave of destruction and intolerance, of flattery and servility replaced the old waves in the name—ironically, the same one as before—of DEMOCRACY. In a quick exchange of roles, the executioners became victims, the victims executioners, the dogmatists became anti-dogmatists, the anti-dogmatists dogmatists, the opposition became the conservatives, the conservatives the opposition. ... And yet the plot remained the same, as in the four historical sequences of D. W. Griffiths' "Intolerance". In the Bulgaria of 1992, nothing but ashes remain from the great burst of cultural and spiritual energy of the Ninth to Thirteenth Centuries.

After all, what can be expected? Is it not inevitable that the economic crisis, though less extreme than Russia's, and the political crisis, though less acute than Yugoslavia's, will place severe restraints on all efforts to remain a philosopher in a non-philosophical age and in a country of the absurd? It has become almost impossible for Bulgarian philosophers to publish books; the commercial market does not want them. *Filosofska Misul* (*Philosophical Thought*), having survived as it were by chance, has changed its name and its ambitions to *Philosophical Alternatives*. People are prepared for anything, because everything depends on the mood of the new directors of the Academy, of the Ministry of Science and Education, and of the government. However, the old ashes of more synthetic, transcendent approaches to knowledge[61] are still alive to aid in the rekindling of a new culture designed—in stark contrast to the words of the Dimitrov directive of 1946—to nurture "the intellectual aristocracy of an elite" rather than just a "democratic" lowest common denominator. Only through accepting some such ideal, the Bulgarian experience suggests, will it be possible to ensure the survival of a genuine philosophical outlook and activity which, instead of following in lockstep with the sociopolitical movements of the time and being at their mercy, remains in touch with the realm of intellect and spirit.

Ivanka Raynova
William McBride

University of Sofia
Purdue University

THE CRISIS OF CONTINUITY
IN POST-SOVIET RUSSIAN PHILOSOPHY[1]

To Reform or to Reconstruct Philosophy?

The changes underway in philosophy in Russia[1] strike a more than casual observer as part of a process the scope of which extends well beyond the confines of institutional or academic philosophy. There is little doubt that it can be characterized as a cultural crisis reaching down to the foundations. For philosophy, like most other disciplines in the humanities and the social sciences in which their own role in culture is a legitimate object of study, this crisis is tantamount to a loss of orientation compounded by doubts about resources and aptitudes required to promote the practice of philosophy as a viable cultural institution. By the same token, however, to observe this process of destabilization is to recognize that there is nothing like a warrant or guarantee that the practice of philosophy belongs essentially to a culture or must/should take this or that form. Whether implicitly or explicitly many Russian intellectuals conscious of their post-Soviet status are raising questions such as: what explains that a culture endows itself with a form of discourse which men call philosophy, and how is it that this discourse gains or loses in importance within a culture? The shift of attitude among Russian *intelligenty* that this questioning highlights is momentous: to pass out of a culture imbued with an articulated world-view in which a practice such as philosophy was essential, to a culture deprived of ideological foundations, anxious for its identity, and thus unsure what place to assign philosophers.

In the period between 1985, when Mikhail Gorbachev came to power, and late December 1991 when the Soviet Union ceased to exist, the culture of so-called "real existing socialism" was gradually dismantled. The process of dismantlement involved the Marxist-Leninist ideology and virtually all of the institutions that had existed in its name, including the Communist Party itself, the leadership of which initially promoted the process and finally submitted itself to its inexorable logic. Nevertheless, with the exception of some events in the political arena, virtually everything that occurred in the process of the self-dissolution of "real existing socialism" took place under the aegis of the central authorities, and can therefore be characterized as an institutional, not a revolutionary or chaotic, process. Until, that is, the events of mid-August 1991, the consequences of which unleashed the series of moves and decisions that by Christmas came to fruition in the collapse of the system.

To say these things is to draw attention to the circumstance that, prior to August, and despite the complexity of the difficulties in which Soviet institutions found themselves, it was still possible to understand the changes going on in philosophy in terms of a process of reform of Soviet philosophy. After August, and especially now that Russia is part of the newly formed Commonwealth of Independent States, it has become senseless to speak of Soviet philosophy at all: not only are its institutions virtually all but dead,[3] but what may have been a process of reform has degenerated into a sense of disorientation among the members of the philosophical community as they wait for decisions concerning their employment by the State (as well as the emerging private institutions).[3]

The specialist of cultural semiotics, the social psychologist, and advocates of the conception of the "social construction of reality" will easily pick out the symptoms of collapsing meaning structures which the "Soviet" social consciousness sustained even as all manner of "personal realities" were honed out of the cultural matrix of "real existing socialism". The consciousness in crisis is caught between recognition of the breakdown of the meaning structures which were its resources and the pressing need to sustain "personal reality" in a disintegrating social setting. The upshot is a crisis of identity directly proportionate to a sentiment of discontinuity fed by a sense of loss often giving rise to resentment, and indeed hopelessness.

How does this all this relate to philosophy? The answer is necessarily complex and hypothetical at the same time. To attempt it I will develop three main subjects:

1) Post-Soviets' own appraisal of the nature of Soviet philosophical practice (*glasnost* in philosophy);

2) an account of the last stage of Soviet philosophy concurrent with the mounting crisis of the *perestrojka* program;

3) an account of the main tendencies of actual philosophical practice with an eye to possible continuities as discussed under (1) and (2).

The hypothetical nature of the answer is due to the quite evident circumstance that very little of the data has come in, in particular that part which is of crucial importance: what post-Soviet Russian philosophers themselves have to say about the bearing of issues central to (1) and (2) on an evaluation of the continuity in their profession or lack thereof in view of the tendencies discernible at present (3). Most of what follows will concern what may be broadly characterized as meta-philosophical issues, that is attitudes to philosophy, its place and role in a culture in the throes of an identity crisis, and the central problem of settling on resources and aptitudes in the absence of which a community of philosophers cannot take form and evolve. The indeterminate state of the present situation can be highlighted by a series of questions about philosophy that are just as pertinent now as they were during the *perestrojka* period when signs of change were rife. Keeping them at the forefront of attention will be crucial to the main issue before us: is post-Soviet philosophy reconstructing itself altogether, or is there some continuity with the past, however described and evaluated? The questions I have in mind are the following:

1) Has post-Soviet philosophy disentangled itself from the "meaning-structures" central to the Marxist-Leninist cultural rationality, including the practices that were designed to transmit and reinforce the ideological dimension of philosophy under real existing socialism?

2) Are themes and problems being given expression that bear witness to philosophers' sensitivity to and articulation of the "consciousness" of a society wholly at odds with its former cultural rationality?

3) Is anything like a new "style" emerging in philosophical discourse that is testimony to a community-wide commitment to an autonomous form of expression freed from ideological constraints and stereotypes?

4) Are new sources of inspiration and conceptual models becoming evident in current research and discussion, in particular methodological orientations in tune with the tone of philosophy pursued in Western professional centers?

5) Does Marxist theory—in whatever guise—still play a role in philosophy, either by impacting central foundational matters or by promoting talk about matters not perhaps of central importance to philosophers elsewhere working out of different traditions (e.g., the ideological critique of consciousness, interest, power, etc.)?

The "Style" of Soviet Philosophical Practice

The sluggish reaction of the Soviet philosophical community to the first stages of Gorbachev's reform process has been documented in some detail (Ignatow 1990, van der Zweerde 1990, 1991, Bykova 1991, Buchholz 1991). The economic *perestrojka* campaign gained in symbolic importance as soon as Gorbachev tied it to the urgent need for "new thinking" which was to be stimulated through the collective examination of conscience known as *glasnost'*. To some extent, the popularity of the *glasnost'* campaign was tactically useful to stifle the grumblings of the conservatives and at the same time to distract attention away from the absence of serious political overhaul. Writers and historians — who were the leading lights of the *glasnost'* campaign during its heyday — were in a comparatively good position to articulate the background conditions of the reform process, since they were perceived as keepers of the nation's memory rather than as the harbingers of "truth". They were thus able to report on the damage done to the nation's morale by bureaucratic and political manipulation, while steering clear on the whole of attacks on the ideological framework of the system (Nove 1989). By comparison, philosophers found themselves in the unenviable position of having to respond to the call for "new thinking" within the limits prescribed by the officially set goals of the *perestrojka*, among others, to revive the spirit of socialist construction after the years of "stagnation" under Brezhnev. *Glasnost'* in philosophy was an exceedingly tricky business, therefore, since by having been absorbed into the official ideological machine philosophers had no evident independent way in the system to lay bare their souls that would not be tantamount to acknowledging that they had often been vessels of a dogma propagated for political effect. Pushed far enough a *glasnost* campaign in philosophy would have to face the judgment that what had passed for philosophy in the Soviet Union was often hardly the genuine article.

This is the social and political backdrop of the "last stage" of Soviet philosophy. Beginning approximately in 1988 philosophers bestirred themselves to supply their version of the "new thinking" in tune with one of Gorbachev's main slogans: that of reinstating the "human factor" as the main value in socioeconomic planning and production. The outcome was what I will call the "anthropocentric turn" in Soviet philosophy. That it ultimately faltered is a consequence of its "ideological" motivation as a response to the "official humanism". This meant that the philosophical establishment continued for a while still to practice its craft in a manner on the whole traditional to Soviet philosophy; rare were the philosophers who turned the appeal for "new thinking" back on philosophical practice as a prime test case for the ideas and theories they were proffering in support of the "new thinking". To understand then the thrust of what I call the "anthropocentric turn" in Soviet philosophy we need to examine first the *Lebenswelt* of the philosophical community, the style and horizon of its specific practices.

Fortunately, there are today a number of descriptions of that *Lebenswelt* which employ several key terms (Ivin 1989, 1990, Nikiforov 1990, Il'in 1991, Tsipko 1990, 1990c, Ojzerman 1989). These include "scholasticism", "dogmatism", "doctrinalism", "authoritarianism", the tendency to "schematism", and "mythologization". In employing language of this kind today's critics of stan-

dard Soviet philosophical practice are engaging in a form of analysis to which
Barbara Staniszkis has given the name "The Ontology of Socialism" in a book
of the same title (Staniszkis 1989). The question she raises is this: how is it that
men managed to create and reproduce a specific form of cultural rationality in
which the dominant patterns of meaning and communication conveyed a sense
of "determination" such that they understood their actions much more as collective responses than as constructive individual probings? Among Soviet theoreticians generally, but also among philosophers who have examined the question,
the answer picks out the virtually intrinsic connection between the political construction of social reality and the propagation of a mythical discourse about the
illusory object of this construction. What was thus obscured and then irretriev-
ably lost was a basis in genuine civilizational values, especially the delicate balance between institutional order and individual action usually identified as the
essence of "modernization" (Krizan 1990, 1991, Offe 1987).

The political construction of social being, called by some Russians "social
creationism" (Ivin 1989, Il'in 1991), is identified as the foremost trait of Soviet
cultural rationality. It is said to depend on the absence of, and indeed the
divorce from, any basis in human affairs; it is less an ideal, than a myth, in a
pejorative sense, since it substitutes fanciful constructions for principles derived
from individual and community action. Finally it is these fanciful constructions
which are clothed in the raiment of political jargon, thus institutionalizing the
break between ordinary social experience and the "official" cultural rationality.
If the resulting system can be called "totalitarian", in the sense that the dominant cultural rationality is explicitly articulated and imposed throughout society
by a political institution, it breeds a typically "dogmatic" form of consciousness.
While it has been characterized in a variety of ways, most writers agree about a
number of traits typical of the "dogmatic" frame of the Soviet mind. One is the
absence of a sense of genuine history, manifest in the tendency to devalue "prehistory" and rewrite "actual" history, both subordinated to a millennial view of
an ever yet to be realized ideal history. With no foundations, an individual is
prepared for self-sacrifice in the name of the mass, humanity, the socialist
future, etc. In this frame of mind, it is essential for the individual to ward off
doubts about the obvious discrepancy between the dominant cultural rationality
and the sorry state of the present. This is effected by exercising the "dogmatic"
option: "always subordinate the facts to the theoretical construction." (Ivin
1989)

One of the most uncompromising accounts of the effects of this mentality
on Soviet philosophy comes from the pen of Alexander Ivin. "The essence of
dogmatism," he writes, "is its intention always to proceed from ideas to facts
and never—from facts to ideas. The dogmatist who has once mastered an idea
uses it as a starting point for his judgments about reality, and is incapable of

noticing the idea's divergence from the changed circumstances. He would not even hesitate to adapt the circumstances in such a way that they acquire (at least in appearance) correspondence to the idea." As Soviet philosophy pandered to the political myth of social construction it engaged in a hollow verbal metaphysics about an imaginary reality. With this in mind, Ivin qualifies mainstream Soviet philosophy, starting in the Stalinist era, as "scholasticism" in the degenerate sense of a pseudo-intellectual enterprise subordinated to the inherently dysfunctional socialist cultural rationality.[5]

The scholastic philosopher in Ivin's description has withdrawn into "the airless space of 'pure', schematic reasoning," and for lack of contact with a real object of inquiry he is defenseless against "dogmatism".[6] The net result is an attitude that is not only less than "civilized" but destructive of disciplined communication in a community of philosophers. Speaking of the past, he writes: "One cannot pass over in silence the absence of personal courage, lack of faithfulness to scientific principles, as well as the indecency characteristic of many philosophers." Very recently, another commentator has written of the principle which in this environment governed the life practice of many: say one thing, think another, and do yet a third. (Zakharov 1991) Often, those who point out such traits of the "Soviet" mind focus on the way they cluster around a central characteristic of socialist cultural rationality which by implication marked the style of philosophical practice too, viz., the ascendancy of the mass over the individual. In a word—collectivism. Properties of individuals recede in importance compared with properties ascribed first to the class, but then, under the terms of the socialist political myth, to the monolith bereft of internal class distinctions.[7] In philosophy, notes Ivin, this collectivistic impetus explains the pervasive mentality of apprenticeship, to underscore perhaps the connection to one of the literal meanings of "scholasticism". It is, however, a debased apprenticeship, involving a "servile subjection to a pattern or scheme, a fear of breaking the circle of routinized topics," and resulting in "an inability to think and behave independently."

One of the most vociferous and widely known critics of Soviet cultural rationality, Aleksandr Tsipko, has engaged in an analysis of the plight of the intellectual in such circumstances that is strangely reminiscent of Ludwig Feuerbach's "transformative critique" of the idea of God. Noting how the Soviet intelligentsia was deprived of the conditions conducive to the pursuit of truth—viz., the expression of doubt, the search for theoretical precision through criticism, etc.—he asks: "How can a man stay healthy in such circumstances? There is only one solution: To endow the one accessible serious thinker—Karl Marx—with all those perfections of which this unfortunate creature is deprived." (Tsipko 1990c, p. 168) As if to echo this judgment, Aleksandr Nikiforov writes about the "[t]housands of lecturers and theoreticians [who] know nothing else but the dogmatism of mythologized Marxism, and can do nothing but propagandize it." (Nikiforov 1990, p. 127) The last remark is pertinent to a question to be examined further below, that of resources and aptitudes in current, post-Soviet thought; but it bears on one further consequence of the collectivism of Soviet intellectual practice. Ivin has noted a somewhat paradoxical state of affairs: depending on the period in Soviet history, that is the degree to which expression of ideological commitment was required of philosophers, many among them preferred to "emigrate" from philosophy to less sensitive domains such as logic, the methodology of science, but also the history of art and aesthetics and, perhaps above all, the history of philosophy. (Ivin 1989) The implication is clear: "philosophy" was left to the dogmatic, mythologized Marxist canon. In point of fact that meant that in abandoning "philosophy" intellectuals were leaving to one side what we might call "foundational issues", especially "pure" ontology and epistemology, which were ideologically sensitive to the highest degree.[8] The areas to which they turned instead, though also ideologically delicate, could often claim contact with counterpart empirical disciplines thus endowing their research with a somewhat "factographical" aspect. This absence of foundational considerations will be of considerable significance presently in assessing the reasons why the "last stage" of Soviet theory, the "anthropocentric turn", remained very much in the mould of traditional Soviet doctrinalism.

Summing up, philosophers in Russia today often describe their previous philosophical practice as dogmatic and scholastic, meaning that:

1) a discursive, analytic style remained underdeveloped: instead of elaborating arguments relying at least in part on conceptual explication and theoretical precision practitioners typically resorted to narrative commentaries reinforced by a "quotadological" technique employing the resources of Marx, Engels, Lenin, and the current first secretary of the party as well as party decrees;

2) foundational, i.e., ontological and epistemological, research, remained underdeveloped: the doctrine "developed" by a series of mechanical applications of the core of historical and dialectical materialist theory to areas about which the "classics" (Marx, Engels, Lenin) had had little or nothing to say, e.g., philosophical aesthetics,[9] meta-ethics, philosophy of language, logic, etc.;

3) to admit influences from without the Marxist pale, philosophers had first to rework concepts and theories in the accepted standardized language of the

doctrine, thus virtually eliminating possible avenues of exchange with their non-Marxist counterparts.[10]

These three characteristics laid the ground for two further traits that pertain to the pervasive collectivist style of Soviet philosophical practice:

4)   the anonymity of expression, what might be described as the absence of the "author" in what was a massive output by an army of workers;[10]

5)   the absence of effective communication among practitioners, as evidenced by the virtually unchanging body of doctrine and the curious absence of definite results arising out of the many discussions promulgated in the pages of the popular and professional press.

With traits such as these in mind Aleksandr Tsipko has drawn a conclusion that appears to be disastrous as far as the continuity of post-Soviet cultural identity is concerned, especially for philosophers:

> Who would dare demonstrate that Marxism enriched Russian culture, raised it to a higher level? No one! But it is very easy to show how the forced ideologization of the nation's spiritual life after the revolution, the forceful imposition of Marxism, ultimately led to a catastrophe. Spiritual life came to a standstill, and philosophy practically died in our country. (Tsipko 1990c, p. 168)[11]

The "Anthropocentric Turn" in Soviet Philosophy

The foregoing account of "typical" Soviet philosophical practice derives in large measure from criticisms by members of the profession—*glasnost'* in philosophy—articulated at a moment (1989, and early 1990) when it was clear to all that Gorbachev's program of reform was failing. Ironically, such open and free criticism coincided with the crystallization of what I called above the "last stage" of Soviet philosophy: the "anthropocentric turn", which was the philosophical counterpart of the ideological theme associated with *perestrojka*,—extolling the "human factor". I want to reconstruct the inner "logic" of this short-lived ultimate stage of Soviet philosophy against the background of the breakup of its institutional basis.

At the end of 1989, after a considerable degree of preparation and fanfare, a collectively authored textbook of philosophy, *Vvedenie v filosofiju* (*Introduction to Philosophy*), was published. (Ignatow 1990, van der Zweerde 1990) As its appearance coincided with far-reaching changes throughout the system of higher learning, in particular the scrapping of obligatory courses in Marxist-Leninist ideology (Buchholz 1990), it seems literally to have fallen stillborn off the press, never in fact to assume the function for which it was destined and in this way at least to influence philosophy.

On the whole, the textbook's authors were of one mind about its purpose: to excite "new thinking" attuned to the socioeconomic transformations under way in the Soviet Union. In their bid to achieve this, the authors latched on to the ideologically promulgated "humanism" and attempted to work out some of its internal intricacies with an eye to the history of philosophy—the first volume—as well as to a number of crucial concepts required for the proposed restoration of the authentic spirit of socialist principles—the second volume.

The central axis of the two volumes is the human being—man. But to say this—and it is little indeed!—is hardly to specify the significance of the anthropocentric turn in Soviet philosophy. One might well ask: man as ... what? The rational animal? Homo faber? Homo ludens? The "subject" or its complex counterpart: the supposedly common referent of the multiple discourses of the modern social sciences and humanities (à la Foucault and the deconstructivists of the post-structuralist reaction)? None of these solutions fits the bill as far as Soviet philosophers of this last period were concerned. For them, the turn to man occurred in terms of a concept that remains as ambiguous and controversial in philosophy today as that of man simpliciter, viz., the person (or in terms which seem to imply a specific dimension of the human being—personality; the Russian word "*licnost*" admits both translations) (Swiderski, 1989, 1991).

To see what these philosophers were getting at one has to read the relevant chapters in the textbook against the background of a number of discussions that had grown in importance in the years since Gorbachev launched his programme of reform. Philosophers had been using the space opened by the retreat from Marxist-Leninist orthodoxy ('Stalinism') to study a number of "categories" that had been, as it were, suspect in the traditional doctrine given their uncertain relation to its social collectivism and determinism. These included above all culture (Swiderski 1988), consciousness (Bakhurst 1991, Mamardasvili 1990, 1991), spirituality (Ksenofontov 1991, Fedotova 1990), and morality (Gusejnov 1991, Apresjan 1991).

The Western reader may well infer that, in relation to this list, the category of the person was being envisaged along lines of, for instance, an existentialist, or religious, or ethical-humanist (rights-oriented) personalism. How far this was indeed the case can be gleaned with more accuracy by contrasting this list with a list of categories belonging to mainstream Marxist-Leninist philosophy. The contrast will help to determine the degree of "negative" correspondence between the lists in relation to what might be called the global qualities sustained by each set of categories.

New categories	Old categories
Person (-ality)	Social subject/man's essence as the "ensemble of social relations"
Culture	Forms of social consciousness in the superstructure
Spirituality (self-integration)	Social morality
Consciousness	Biosocial reflection

The consistent occurrence of "social" among the "old categories" identifies the global feature which, in orthodox Marxism-Leninism, characterizes all aspects of human existence, viz., "social being". However, the social being in question has nothing to do with an intrinsic, constant feature of a human nature exemplified in a variety of social forms. Rather it is best understood in a relationist, indeed holist, sense as conveyed by Marx's admonition to Feuerbach: the "human essence" is no abstract nature inhering in each individual, it is rather the ensemble of the social relations. Thus instead of saying, from this point of view, that man is conscious or that man is moral the Marxist prefers to say man has a consciousness or man has a morality, meaning thereby that it is imperative to know what (which) consciousness or morality is meant, and to answer not in psychological ("personal") terms but in terms of specific so-called forms of social consciousness and their "determinants" (the factors governing the structure of social relations). In other words, in the picture arising out of the "old categories", one could say that man's nature/essence lies outside of him, in a collective structured by economic and ideological relations governed by "laws" that Marx claimed operated independently of men's wills. Most importantly, as this structured collective has undergone repeated transformations, there is no basis to the claim that human nature is constant; on the contrary, it is thoroughly historical, being in the end but the abbreviated name of specific forms of social existence.

By contrast, against the backdrop of the "official humanism", the "new categories" seem to exhibit a picture of the human being at odds with the collectivist thrust of the "old categories". Nominally, the anthropocentric turn presaged a recovery of individualism as the "global quality" projected by the concepts brought into play by the philosophers involved in "new thinking". However, although individualism is a nice slogan, we are hardly very far along when we conclude that "individualist personalism" is being defended.

To see why, let me first note, after J. M. Bochenski, that in orthodox Soviet philosophy social collectivism has an ontological ring that is almost certainly due to Engels' transposition of Marx's social relationism to natural processes in order to explain the properties of bodies.[12] In Soviet philosophy the effect was to ordain the domain of human being as a sub-domain in the cosmos and as such to subordinate its elements to a single set of dynamic processes that Engels' dialectical laws (*pace* Hegel) are said to capture. Hence, the classic Soviet view of man is, to use Bochenski's term, decidedly "cosmocentric".

Now looking at the list of "new categories" one might well think of "cosmocentric" philosophies other than Soviet dialectical materialism which managed quite well to accommodate the "person". For instance, the ontology of Nicolai Hartmann, in which the categorial specificity of the human being qua "person" does not preclude, but on the contrary presupposes, its supervenience ("emergence") on ontically more fundamental domains. (Hartmann 1953) Why then do I claim that the shift in Soviet thought presaged anthropocentrism?

A less than casual reader will note that, in the table above, morality is not listed among the "new categories". In orthodox Marxist-Leninist thought, to speak of morality was to refer not to a facet of human nature (to reiterate a point made above) but, on the contrary, to a manifestation or form of class interest that was said to undergo change and finally disappear as class interests disappeared in communist society. Like essence, therefore, morality in orthodox doctrine had no positive, constant quality or nature. It is appropriate, therefore, that the list of new categories contrasts not morality but "spirituality" (*duchovnost'*) to social morality; spirituality is the name given to an immanent disposition in virtue of which an individual unifies his many powers and abilities, etc., in a wholly personal, unique manner. (Kagan 1985, Fedotova 1991, Ksenofontov 1991) And this personal "order"—the self integrating [= "consciousness"] resources for meaningful action [= "culture"]—is the basis of genuine morality. As such, therefore, morality, and not individualism, is the global quality projected by the set of new categories designed as the philosophers' answer to the appeal for "new thinking" about the "human factor".[14]

The spirit if not quite the letter of this conclusion is evident throughout the many systematic chapters of the second volume of the textbook. It is especially evident in the discussion, or rather the lack thereof, of the so-called "basic question of all philosophy": to be or not to be a materialist.[15] As one of the authors of the textbook avers, the leading philosophical question should be what is man all about. And to give weight to her considerations she draws on Kant for whom, as she recalls, philosophy was destined to answer three questions: what can man know, what can he do, and what can he hope for? (*Vvedenie* [Kozlova, M.] 1990) One can take from this invocation of Kant that the author abhors dogmatism (the Marxist-Leninist cosmocentric *Weltanschauung*) and recognizes the "practical" vocation of philosophizing (as contrasted with the scientistic rationalism of received Soviet philosophy).

In short, the anthropocentric turn in Soviet philosophy seems to have been tantamount to the acceptance of what may be called "moral personalism". I write "seems to have been" not only in light of my earlier remark that the textbook, in which this personalism received its fullest expression to date, not only failed to function in its intended role, but also because in many respects the "anthropocentric turn" itself remains schematic and indeterminate. So saying we return to the underlying questions about philosophers' resources and aptitudes in the context of Soviet philosophical practice.

The Inherent Limitations of the Anthropocentric Turn

Today, philosophers in Moscow rather ruefully acknowledge the "dialectical dependence" of the anthropocentric turn on the spirit, and in many ways still the letter, of Marxism-Leninism.[16] At least four considerations sustain this evaluation. First, to use a familiar analogy, it might be said that the new "paradigm" did not take shape as a response to the inability of the standing conception to deal with anomalies encountered with increasing frequency in the chosen area of investigation. Instead, philosophers were responding to the bidding by the keepers of the ideology to engage in "new thinking" for the sake of the official humanism promulgated to reinvigorate the social psychology. Second, it is widely claimed today that the anthropocentric turn in Soviet thought exploited resources that had been developed in the philosophical "underground" during the sixties. At that time a group of philosophers and sociologists began explicitly to oppose Marx to the established Soviet doctrinal monolith.[16] In this respect, therefore, the moral personalism of the new humanism carried an additional ideological charge: it was an implicit claim about the "authentic" basis of Marxism as opposed to its distorted official face. Third, despite the attractive ring of the moral personalism projected throughout the pages of *Introduction to Philosophy* as well as in lead-up articles about culture, consciousness, spirituality, morality, etc., there is little "substance" in the arguments. What is lacking is foundational work that would have put pressure on the received ontological and epistemological doctrines of Marxist-Leninist doctrine. And this observation leads to the fourth point: the new "paradigm" emerged in the absence of a thoroughgoing review, least of all a critique, of the main doctrinal tenets of Soviet dialectical and historical materialism.

How far philosophy was still part of the ideological establishment at the end of the last decade can be measured by the contrast between the moral personalism touted in the pages of the professional literature (including the aforementioned textbook) and the kind of virulent vilification of the Communist mentality set out in the so-called "thick" literary journals by acclaimed publicists (e.g., Tsipko, Kljamkin, Butenko, Migranjan, Lisichkin, *et al.*). On one

side the philosophers were extolling the virtues of humanism, while on the other
the publicists were mincing no words in vituperating the so-called humanist
content of the communist ideal that had been invoked so often as the deeper
sense of the miserable lot of the Soviet nation. The contrast is especially striking in the matter of foundational issues, e.g., the question about human nature.
Such publicists as A. Tsipko felt no compunction in attacking the general
Marxist, and not just Marxist-Leninist, thesis concerning the historical mutabili-
ty, inconstancy of human nature and the use to which the thesis was put by successive Soviet regimes (Tsipko 1990). In the meantime, philosophers remained
strangely silent on the matter, contenting themselves with talk about the moral
dimension of the human spirit.

True, some did invoke Kant, citing his doctrine of the categorical imperative as the basis of genuine moral behaviour (Solov'ëv 1988, 1991a,b).
However, no one confronted the question whether, in appropriating this much of
Kant's practical philosophy, they were responsible, so to say, to the remainder,
in particular to the circumstance that in as much as Kant speaks of the "person"
at all he would no doubt locate personhood with "absolute freedom" in the
noumenal realm. At the very least, therefore, personhood could not be grounded
in the category of substance which in the Kantian perspective is a "naturalistic"
category reserved for the empirical sciences. Others placed so much emphasis
on what they dubbed the spiritual dimension of the person—the capacity to inte-
grate action and experience around a core of values for the self—that a comparison of their position with Max Scheler's personalism seemed justified. For
Scheler the person is the ever reconstituted unity of her acts, dynamic and virtual in being, and thus incompatible with substance, which Scheler like Kant
(notwithstanding the many differences between them) treats as a naturalistic
category alien to the spiritual nature of the person. Were the Soviet philosophers
in question prone to accept Scheler's ontology of the person and what goes with
it, the stratified picture of the structure of the world (otherwise developed by
Nicolai Hartmann)? There is no telling one way or the other, since the foundational issue of the ontology of the person remained a dangler. (Swiderski 1992)

One can guess, however, that to the extent that the new paradigm was an
implicit statement in behalf of the kind of ethical humanism that had been
attributed to Marx by philosophers in the sixties, it conflicted with mainstream
Marxism-Leninism.[18] But so long as the cosmocentrism of the latter had not
been challenged—and as of this date no review of the doctrine has been undertaken—it was easier to make allusions to a variety of sub-themes that had
grown out of discussions made possible by an earlier concern for the "authentic
Marx"—the "thaw" of the fifties and early sixties. A thumbnail sketch of those
themes can be readily devised to show how a personalist orientation would have
been quite compatible with them.

The allegedly "humanistic" young Marx was invoked in the late fifties in the setting of a discussion of aesthetic theory concerning the nature of aesthetic qualities (properties). (Swiderski 1979a,b) His early writings inspired those who wished to scale the aesthetic to the proportions of the human being's place in the world, viz., as the labourer who "humanizes" nature. The discussion around this matter could well be seen in Kantian terms—but à la Vico and transposed into the Marxian theme of humanization: in humanizing the world, do men not thereby also set the limits within which their cognitive powers are effective? The issue reappeared in a discussion of values in the mid-sixties, in particular in the thesis that values are objects in a relational, "subject-object" mode of existence of which the Marxian description of the commodity was accepted as the paradigm example.[19] The context of this problematic was, however, widened to become a general theory of culture very much reminiscent of German philosophies in which culture was hypostasized as a realm of "objective spirit". Certain writers appeared to invert the order of categories laid down in classical Marxism-Leninism: to the question about the being of the social (i.e., the structure of social relations) they answered that it was "cultural" in essence and thus a resource, and not merely the product, of human actions.[20]

The point here is that Soviet philosophers could continue to speak about humanized nature, value, culture, and so forth without raising suspicions among the ideological watchdogs that they were surreptitiously evincing canonical historical materialism so long as they also spoke in terms of collectivist, social categories of activity, like "material-transformative practice", "social production", and the like. The category of individual action was unmanageable since in the setting of Marxist-Leninist collectivism it was virtually spurious[21]; in what the writer Platonov once described as the "orgy of humanism" there was no question but that the "subject" of activity is humanity as a whole concretely manifested in its "mediated" forms: classes and successive social formations, with the proletariat finally emerging as the self-identical subject and object of history.

Given this background, it is quite plausible that when the personalism described above came to expression, its brokers could presumably rely on their more mature readers' associations to see in it what was in fact an evocation of a theory—and not the theory itself—of the human agent as responsible in the first place neither to Humanity nor to Society, but to herself.[22]

Would matters have been easier had Soviet philosophers of the late *perestrojka* stage directly confronted Marxist-Leninist doctrine and scrapped it piece by piece? It has to be recognized that this would be no mean undertaking. Many have demonstrated the complex nature of the doctrine, the heterogeneous nature of the elements that make it up, their diverse origins, and especially their different functions.[23] Only recently has there been a spate of attempts to criticize

Marxism at arm's length, so to speak, chief among which is an as yet only partially published discussion among philosophers, cinematographers, and artists entitled "Marxism: Pro and Contra" (also known by the titles "Is Marxism Dead?" and "The Emancipation of the Spirit").[2] Yet even here the confrontation is over what might be called the "general spirit" of the doctrine as a world-view, and very rarely over specific theses examined from the perspective of, say, a conceptual analysis. Why is this so?

Part of the answer consists in noting that the doctrine appears each time in a different light when it is examined in its relation to Marx, Lenin, and Stalin—the trio most often cited in this regard. The matter is the simplest when we start with Stalin. To have attacked and renounced him at the start of the *perestrojka* campaign was relatively straightforward; after all he had already been the butt of criticism in 1956 and his crimes once again became the object of something approaching a cultural industry during the height of *glasnost'* in 1988 and 1989. But even when all affirm that he concocted the doctrine of Marxism-Leninism (that some prefer to name Leninism-Stalinism) they have not always pushed the matter of attributions to its roots: where and with whom lies the source of the "Soviet" experience? To answer "Lenin" has always been a tricky business (Dahm 1990; Taras 1990; Ignatow 1990). So long as the Party existed, to criticize Lenin was to engage in an enterprise beset with risks, since, far from being regarded merely as a political leader in the narrow sense, the man had become the cherished symbol of the socialist myth, and thus the mainstay of Soviet cultural rationality represented by the Party's self-image as the chief architect of communism. To undermine Lenin was tantamount to cutting the ground out from beneath the nation's feet, or as some put it (who, in wishing to stress the continuity of Soviet and Russian culture, cited Pushkin), it would be tantamount to barbarism. What to say, then, about Marx? The irony here is that any criticism today of his doctrine has to face the fact that he has been continually set off against "parts" of himself: the young against the old, the scientistic economist of *Capital* against the romantic ethical humanist of the *Paris Manuscripts*, the champion of inexorable laws of social development against the prophet of revolution in the name of a realm of liberty in which man is the root of man, etc. Where is the connecting thread that would allow anyone to pick out the Marxian "idea" which when criticized would bring down the entire world view? Should we impugn Soviet and post-Soviet philosophers for their failure to discover and break this thread when we in noncommunist lands, with no a priori ideological commitment to the doctrine or a history of political subjugation to it, have for so long disputed the question about the key to the unity—or lack thereof—of the doctrine?

I said that this complexity of origin and function is part of the answer to the question why there is such an anaemic approach in the critique of the Marxist-

Leninist doctrine. The other part, more concrete and at the same time more telling with respect to the question about the absence of foundational research, is that already evoked earlier: by dint of rote repetition of canonical forms "the thousands of lecturers and theoreticians" who, to cite Nikiforov again, "know nothing else but the dogmatism of demythologized Marxism," have neither the resources nor the aptitudes to engage in the kind of critique that philosophy requires. The massive intrusion of the imaginary world of the social mythology into all the disciplines of the humanities effectively stunted the development of the kind of critical acumen promoting conceptual innovation and theoretical revision in a milieu of untrammeled communication. Another philosopher complains that the difficulties of articulating and thus criticizing the pervasive ills of the dogma are due in large measure to the "poverty of our conceptual lexicon for such things as social classes, the core of which took form in the middle of the last century." (Solov'ëv 1990, p. 163) Recognition of this lack is compounded by the acknowledgement that, for all the talk about coming to grips with Marxism, or even simply abandoning it, it is a deeply entrenched component of the cultural rationality. The philosopher just cited sums up the matter in this way. Writing about "Stalinism" as a structure of consciousness he explains that "… it is not a matter of economics as distinct from politics, of government as distinct from the people, even of social being as distinguished from social consciousness. It is a matter of the very being of consciousness, of such massively widespread modes of understanding which have entered deeply into everyday practice, have taken on a material, virtually thing-like solidity, and therefore obstinately resist 'all reason', all rational-critical proofs, demonstrations of the 'new thinking'. Looked at one way, these are mental representations, ideas, attitudes, characteristics of mind and spirit. Looked at in another, however, they turn out to be characteristics of people's factual situation, of their activity and communication—something that is virtually a part of their bodily [telesno] existence." (Solov'ëv 1990, p. 162)

To admit such things now, after the demise of the Soviet system, is to admit ipso facto that the "soil" in which latter-day Soviet philosophers were aspiring to cultivate "moral personalism" was hardly apt to nurture it. It is also to recognize that between the old "New Soviet Man" and his erstwhile successor, whatever be his outlook on the world, there is not likely to be any continuity and cultural identity.

W(h)ither Post-Soviet Philosophy?

Much of the conversation making the rounds in the corridors of the Institute of Philosophy in Moscow is pessimistic in tone, be it about the survival of the Institute—and by extension, as some see it, of philosophy as such!—or the fate of Russian cultural identity. A kind of informal consensus exists over an unwritten "check list" of the sorts of items that make up a "modern civilization" and that are said to be absent in post-Soviet Russia. It is an impressive list: civil society, democratic institutions, a functioning market, a law-governed state, as well as all those attitudes, mental representations and the like typically paired with such things in (idealized descriptions of) societies in which they can be said to exist, above all a moral frame of mind responsive to conscience and attuned to rights, duties and obligations in the sphere of civil society.

It is not easy to decide whether to describe a person who, on the basis of this kind of assessment, writes about post-Soviet Russia as a social ruin deprived of civilization as a post-romantic succumbing to *Weltschmerz* or an anti-post-modernist hankering for some great myth of cultural continuity, progress, national self-identity, and the like, including Marxist versions thereof. The old refrain about Russia being too underdeveloped in all those ways Marx's theory required for a society to pass from the capitalist to the socialist formation, has come back to haunt those who condemn the Soviet experiment, hope to save some sense of Russia's cultural worth, and yet continue to admire the socialist ideal. "But how can one be a Marxist," laments Vadim Mezhuev (Mezhuev 1990, p. 31), "where even this, in Marx's opinion, relative, historically restricted, and imperfect degree of freedom characterized by the institutions of private property, the market, and parliamentarism remains still ever distant and only desirable? What good is the idea of socialism for a nation that has yet to attain the level of normally civilized society?"

The same writer ruefully admits in this and other texts how difficult, indeed impossible, it is to imagine the revival of the socialist idea in an atmosphere of loathing directed to its Soviet form as this has been applied by violent means in what he repeatedly characterizes as "pre-civilizational" circumstances. (Mezhuev 1991) What, then, of philosophy and its possibilities in the light of the general cultural malaise?

So far philosophers have been spared the ignominy, on the institutional plane, that has been the fate of their formerly East German counterparts. With the unification of the German State commissions from the former Federal Republic have examined the credentials of professors of Marxism-Leninism and in many cases dismissed them from their posts virtually purging entire departments of their personnel. The implied comparison is a bitter one, but it has to be admitted that, were such independent commissions established in post-Soviet Russia, their results would not always be favourable to the parties screened. In point of fact, as one respected figure in the philosophical establishment told me, there is no guarantee that "good" philosophy, that is to say, philosophizing carried out with high quality resources by competent men and women, will survive in Russia.

The scenario he sketched had as much to do with personalities as with the uncertain future of institutions, due to the disappearance of all-union organs like the Academy of Science under whose wing fell the Institute of Philosophy in Moscow. But the matter goes deeper, right to the "civilizational" profile of the philosophical profession in post-Soviet Russia. "In the West," my contact pointed out, "the best philosophy is practiced in the universities and is thus intrinsically connected with teaching. With us, on the contrary, the best philosophy existed in the institutes of the Academy of Sciences, and these were given over to research, not teaching. The universities were beds of Marxist-Leninist dogma and the personnel entrusted with the task of transmitting the dogma were generally philosophically 'uncivilized'." What does the future hold? My respondent fears that if finances fail the Institutes may close, or at the very least suffer considerably through layoffs; whereas it seems that the universities are guaranteed, even though it can hardly be expected that philosophy falls among the economic priorities associated with their restructuring. Serious philosophers, those in possession of the requisite resources and aptitudes to engage in competent discussions, may well "disappear" from the institutional scene and practice the art in the manner of a *Freiberuf* or when time allows.[25] For his part, the director of the Institute, V.S. Stepin, is trying to head off any such "scandal" by urging the Russian government under Yeltsin to accept his plan to turn the Institute into a kind of teacher-training college for philosophy teachers in all centres of higher learning. At the present writing the fate of this proposal is still uncertain.

Against this background of cultural upheaval and institutional collapse, it is hardly surprising that to the extent that it is possible to speak of tendencies in current philosophy the more "visible" among them revolve in one way or another around the question of "culture", i.e., Russian culture. What this may mean is a question best addressed by surveying the tendencies I have in mind.[26] The first and thus far most prominent is (1) the return to the indigenous tradition of Russian religious philosophy (2); the second is tantamount to a Russian form of post-structuralist deconstructivism that mixes European post-modernist currents with Russian culturological thinking; and (3) the third is an as yet fledgling attempt to instill recognition of moral and legal principles underpinning civil society. On the whole, barring some as yet indeterminate aspects in the first tendency, I think that it is unlikely that the future development of philosophy in Russia will be continuous with its pre- and post-revolutionary past and with the kind of traits that were then characteristic of it.

Ad (1) The "boom" in pre-revolutionary but also post-revolutionary émigré religious thought has taken dramatic proportions. No self-respecting journal (philosophical or otherwise) anxious to secure a permanent readership in this day of media mania in Russia, no large or small publishing house worried about rising costs, least of all no newspaper with a claim to be an opinion-maker, can afford to turn a cold shoulder to the public's demand (long-lived or not) to bask in the theosophical and historiosophical illuminations of this now legendary tradition.[27] Which is also to say that the renaissance goes well beyond professional philosophical circles.

In the latter there does not exist unanimity as to how best to recover this tradition. There are those for whom it should be recuperated *in toto*, i.e., not only in spirit but in doctrine as well, as the veritable essence of Russian cultural identity (e.g., Jurij Borodaj 1990), whereas others adopt a more reserved approach to their philosophical forebears in view of the radically altered cultural climate (cf. Barabanov 1990, 1991; Akhutin 1991).[28] The issues dividing these "camps" inevitably bring to mind the debates that pitted so-called Slavophiles against their Westernizing opponents throughout the nineteenth century, debates which for philosophers came to rest on V. S. Solov'ëv's and N. Berdjaev's "Russian Idea." Is authentic Russian civilization and culture specific and distinct from that of Western Europe by virtue of its communitarian Orthodox theology which embraces all aspects of social existence and its cultural forms? It has been pointed out how thoroughly eschatological the affirmative answer to this question has been, and how, as a result, its philosophy is really theosophy, a revelation of the incarnation of spirit in history, and not metaphysics. (Barabanov 1990). At the same time, for many the attraction of the "doctrine" lies in its advocation of "spiritist personalism" (witness the centrality of the concept of the God-Man); there can hardly be a more uncompromising refusal to countenance but the slightest doubt that perhaps man is not an unconditionally free being.[29] By the same token, however, others wonder about the social and political pertinence of such a theosophically inspired humanism.

> Is is true that Russian religious-philosophical thought of the past has 'profoundly resolved' all questions which have risen up before us today? Is it true that all that is left for us is to draw on it in handfuls? And how to face the fact that in this entire philosophy there was precisely nothing which could help to reverse the catastrophe of Russia's previous attempts to break through to political modernization? How to account for the shattering defeat it suffered confronted with the practical realities of the twentieth century? What to make of the fact that it speaks to us only now — after decades of deafening silence? In other words, what about its striking non-practicality which condemns it to utter defeat? Can we really take it on now as a pathmarker, in our present attempt to break out, when our own lives and the future of our children are at stake?" (Janov 1991, p. 81)

Whatever the outcome of debates over such large-scale cultural issues,[30] there is also the question about the impact of this revival on the practice of philosophy, on the way it helps or hinders the development of aptitudes which, as we have seen, many today consider to be woefully underdeveloped. An uninitiated reader is hard put to deny his impression that a "typical" text of the Russian philosophers in question often reads more like an inspired narrative, imbued with deep conviction and profound allusions—"Russian philosophy as literature"—than like the discursively structured treatises of mainstream Western academic philosophy. This reader might well conclude that the tradition lends itself poorly to use in promoting and refining the conceptual-analytic skills so highly prized in Western academic philosophy. Of course, the Russians have not been blind to this difference; Piotr Chadaaev, for some still the most original thinker their culture has known, did not flinch when he wrote: "We know nothing about the syllogism of the West." It remains to be seen how much of a virtue this will continue to be. (Cf. Poljakov 1991 for one of more balanced accounts of the specificity of Russian philosophy in the nineteenth century.)

Ad (2) It is much harder to describe and assess the second tendency if only because it has no single focal point. One can cavil by pointing out that those who follow this post-Soviet deconstructivist path often draw inspiration from a tradition that existed at the fringes of official Soviet doctrine for the social sciences and humanities. I have in mind Bakhtine and Vygotsky, who are well-known in the West, as well as a number of their current disciples or spiritual heirs, such as V.S. Bibler[31] (and perhaps the recently deceased M. Mamardasvili). One can also add that texts written by current post-Soviet philosophers in this vein often abound with references to above all the French deconstructivist movement, be it in philosophy, psychology, sociology, or what one will. In this last respect not a few of the themes developed by the French movement have been at the centre of attention of the on the whole youthful post-Soviet deconstructionists.[32]

My present inclination is to suggest that what is afoot is a conception of culture as communicational activity along lines that "discourse ethicians," cultural semioticians, social psychologists practicing some form of ethogenic analysis or "social-construction-of-mind-in-action" theory, would recognize while perhaps noting certain peculiarities associated with the Russian input, in particular the Bakhtinian[33] and Vygotskyian elements (cf. Kozulin 1991). From the philosophical perspective, if this characterization stands up to further scrutiny, it suggests a thoroughly contemporary attitude: the primacy of interpretation, a stand often linked with pragmatism to the exclusion of all manner of essentialisms and foundationalisms.

A cursory review of the themes subjected to closer examination is suggestive: totalitarianism (*Totalitarizm* 1989), bureaucracy (*Bjurokratija* 1991), power (Podoroga 1991b), terror, science/scientism as a form of cultural rationality, the social hermeneutics of speech acts, of images (Podoroga 1991a), the social colonization of the body, feminism (Klimenkova 1991), literature as politics, mythical consciousness, historical consciousness, etc.[34] In the post-structuralist current, virtually all the items on this list are seen to have the peculiarity of naming themselves, so to speak, i.e., as elements of discursive formations they are as much categories inherent to—constitutive of—specific discourses as the very "objects" (or intrinsic parts thereof) which the discourses elaborate. Philosophers have wondered how nominalist "discourse-analysis" is, and thus if it is indifferent to the question whether the behaviour of discourses is constrained by extra-discursive considerations—by "objectivity". However, for the Russian writers I have in mind, this narrow epistemological problem is virtually exemplified in the social setting in which they situate the discourses to which the kinds of categories listed above belong viz., Soviet cultural rationality (described as the "political construction of social reality" in section II above).

Writing, for example, about the collectivism of Soviet culture one writer advances the view that it perpetrated the illusion of "collective bodies" which are misfortunate enough to be invisible even though great stores of energy were expended to catch a glimpse of them. A prime example is painting in the Socialist Realist canon. The artist's gesturing has to be sustained by talk, but about what? "The invisibility of such bodies is guaranteed . . . by the domination in culture of an all-inclusive [totalizing] verbal vision, which is able to see everything on the condition that it sees nothing in isolation, does not remark the irreducibility of concrete bodily forms [to one another]. The unceasing subordination of the world to speech turns into a magical verbalism, discourse becomes talk that knows nothing external in relation to itself." (Riklin 1991, p.10) The illusion of meaningful talk is sustained by the exercise of power, the only basis of which in such a "magical world" is terror.

All the same, however, it is unclear whether these analysts of the cultural rationality of the Soviet system construe their findings as philosophy. After all, in the first place, the critical light of this method cannot spare the philosophy practiced in the system; thus at the very least a shift to a meta-philosophical attitude is to be expected. But given what the analysis may be expected to show about that practice and its conditions (e.g., discourse sustaining the political construction—by forced collectivization—of social reality) can it be plausibly assumed that the meta-philosophical attitude would be readily abandoned in favour of constructive analysis attuned to the "things themselves"? Expectations of this kind may well falter when confronted with the "deconstructionist" spirit pervading this research: nominalism, anti-foundationalism, anti-essentialism, pragmatism, meta-discourse, the search for discontinuities, etc. It looks as if the "things themselves" are better examined as discourse-relative, as "cultural posits" or the like.

What could motivate a renewed concern for the resources and aptitudes of philosophizing attuned to foundational questions in all traditionally cultivated areas? This is the place to suggest, at the very least, the role Western philosophers can play in instilling in their Russian counterparts a sense of philosophizing that might be characterized as "culturally indifferent" (not naive) without thereby suggesting that philosophers enjoy a view of the world "from nowhere".

Ad (3) To be sure the "Western philosophers" in question need not be living, even though the role they play in current Western philosophy makes it possible to say that they are "alive and well". … One such figure is Kant, whose significance for Russians today fortunately goes beyond the remark that made the rounds among intellectuals in the last years of the Soviet Union—"Kant, our countryman". The philosopher from Königsberg has a central place in what is perhaps the single area in post-Soviet philosophy in which the need for foundational research is openly recognized: ethical and political theory.[35] I wrote above that there is near consensus among intellectuals of all leanings that Russia has yet to accede to the social and political form of existence which will ensure its right of entry to the pantheon of "civilized" nations. However overdramatic it may be, this kind of declaration does at least convey the conviction—and the worry!—that in Russia, due to the systematic deprivation of the populace of institutional forms of civil society, a consciousness of rights and obligations, of commitment to self-appropriated maxims of behaviour, as well as a sense of tolerance and dialogue is on the whole in a primitive state. To this must be added the virtual ignorance of the Western tradition in ethical, political, and juridical theory and the way it has influenced policy and institutional change.[36] Thus, talk about (re)building civil society and promoting a constitutional order based on the principle of law appears to many intellectuals to be naive, virtually utopian, so long as the corresponding "ethical-political" consciousness is absent and indeed still blocked by the cultural lag of the deeply entrenched "Stalinist" mentality. Accordingly, the foremost task is seen to be that of "education" of the ethical and political consciousness. A noble ideal perhaps, but how to go about realizing it when the competence is missing, the educational institutions do not exist, and there is little or no consensus at the level of mass opinion and its spokesmen as to the future shape of post-Soviet political and socioeconomic life?

For philosophy the matter is of extreme urgency. At present, steps have been taken to establish a department of Political Science at the University of Moscow to comprise, among other sectors, a chair of Political Philosophy.[37] The person who has been named to the chair has taken pains to insist that, if it is to succeed, the process of education to an ethical-political consciousness and thus the piecemeal constitution in Russia of a *civil society* must aim to recover and renew the positive features of Russian national civilization. The choice of the expression *civilization* is significant: had he written about the *culture* of Russia instead he would have awakened all the associations with the Russian Idea, whereas his purpose is to insist that the best moments in Russian society coincided with periods when it followed the path of natural self-movement, i.e., when its members could rely on their own capacities to raise and pursue goals important to them. To recover this natural-historical civic consciousness requires 1) implanting the concept of the *ordinariness* (as opposed to the sense of mission, or calling) of Russian national life; 2) adopting a stable, realistic regimen of development that respects common sense and forsakes utopian projects; 3) instilling a sense of continuity in the production of life that will be conducive to promoting dynamic growth in all socioeconomic sectors; and 4) overcoming the ideology of the construction of reality with political (doctrinal) recipes. (Il'in and Il'ina 1991, pp. 57-58)

If there is a paradox here it lies in calling for education of the civic consciousness while simultaneously advocating what amounts to a defense of *laissez faire* in the local institutionalization of social life. This remark is not intended as a criticism, but it is difficult to suppress a sense of irony when considering the creation of chairs of political theory and philosophy in circumstances where the adepts admit that few appreciate their value. How else can they be effective other than by imposing themselves, so to speak, on students, the general public, and of course politicians? In these circumstances can a civil society arise spontaneously without recourse to political means that initially stand outside it? Can we escape the conclusion that there are intellectuals who have the knowledge to act in the name of the general social good? But this does sound rather familiar ... and recalls a long continuous tradition in Russian society and politics.

The alternative, from the philosophical standpoint, is expressed in the slogan *"Vorwärts zu Kant!"* The heroic ring expresses its author's conviction that Kant has survived unscathed as a moral philosopher despite the many attempts to put down his doctrine (Solov'ëv 1991a, b). Ethics and politics fall together in Kant's view of man thanks to his insistence on the moral autonomy of the individual. But in this philosopher's opinion we cannot abstract the moral nature of the individual from the civilizational process itself. He notes that, in the context of the doctrine, Kant's phrase, *"Nature's task for the human species,"* lends itself to interpretation ... as a judgment on the cosmic nature and, accordingly, the cosmic destiny of humanity consisting in the creation of culture. Autonomous morality and law reflect the formal framework of its being without which cosmogenesis cannot be considered complete. (Solov'ëv 1991a, p. 49) Leaving aside the overtly speculative side of this interpretation, what can we conclude about it in the context of post-Soviet culture and the present state of philosophy? The answer can only be that the author admits the cultural break, acknowledges how idle it would be to seek continuity in a tradition that has ravaged "nature's task" for humanity by consistently suppressing the consciousness of right as conscience and as formal law; (cf. Solov'ëv 1990).

At the end of the first section I formulated five questions that turn about the ambiguous situation of post-Soviet philosophy: reconstruction or some form of continuity with the past. The foregoing appears to allow some tentative answers:

(1) Marxist-Leninist cultural rationality is in a state of disarray but also abeyance; among philosophers we have seen only the beginnings of a settling of accounts with the cultural rationality of "real existing socialism", an examination of conscience that will have to comprise the role of philosophy among the other social scientific and humanistic disciplines, the organization of curricula in universities, etc., and the restructuring of departments, Institutes, and literary organs of the philosophical community.

(2) The rebirth of the Russian pre-revolutionary and *émigré* tradition, the emergence of what I have labelled Russian "deconstructionism", and the growth of interest in ethical-political thought are all signs that philosophers are attuned to the cultural crisis; but on the basis of the materials presently available it is difficult to say whether their efforts in these areas mitigate or only deepen the crisis of cultural identity. The debates among them show the degree to which the issue of continuity is problematic, reaching all the way to the question about the viability of philosophy as a cultural force.

(3) There seems to be no new emerging common "style". However, it is too soon to say whether this is testimony to pluralism or uncertainty. But should we expect those who advocate a retrieval of the spirit and letter of Russian philosophy to find a language in common with those "deconstructivists" who may be inclined to see the latter as yet another attempt to "re-ideologize" the cultural atmosphere, thus reinforcing their own suspicions about philosophical discourse? In another vein it needs to be acknowledged how far Russian philosophers have come in overcoming dogmatism and anonymous collectivism, and, as if in concerted opposition to those in the West who had solemnly "buried the author" within the indeterminate perimeters of inter- textuality, given importance to the individual "voice" (e.g., Bakhtine, Mamards- vili, Bibler, Losev).

(4) By most accounts, contact with Western philosophy is still sporadic and unsystematic. Of the tendencies I have surveyed, the "deconstructionist" line has gone beyond historical research and virtually asserted its association with the spirit of a variety of post-structuralist, post-modernist continental thinkers. As I have insisted, however, this move suits the ambiguous situation of post-Soviet philosophizing in which foundational issues have yet to return to cerntre-stage; so far historical studies alone keep them before philosophers' minds.

(5) The problem-field typically associated with mainstream Marxist philosophizing has disintegrated and for the present there seems to be no interest in reevaluating the Marxist input to central issues in the philosophical repertoire. This is a matter that is affected by and contributes to the unfocused attitudes to

the "Soviet" experiment in light of the current crisis, as suggested under (1) above. It may be some time before we see a history of Marxist-Leninist philosophy written by those whose professional existence was inextricably bound up with it.

Edward M. Swiderski

University of Fribourg, Switzerland

REFERENCES

Akhutin, A. V. 1991 "Sophia and the Devil" *Soviet Studies in Philosophy* 29, 4: 59-89.

Apresjan, R. G. 1991 "Priroda morali" (The nature of morality), *Filosofskie nauki* 12: 53-64.

Bakhurst, David 1991 *Consciousness and Revolution in Soviet Philosophy. From the Bolsheviks to Evald Ilyenkov.* Cambridge: Cambridge University Press.

Bakstanovkij, V. I. and Ju.V. Sogomonov 1991 "Politiceskaja etika: duch sopernicestva i sotrudnicestva" (Political ethics: the spirit of competition and collaboration), *Filosofskie nauki* 12: 3-15.

Barabanov, E. V. 1990 "Russkaja Idea v eschatologiceskoj perspektive" (The Russian Idea in an eschatological perspective) *Voprosy filosofii* 8: 62-73.

___ 1991 "Russkaja filosofija i krizis identicnosti" *Voprosy filosofii* 8. 102-116.

Bibler, V. S. 1991a *Mikhail Mikhailovic Bakhtin. Poetika kul'tury.* Moskva: Progress.

___ 1991b *Kant-Galilej-Kant.* Moskva: Mysl'.

___ 1991c *Ot naukoucenija k logike kul'tury* (From the theory of science to the logic of culture). Moskva: Politizdat.

Bjurokratija i obscestvo 1991 (Bureaucracy and Society) Moskva: Filosofskoe obscestvo.

Blakeley, Thomas 1961 *Soviet Scholasticism,* Dordrecht: Reidel.

Bochenski, J. M. 1963, *Soviet Russian Dialectical Materialism.* Dordrecht: Reidel.

Buchholz, Arnold 1990 "The on-going destruction of Marxism-Leninism" *Studies in Soviet Thought* 40, 1-3: 231-240.

___ 1991 "Vom Ende des Marxismus-Leninismus" *Studies in Soviet Thought* 42, 3: 259-294.

Bykova, Marina 1990 "Die Perestrojka in der sowjetischen Philosophie: Mythos oder Realität?" *Studies in Soviet Thought* 40, 1-3: 73-88.

Charcev, A. G. (ed.) 1966 *Problema cennosti v filosofii* (The Problem of Value in Philosophy) Moskva: Nauka.

Dahm, Helmut 1990 "What restoring Leninism means" *Studies in Soviet Thought* 39, 1: 55-76.

Fedotova, V. G. 1991 *Prakticeskoe i duchovnoe osvoenie dejstvitel'nosti* (The Practical and Spiritual Appropriation of Reality) Moskva, Nauka.

Gusejnov, A. A. 1991 "Zur Geschichte und aktuellen Situation der Ethik in der Sowjetunion" *Studies in Soviet Thought* 42, 3: 195-206.

Hartmann, Nicolai 1953 *New Ways of Ontology* Chicago: Henry Regnery.

Ignatow, Assen 1990 "Perestrojka der Philosophie?" *Studies in Soviet Thought* 40, 1-3: 7-54.

Il'in, V. V. and T. A. Il'ina 1991 "Garantija social'noj ziznesposobnosti - preemstvennost'" (The guarantee of social vitality—continuity) *VMGU* Ser 12: Social'no-politiceskie issledovanija 3: 5333-60.

"Is Marxism Dead?" 1991 *Soviet Studies in Philosophy* 30, 2: 7-74 (translated from *Voprosy filosofii* 1990, 10: 19-51).

Ivin, Aleksandr 1989 "Intellektual'nyj konsensus istoriceskoj epokhi" (The intellectual consensus of a historical period) "Ne naukoj edinoj" Moskva: IF ANSSSR. 24-56.

___ 1991 *Modern Scholastics*. Unpublished manuscript, Moscow.

Janov, Aleksandr 1991 "Filosofija pobezdennych" (The Philosophy of the Defeated) *Strannik. Literatura. Iskusstvo. Politika* 1: 80-85.

Kagan, M. S. 1985 "O duchovnom" (On the Spiritual) *Voprosy filosofii* 9: 91-102.

Klimenkova, T. A. 1991 *Ot fenomena k strukture* (From the Phenomenon to Structure) Moskva: Nauka.

Kołakowski, Leszek 1977 *Main Currents of Marxism* vol. 3. Oxford: Clarendon.

___ 1980 *Le marxisme de Marx, le marxisme d'Engels. L'esprit révolutionnaire* (suivi de *Marxisme: utopie et anti-utopie*) Bruxelles: Editions complexes. 133-157.

Kozulin, Alex (ed.) 1991 "Lev Vygotsky and Contemporary Social Thought" *Studies in Soviet Thought* 42, 2 (special issue).

Krizan, Mojmir 1991 *Vernunft, Modernisierung und die Gesellschaftsordnungen sowjetischen Typs. Eine kritische Interpretation der bolschewistischen Ideologie* Frankfurt a. M.: Lang.

Ksenofontov, B. I. 1991 "Duchovnost' kak ekzistencial'naja problema" (Spirituality as an existential problem) *Filosofskie nauki* 12: 41-52.

Lapin. N.I. 1991. ed. *Filosofskie soznanie: dramatizm obnovlenija* (The Philosophical Consciousness: The Drama of Renewal) Moskva: Politizdat.

Mamardasvili, M. M. 1990 *Kak ja ponimaju filosofiju* (How I Understand Philosophy) Moskva: Progress.

___ 1990 "Soznanie kak filosofskaja problema" (Consciousness as a Philosophical Problem) *Voprosy filosofii* 10: 1-14.

___ 1990 "Marksizm: problemy, protivorecija, perspektivy" (Marxism: problems, contradictions, and perspectives).*VMGU* ser. 12, *Social'no-politiceskie issledovanija* 5: 3-71.

___ 1991 "Problema celoveka v filosofii" (The Problem of Man in Philosophy) in I. T. Frolov (ed.) *O celoveceskom v celoveke* (On what is human in man) Moskva: Politizdat.

___ 1991 "Marksizm v izmenjajuscimsja mire: samoanaliz, ocenki, perspektivy" (Marxism in a changing world: self-analysis, evaluations, perspectives) *VLGU* Ser. 6: *Filosofija* , 2: 3-58.

Mezhuev, Vadim 1991 "Est' li buduscee u socializma?" (Does Socialist have a future?) *Svobodnaja mysl'* (formerly *Kommunist*) 14: 6-15.

Nikiforov, Aleksandr 1990 "Perezivet li marksizm perestrojku?" (Will Marxism survive perestrojka?) *Obscestvennye nauki* 3: 115-128.

Nove, Alec 1989 *Glasnost' in Action. Cultural Renaissance in Russia.* Boston: Unwin Hyman.

Offe, Claus 1987 "The utopia of the zero-option. Modernity and modernization as normative political criteria" *Praxis International* 7, 1: 1-24.

Ojzerman, T. I. 1989 "Dialektika i socialisticeskij pljuralizm" (Dialectics and Socialist Pluralism) *Socialisticeskij pljuralizm. Voprosy teorii i praktiki* Moskva: MGU, 20-36.

Panin, A. V. 1990 "Contribution to a review discussion of Vvedenie v filosofiju" *Voprosy filosofii* 8: 170-171.

Pechenev, V. 1990"Perestrojka i nravstvennost'" (Perestrojka and morality) *Voprosy filosofii* 7: 5-25.

___ 1991 "Change so as to preserve oneself and one's nature" *Soviet Studies in Philosophy* 29, 1: 55-69.

Podoroga, Valery 1991a "Znaki vlasti (zapisy na poljakh)" (Signs of Power. Marginal Notes) *Kinoscenarii* 3-4: 176-191.

___ 1991b "The Eunuch of the Soul: Positions of Reading and the World of Platonov" *The South Atlantic Quarterly* 90, 2: 357-408.

Poljakov, L. V. 1990 *Metodologiceskie vvedenie v istoriju russkoj filosofii XIX.* (A methodological introduction to the history of Russian philosophy in the nineteenth century) Moskva: Rossijski otkrytyj unet.

Ryklin, Michail 1991 "Porazenie zrenija. Pjat' razmysleniji o recevoj kul'ture" (The destruction of vision. Five considerations about the culture of speech) *Paralleli* 2: 4-32.

Solov'ëv, E. Ju. 1988 "Individ, individual'nost', licnost'" (The individual, individuality, the person) *Kommunist* 17. 49-63.

___ 1989. "Licnost' i pravo" (The Person and the Law) *Voprosy filosofii* 8: 67-90.

___ 1990. "Pravovoj nigilizm i gumanisticeskij smsyl' prava" (Legal nihilism and the humanistic meaning of the law) *Kvintessencija. Filosof. al'manach.* Moskva: Politizdat. 162-235

___ 1990 "Soznanie v sociokul'turnom izmerenii" (The socio-cultural dimension of consciousness). Moskva: IF AN SSSR.

___ 1991a *Epokha rannykh burzuaznykh revoljucij i moral'naja filosofija I. Kanta.* Doctoral Lecture.

___ 1991b "Sowjetische Kant Forschung gestern und heute" *Mare Balticum. Ostseegesellschaft e.V.* 21-23.

Staniszkis, Jadwiga 1989 *Ontologia socjalizmu* Warszawa: In Plus ("Krytyka").

Suchov, A. D. 1989 *Russkaja filosofija. Puti razvitija* (Russian philosophy. Paths of Development) Moskva: Nauka.

Swiderski, E. M. 1979a *The Philosophical Foundations of Soviet Aesthetics. Theories and Controversies in the Post-War Years.* Dordrecht: Reidel.

___ 1979b "Options for a Marxist-Leninist Aesthetic" *Studies in Soviet Thought* 20, 2: 127-144.

___ 1988 "The Category of Culture in Soviet Philosophy" *Studies in Soviet Thought* 35, 2: 88-124

___ 1989 "How the Category of the Person is Accommodated in Soviet Philosophy" in *Identität: Evolution oder Differenz?/Identité: Evolution ou différence?.* Fribourg: Editions universitaires St. Paul, 55-78.

___ 1992 "From the 'Social Subject' to the Person in Recent Soviet Philosophy" forthcoming in *Philosophy of the Social Sciences.*

Taras, Raymond 1991 "The Makings of a Leninist: Gorbachev on Dogmatism and Revisionism" *Studies in Soviet Thought* 42 1: 1-28.

Tolstykh, V. and A. Gusejnov 1991 *Osvobozdenie ducha* (The Emancipation of the Spirit) Moskva: Politizdat.

___ *Totalitarizm i socializm* 1990 (Totalitarianism and socialism) Moskva: IF ANSSSR. 145 pp.

___ *Totalitarizm kak istoriceskij fenomen* 1989 (Totalitarianism as a historical phenomenon) Moskva: Filosofskoe obscestvo.

Tsipko, A. 1990 *Die Philosophie der Perestrojka. Die Grundlagen der Reformpolitik M. Gorbatschews.* München: Hene.

___ 1990a "Man Cannot Change His Nature" *Soviet Studies in Philosophy* 29, 1: 27-54.

___ 1990b "Protivorecija ucenija Karla Marksa" (The Contradictions in the Doctrine of Karl Marx) *VMGU*: Ser. 12. *Social'no-politiceskie issledovanija* 2: 35-51.

___ 1990c "Dvoemyslie 'ortodoksov' ili dolgij put' z zdravomu smyslu" (The double-thought of the orthodox or the long road to common sense) in V. Tolstykh (ed.), "Marksizm. Za i Protiv". Unpublished proceedings of the Club *Svobodnoe slovo*, Moscow.

van der Zweerde, Evert 1990 "Die Rolle der Philosophiegeschichte im 'Neuen philosophischen Denken' in der UdSSR." *Studies in Soviet Thought* 40, 1-3: 55-72.

___ 1992 "Preparing for the Renaissance" forthcoming in: M. Urban (ed.). *System Change and Ideology in the Soviet Union.* London: Macmillan.

Vvedenie v filosofiju 1989/1990 (Introduction to Philosophy, 2 volumes) I. T. Frolov (ed.). Moskva: Politizdat.

Zakharov, Igor 1991, "Time of the New Troubles." *The Guardian: Europe:* December 27, p. 21.

Zimovec, Sergej 1991, *Fenomen totalitarizma (Social'no-filosofskij aspect)* (The Phenomenon of Totalitarianism. The Socio-philosophical Aspect) Avtoreferat dissertacii. Moskva: IF ANSSSR.

THE NEW EUROPEAN PHILOSOPHY

There is a somewhat crude but still serviceable distinction between "Anglo-Saxon philosophy" on the one hand and "Continental philosophy" on the other.[1] The former sees the discipline of philosophy as being in the first place a technical enterprise, in some ways comparable to physics or mathematics (for example, in that it is largely confined to universities). The latter places greater emphasis on a conception of philosophy as an enterprise enjoying a wider social and political relevance. Thus on the Continent philosophy has been, and is still, more closely intertwined with religion and literature, with journalism and ideology, than is the case in the English-speaking world. What counts as "philosophy" in the two cultures is accordingly somewhat different: much of the work of Habermas, for instance, would be classified in England or America not as philosophy but as sociology or as social or political criticism.[2]

The philosophers of Eastern and Central Europe have for some time constituted a third group, skew to the two just mentioned, though incorporating elements of each. As a result of recent political events, such philosophers are now confronted with a unique opportunity—the opportunity to rebuild their philosophical culture, as it were, from the ground up. The necessity of such rebuilding is faced to different degrees and in different ways in the different parts of post-Communist Europe. In Poland, above all, there is a certain continuity. But there, too, new institutions and associations are being founded and old ones closed; new journals are being established and new curricula fashioned and taught; new faculty is being appointed while politically discredited members of the formerly Communist academic structures are being encouraged to retire.

What, then, are the choices by which philosophers in post-Communist Europe are confronted? One very real alternative, particularly against the background of a conception of philosophy as a discipline enjoying wider social and political relevance, is a sort of *national* philosophy: a philosophy in Hungarian, for example (and analogously for Croatians, Rumanians, Bulgarians, and so on)—a philosophy which would address the problems which Hungarians face, problems rooted in Magyar culture, language and history; a philosophy which would do full justice to the thesis—embraced by many philosophers—to the effect that one cannot do really good philosophy except within one's own language and culture. A development along these lines will surely be taken seriously by many intellectuals of standing in Russia. In Hungary, or Slovenia, however, one disadvantage of such a course is obvious: it would result in a philosophy which almost no one outside the given countries would understand or care about, simply because there is almost no one outside the given countries who reads Hungarian or Slovenian and who is sufficiently attuned to the local culture and history to find more than curiosity interest in the products of a philosophy of the suggested sort.

At the opposite extreme, as it were, is professionalism *à la* Princeton or Pittsburgh: the deliberate cultivation of a technical, scientific philosophy addressing problems of a universal or abstract character. This is the course which has been adopted already, for example, by many of the best philosophers in Finland, itself one of the most sophisticated philosophical cultures in Europe. Thus Finnish philosophers take it as a matter of course that they must publish and lecture in English, that their students must read philosophy in English, and that they must compete and collaborate intensively with philosophers and institutions abroad. The result is a philosophical culture with an international reputation that is second to none. But it is also a philosophy which has sacrificed its local character for the sake of technical competence.

A third alternative (or family of alternatives), which some might be disposed to regard as a sort of compromise between these two extremes, would consist in the forming of alliances not with Anglo-Saxophone philosophy but rather (as at various times in the past) with Germany or France. (This alternative is indeed in process of being imposed upon the philosophers of the former German Democratic Republic by *force majeure*.)

The necessity to make a choice between the mentioned groups of alternatives is, I believe, a real existential problem facing some hundreds of young philosophers in Eastern and Central Europe today. Should young Hungarian philosophers, for example, learn English, devote their attention to English-language philosophy journals, train themselves to meet the exacting (and sometimes stifling) writing and lecturing standards dominant in the Anglo-Saxon world? Or should they rather learn German or French? Germany is, to be sure, a still- thriving philosophical culture, though as already suggested, there is a sense in which German philosophers have manifested an increasing tendency to abandon the classical concerns of philosophy in favour of something more like critical sociology. Moreover, it seems that there are at the moment few German philosophers—and this for several independent reasons—who are making serious contributions to philosophy which are of international standing.

What, then, of France? Contemporary French philosophy does, it is true, consist of much more than the absurd Dadaistic clowning of Derrida and his ilk. Yet still, it seems that Derrida is to some degree representative of the style and mores of current native French philosophy, and this implies that France, too, faces serious obstacles if it wishes to draw upon its own resources in order to make contributions to philosophy of international consequence. Indeed many young French (and Italian and Swiss and Spanish) philosophers are beginning to embrace at least some aspects of the approach to philosophy that is dominant in the Anglo-Saxon world, in part as a response to the excesses of *la pensée 68*.[3]

Of course in each post-Communist philosophical community different individuals will make different choices (so that the extremes will to some extent cancel each other out). Moreover, some will try to bring about new sorts of syntheses between philosophical currents and traditions hitherto seen as incompatible, thus applying methods normally seen as belonging to one philosophical culture to the problems thrown up by another. The fact that new choices will be made and new philosophical cultures nurtured in the countries of Eastern and Central Europe must, however, have a serious cumulative effect. Indeed I would go so far as to claim that philosophers outside post-Communist Europe—including Anglo-Saxon, German and French philosophers—are themselves destined to be affected by the decisions which are made by philosophers in Poland or Hungary or the Czech Republic in the coming years. For new sorts of collaboration between East and West will influence also the Western philosophers who become involved therein. The concept of "Continental philosophy," like the concept of Europe itself, will be to this extent transformed.

The New European Philosophy

Much of what until recently passed for "advanced European philosophy" in Paris and its intellectual suburbs has, surely, reached a point of no return in degree of absurdity and willful obfuscation. (Or, as its more candid adherents will admit, it is not "philosophy" at all, but a sort of literary or cultural criticism.) The philosophy of formerly Communist Europe, in contrast, is destined to enjoy a new lease of genuine philosophical life: *the centre of gravity of European philosophy is set to move east.*

From this point of view it is important to bear in mind that the countries of Eastern and Central Europe are in fact able to draw upon rich philosophical cultures of their own, cultures which go back much further than the Marxist-Leninist philosophy which has enjoyed a certain institutional dominance in these countries since the 1940s and '50s. Here I am interested above all in the philosophical culture of Central Europe—of Poland, the Czech Republic, Croatia, Ukraine, etc. This culture, which is rooted in a wider Latin culture (as contrasted with the Byzantine roots of much Russian philosophy), may be said to have been initiated with the founding of the Charles University in Prague in 1348. It embraces (to mention just one, albeit prominent, example) the Bohemian logician-priest Bernard Bolzano, whose *Theory of Science* of 1837 can be seen in retrospect as one of the earliest contributions to that exact or scientific philosophy which in the Anglo-Saxon world constitutes the contemporary mainstream.[4]

This native Central-European philosophical culture has in the last 100 years been marked above all by the thinking of Franz Brentano, the founder of modern Austrian philosophy, whose pupils Kasimir Twardowski, Alexius Meinong, Christian von Ehrenfels, Edmund Husserl, Carl Stumpf Anton Marty, and T.G. Masaryk shaped the philosophical cultures of, especially, German-speaking Europe and the Habsburg lands in the decades around the turn of the present century (a time when philosophers working on the Continent still enjoyed friendly and collaborative relations with their English-speaking counterparts).[5] Brentano was at least in part responsible also for the fact that philosophy in Central Europe—in Vienna, Prague, Lemberg, Trieste, Laibach and Graz— enjoyed friendly relations with the sciences (above all with empirical psychology), and with logic and mathematics. He and his followers can to this extent be seen to have prepared the ground for that alliance between science and philosophy which was Vienna -Circle positivism.[6]

There are some, above all in the Czech Republic and in Poland, who never broke with these Bolzanian-Brentanian roots of Central European philosophy. They were thereby able to preserve the continuity of this older tradition. More of the brightest Polish and Czech and Hungarian and Slovenian and Croatian philosophers are now, or will in time be, in a position to do the same, in ways which are destined to bring about a renewed collaboration with their Anglo-Saxon counterparts.

Part and parcel of the changes which result will, I believe, be a new pattern of alliances on the Continent of Europe between philosophy and other disciplines, including mathematical logic, linguistics, psychology, and so on. But it will involve also the establishment of a new or extended canon of "Continental philosophy", a new list of exemplars or paragons (new intellectual "masters" if one will), embracing figures beyond the usual confines of Sartre, Merleau-Ponty, Habermas, Gadamer, etc. to include also Poles, Czechs, Hungarians, Slovenes—new philosophical heroes who can be seen as part of a continuing tradition of philosophy stretching from Bolzano and Brentano to the present day. Husserl has already been mentioned in this respect, not, however, or not exclusively, as the initiator of the tradition which includes Heidegger, Sartre, *et al.*, but rather as a philosopher of mathematics and logic, a thinker born in Moravia and educated in Vienna, the teacher of Roman Ingarden and of Adolf Reinach.[7] Other thinkers worthy of being mentioned in this connection are Aurel Kolnai, Michael Polanyi, Roman Jakobson, Max Scheler, Stanisław Leśniewski, Tadeusz Kotarbiński and Josef Bocheński.

In tandem with these developments there will arise also, I believe, a new or extended conception of what exact or scientific (or "analytic") philosophy is. The latter has hitherto been seen in Continental Europe as a rather narrow affair, allied of its very nature to positivistic, reductionistic and materialistic tendencies and somehow excessively oriented around formal logic and natural science at the expense of concerns with, for example, politics, law and culture. If, however, Brentano and Twardowski, Reinach and Polanyi are included as part of a single tradition along with Frege, Russell, Wittgenstein and Carnap, then this tradition itself begins to bear a richer aspect. It is no longer exclusively oriented around language or logic, but manifests also a psychological sophistication that modern analytic philosophers are only now beginning to acquire, in part as a result of the influence of developments in cognitive science. It is marked by a concern not so much, or not exclusively, with questions of "reducing" one domain to another, but rather with the explanation of how the different domains of reality (above all of logic, language, thought and action) hang together. Analytic philosophy in this wider sense is distinguished not by positivism or reductionism but rather by its concern with a certain sort of clarity, the clarity of *argument*, and thus by a certain sort of philosophical style, analogous in some ways to that of textbooks of mathematics or physics (though not necessarily always in such a way as to involve the use of any specific formal machinery).[8]

Marxism, Economics and Logic

In what respects, now, might Western European and especially French and German philosophy be affected by the developments I have mentioned? Note, first of all, that for all my comments above as to the wider social and political relevance of "Continental" philosophy, there is one respect in which Anglo-Saxon philosophers, too, can point to certain not insignificant achievements in this regard. For we can register in the Anglo-Saxon world more than two centuries of fruitful interaction between philosophy and *economics*, and collaboration of a similar sort was a characteristic feature also of the intellectual world of Central Europe at least in the half-century beginning in 1871.[9] In post-war France and Germany, in contrast, the possibilities for such collaboration have been usurped by the single all-embracing figure of Marx (and I venture that it will be very difficult for intelligent philosophers in post-Communist Europe to take the economic ideas of Marx seriously in the years to come). One can point, indeed, to a long-standing alliance between Anglo-Saxon and Central European intellectuals working on the borderlines of philosophy and economics,[10] an alliance which includes (in no particular order): Friedrich Hayek, Lionel Robbins, Alfred Schütz, Felix Kaufmann, Frank Ramsey, Karl Popper, Fritz Machlup, George Stigler, James Buchanan, John von Neumann, Herbert Simon, Ludwig von Mises, Michael Polanyi, John Neville Keynes, John Rawls, William Stanley Jevons, Carl Menger, Karl Menger, Jr., G. L. S. Shackle, Robert Nozick, Friedrich von Wieser, Christian von Ehrenfels and Gary Becker—and which has no counterpart as far as the philosophical traditions of France and Germany are concerned.

Contemporary French and German philosophy is marked, finally, by a similar deficit also as far as *logic* is concerned. Certainly there have been individual French and German logicians of genius. Yet there are few serious and creative communities of logicians working within the departments of philosophy of French and German universities today, and therefore also little serious interaction between logicians and those working in other branches of philosophy. And again: conditions in Eastern and Central Europe are quite different also in this respect. It is above all in Poland, of course, that we find the most important traditions of both philosophical and mathematical logic (and the most open and creative philosophical culture of Communist Europe). Yet other Eastern and Central European countries, too, can boast communities of logicians of no small standing. My conjecture, therefore, is that Continental philosophy is destined to evolve at least incrementally also in a logical direction—not least in the sense that future generations of philosophers in Continental Europe will become increasingly accustomed to treating philosophy as a discipline, open to neighbouring sciences, and subject to certain minimal standards of clarity and rigour.

Barry Smith

State University of New York at Buffalo

NOTES TO CHAPTER ONE (pp. 3-12)
Tradition and Bureaucratic Lore: Lessons from Hungary

1. *Geschichte und Klassenbewußtsein*, Berlin: Malik-Verlag, 1923.
2. *Három nemzedék: Egy hanyatló kor története*, Budapest.
3. Georg Lukács, *Dostojewski: Notizen und Entwürfe*, ed. by J. C. Nyíri, Budapest: Akadémiai, 1985.
4. "Az individualizmus csődje," *Huszadik Század* (1915).
5. *Hungary 1956*, London: Allison & Busby, 1976, p. 18.
6. Most notably in the essays "A magyar demokrácia válsága" ["The crisis of Hungarian democracy"], *Valóság* 1945; *Az európai kisállamok nyomorúsága* ["The misery of European small-states"], Budapest 1946; "Eltorzult magyar alkat, zsákutcás magyar történelem" ["Distorted Hungarian character, stranded Hungarian history"], *Válasz* 1948.
7. The last five sentences I am quoting from my paper "Some Marxian Themes in the Age of Information," in: J. C. Nyíri, ed., *Perspectives on Ideas and Reality*, Budapest: 1990, pp. 55-65. When the paper, written in the first half of 1988, appeared in a Hungarian translation (*Világosság* 1989/4), it found no echo at all. As a friend said: he tried to read it, but was put off by the term "Marxian" in the title.
8. *Die Zerstörung der Vernunft*, 1954.
9. As Tibor Hanák puts it: "die stellenweise grob geführte Auseinandersetzung mit dem Irrationalismus bot den kommunistischen Ideologen wenigstens die Möglichkeit, einen Großteil der bürgerlichen Philosophie kennenzulernen." And: "auch wenn [Lukács] die immanente Kritik nur inkonsequent benützte, ermutigte er offen zu ihrer Anwendung." (Hanák, *Lukács war anders*, Meisenheim am Glan: Anton Hain, 1973, p. 114.)
10. He had a manuscript of his *On the Ontology of Social Reality* ready by 1968.
11. An illuminating document of the divergences between Lukács and his circle is the "Notes on Lukács' Ontology" (*Telos* 1976), written by Ferenc Fehér, Ágnes Heller, György Márkus, and Mihály Vajda. "We remain unshaken in our demand," runs a passage in the introduction to these notes, "to transcend the bourgeois state of the world and convinced that this transcendence can and should be achieved with Marx as a starting point . . . [W]e had sought a 'philosophy of practice'. Here it is unnecessary to describe in detail the close connection between this striving and the fact that we were students of the author of *History and Class Consciousness*, whose radical rejection of his masterpiece we never shared."
12. An exception here is the treatise *Kritikai előtanulmányok egy marxista tudományfilozófiához* ["Towards a Marxist philosophy of science: Critical preliminary studies," 1972] of György Bence, a younger member of the Lukács school. The central issue Bence addresses is that of the autonomy of technological change. On the basis of some very impressive analyses he condludes that "empirical technology has its own indubitable, inner dynamics, this dynamics can overcome—through the conflict of causal insights and social recognition—substantial social obstacles, and is as such one of the most independent, or perhaps *the* most independent, variable of

social development." To the detriment of Hungarian philosophy, this outstanding treatise could not make an impact. In 1973 the party boss responsible for ideological issues, György Aczél, launched an attack against the Lukács school. Bence's work remained unpublished (it finally appeared in 1990) and was for a long time generally neglected.

13. György Bence—János Kis—György Márkus, *Lehetséges-e kritikai gazdaságtan?*

14. In *Bexzélő*, Nov. 2, 1991, p. 21.

15. Princeton: Princeton University Press, 1982, p. xxii.

16. *Ibid.*, pp. 65f.

17. *Ibid.*, p. 212.

18. *Ibid.*, p. 97.

19. *Ibid.*, p. 92.

20. As István Csurka, now vice-president of the Forum, said in a broadcast talk on January 14, 1990: "As long as in Hungary it is possible to socially disgrace Hungarians of a popular-national spine [*nép-nemzeti gerincű magyarok*] with a flood of slander, as long as the basis of distinction is the belonging to a clique, to a sect, as long as what comes from the people [*ami népi*] is suspect from the start, as long as a dwarf minority can make a whole society accept that only *its* truth is the truth, . . . and as long as this tendency—made to look Hungarian, now said to be radical, liberal—feeds from the same Marxist-Lukácsist left-wing roots as in the Kádár-Aczél era, there is no hope for the great popular masses of Hungarians to have a sense of well-being in their own homeland. Wake up, Hungarians!" Some weeks ago it was the Young Democrats—a liberal-libertarian party having 21 seats in the Hungarian parliament—that Csurka attacked as "uprooted" and "turning against Hungarian traditions" (*Népszabadság*, February 14, 1992).

21. *Der Einfluß der herrschenden Ideen des 19. Jahrhunderts auf den Staat*, vol. I-II, Vienna, 1851, and Leipzig, 1854. For a brief description, see my "Intellectual Foundations of Austrian Liberalism," in: W. Grassl and B. Smith, eds., *Austrian Economics: Historical and Philosophical Background*, London: Croom Helm, 1986, pp. 119–23, compare also my "From Eötvös to Musil: Philosophy and Its Negation in Austria and Hungary," in Nyíri, ed., *Austrian Philosophy: Studies and Texts*, München: Philosophia, 1981, pp. 15ff.

22. Szekfű, *Három nemzedék*, Budapest: 1920, p. 57.

23. *Ibid.*, p. 58.

24. *Ibid.*, p. 59.

25. *Three Generations*, 2nd ed., Budapest: 1922, p. 5.

26. Gyula Szekfű, *Magyar Történet: A tizenkilencedik és huszadik század* ["Hungarian history: The nineteenth and twentieth centuries"], Budapest, 1936, p. 352.

27. Cf. esp. his series of essays *Valahol utat vesztettünk* ["Somewhere we have lost our way"], 1943–44, repr. in Szekfű, *Forradalom után* ["After the revolution"], Cserépfalvi, 1947.

28. I am here following Miklós Lackó, "Szekfű Gyula és kortársai" ["Gyula Szekfű and his Contemporaries"], *Valóság* 1983/8, pp. 18f.

29. *Journal of Folklore Research* 21/2–3 (1984), p. 137.

30. *Ibid.* The quote is from Kodály, "Népzene és Műzene," in: *Úr és paraszt a magyar élet egységében* [Lord and peasant in the unity of Hungarian life], Budapest: Magyarságtudományi Intézet, 1941. "From my youth I still remember," Hofer here

adds, "how members of the so-called middle class claimed that the tunes Bartók collected were Rumanian or something else, but not real Hungarian tunes," *ibid.*

31. Deutsch, *Nationalism and Social Communication: An Inquiry into the Foundations of Nationality*, London, 1953, p. 71.

32. The pioneering work of the historian István Hajnal notwithstanding. In his paper "A technika fejlődése" ["The development of technology"], *Domanovszky Emlékkionyv*, 1937, Hajnal gave an original analysis of "tradition" in the sense of a *handed-down craft*, while in his "Írásbeliség, intellektuális réteg és európai fejlődés" ["Literacy, intellectual class, and European development"], *Károlyi Emlékkönyv*, 1933, he had singled out *writing* as the vehicle of rational thinking, literacy as the basis of modern, post-traditional times. A French translation of this latter essay, published under the title "Le rôle social de l'écriture et l'évolution européenne" in 1934 in *Revue de l'Institut de Sociologie* (Bruxelles), is referred to in Harold A. Innis, *The Bias of Communication*, University of Toronto Press, 1951. That Marshall McLuhan was greatly influenced by Innis is of course well known.

33. It might be in order to give a brief survey of this literature here. The best overall study of the connotations of "tradition" is an essay by Dan Ben-Amos, "The seven strands of *tradition*: varieties in its meaning in American folklore studies" (*Journal of Folklore Research* 21/2–3 [1984]). As befits a folklorist, Ben-Amos stresses the element of oral tradition, but also covers a variety of other aspects. The modern tendency to construe traditions as *customs* is reflected in H. B. Acton's excellent "Tradition and Some Other Forms of Order," *Proceedings of the Aristotelian Society*, N. S., vol. LIII (1953). A useful analysis, distinguishing traditions from customs, is "The Nature of Tradition" by D. M. Armstrong, in his *The Nature of Mind*, Harvester Press, 1981. That customs as traditions must involve a kind of specific *consciousness* is stresed in Max Radin's "Tradition," in: *Encyclopaedia of the Social Sciences*, New York: Macmillan, 1935, vol. 15, compare also J. G. A. Pocock, "Time, Institutions and Action: An Essay on Traditions and Their Understanding," in: Preston King and B. C. Parekh, eds., *Politics and Experience*, Cambridge: Cambridge University Press, 1968. This is the element worked out in the classic paper by Edward Shils, "Tradition and Liberty: Antinomy and Interdependence," *Ethics* LXVIII/3 (April 1958). Shils here emphasizes that traditions foster social cohesion, but contrasts the adherence to "normal tradition" with *traditionalism*, which is "the self-conscious, deliberate affirmation of traditional norms, in full awareness of their traditional nature and alleging that their merit derives from that traditional transmission from a sacred origin. This is a revivalist, enthusiastic attitude. It is always dogmatic and doctrinaire . . . it does not discriminate between the workable and the unworkable. . . ". Normal traditions, Shils stresses, are an indispensable basis of *liberal values*. "The traditional affirmation of liberty," he writes, "resembles any other traditional affirmation. As such it draws strength from the traditional outlook in other spheres, e.g., the respect for family traditions and for religious traditions, however widely these might differ in content from the tradition of liberty. The disruption of non-liberal traditions in a free society might well have a disruptive effect on the traditions of freedom in that society." A rather different picture emerges from Shils's book *Tradition*, London: Faber and Faber, 1981. Shils here emphasizes the technical terms "substantive tradition" ("traditions which maintain the received") and "substantive traditionality" ("the appreciation of the accomplishments and wisdom of the past and of the institutions especially impregnated with tradition"), retaining, for the term 'tradition' itself, the widest possi-

ble meaning: "Tradition means many things. In its barest, most elementary sense, it means simply a *traditum*; it is anything which is transmitted or handed down from the past to the present." The idea that without an adherence to traditions there can be no liberty goes back, of course, to Burke; and it was given a memorable expression by F. A. von Hayek in his 1945 talk "Individualism: True and False" (in Hayek, *Individualism and Economic Order* [1949], London: Routledge & Kegan Paul, 1976). Hayek's view is criticised in the paper by H. B. Acton referred to above. The themes of Shils's "Tradition and Liberty" paper are taken up in numerous writings by S. N. Eisenstadt, see e.g., his "Intellectuals and Tradition" (*Daedalus*, Spring 1972—tradition, Eisenstadt here writes, should be seen as "the reservoir of the most central social and cultural experiences prevalent in a society, as the most enduring element in the collective social and cultural construction of reality"), see also his "Post-Traditional Societies and the Continuity and Reconstruction of Tradition" (*Daedalus*, Winter, 1973). An analytically better-founded view is presented by Eric Hobsbawm (see his "Introduction: Inventing Traditions," in: Hobsbawm and Ranger, eds., *The Invention of Tradition*, [Cambridge: Cambridge University Press, 1983]). The philosophical problem of traditions is well brought out, in the wake of Nietzsche, in the German discussions. See esp. Max Scheler, *Die Stellung des Menschen im Kosmos*, 1928 ("Conscious 'recollection'," as Scheler has it, "means the dissolution, indeed the actual extinction of a living tradition"); Carl August Emge, "Zur Philosophie der Tradition," in: H. Wenke, ed., *Geistige Gestalten und Probleme*, Leipzig: 1942; Josef Pieper, "Über den Begriff der Tradition," *Arbeitsgemeinschaft für Forschung des Landes Nordrhein Westfalen: Geisteswissenschaften*, Heft 72, Köln: Westdeutscher Verlag, 1958. A lucid treatment of the theological issues pertaining to the notion of tradition is August Deneffe, S.J., *Der Traditionsbegriff*, Münster/Westf, 1931.

34. "Wittgenstein új tradicinalizmusa" ["Wittgenstein's new traditionalism"], *Világosság* 1975/1. An expanded English version appeared in *Acta Philosophica Fennica* 28/1-3 (1976), pp. 503-12. A characterization of German neo-conservatism in particular was included in a later paper of mine: "Wittgenstein 1929-1931: A visszatérés" ["Wittgenstein 1929-1931: The turning back"], *Magyar Filozófiai Szemle* 1981/2, Engl. transl. in: Stuart Shanker, ed., *Ludwig Wittgenstein: Critical Assessments*, vol. 4, London: Croom Helm, 1986, pp. 29-59.

35. "Szabadpiac és tekintélyelvü társadalom: Angolszász liberális-konzervatív elméletek" ["The free market in an authoritarian society: Anglo-Saxon liberal-conservative theories"], *Világosság* 1981/8-9. "The gradual adoption of classical liberal or 'libertarian' ideas by post-war conservatives," I here wrote by way of introduction, "is still regarded today in many quarters with suspicion, and indeed bewilderment. However a conservative interpretation of classical liberal notions is neither historically unprecedented, nor *prima facie* implausible. After all, the spontaneous order of a free market might very well appeal to the conservative taste for the naturally grown, while state intervention and central planning arouse the conservative abhorrence of the artificial and the blueprint; division of labour can easily be construed as an aspect of the social variety and hierarchy conservatives have always found desirable; material inequality seems normal in a world of inevitable frustration and suffering, whereas the idea of redistribution and of the welfare state must necessarily run counter to the conservative's conviction that an earthly utopia is unrealizable."

36. Cf. esp. "Öt nemzedék" ["Five generations"], *Magyar Nemzet*, Jan. 1, 1982,

and *Am Rande Europas: Studien zur österreichisch-ungarischen Philosophiege-schichte*, Wien: Böhlau, 1988 (Hungarian version: *Európa szélén: eszmetörténeti vázlatok*, Budapest: Kossuth, 1986).

37. "A hagyomány filozófiájához" ["On the philosophy of tradition"], *Világosság* 1988/8–9.

38. In the *Beszélő* samizdat journal. The essay was republished in *Kritika* in February 1990. An English translation has now appeared in *East European Politics and Societies*, 5/1, Winter 1991.

39. For this view of traditions, see esp. Jack Goody and Ian Watt, "The Consequences of Literacy," 1963, in: Goody (ed.), *Literacy in Traditional Societies*, Cambridge: Cambridge University Press, 1968, as well as Eric Havelock, *The Muse Learns to Write: Reflections on Orality and Literacy from Antiquity to the Present*, New Haven: Yale University Press, 1986. For more detailed references, cf. the chapter "Historical Consciousness in the Computer Age," in: Nyíri, *Tradition and Individuality*, Dordrecht: Kluwer, 1992.

40. See the classic discussion by Ernest Gellner in his *Thought and Change*, London: Weidenfeld & Nicolson, 1964, pp. 164ff. Cf. also K. W. Deutsch, *op. cit.*, pp. 75f.: "the rise of industrialism and the modern market economy . . . offer economic and psychological rewards for successful group alignments to tense and insecure individuals—to men and women uprooted by social and technological change, exposed to the risks of economic competition. . . . In a competitive economy or culture, nationality is an implied claim to privilege. It emphasizes group preference and group peculiarities, and so tends to keep out all outside competitors."

41. Dorson, "Folklore in the Modern World," in: R. M. Dorson, ed., *Folklore in the Modern World*, The Hague: Mouton, 1978, p. 42.

42. "As a nationalist strategy, folklore would restore the old peasant values of community bonds being weakened by urban impersonality," *ibid.*, p. 43.

43. Wilson, *Folklore and Nationalism in Modern Finland*, Bloomington: Indiana University Press, 1976, p. 205.

NOTES TO CHAPTER THREE (pp. 17–28)
Conservatism, Philosophy and Eastern Europe

1. Elie Kedourie, "Diversity in Freedom: Conservatism from Burkean Origins to the Challenge of Equality," *The Times Literary Supplement*, January 10, 1992.

2. Michael Oakeshott, "On Being Conservative" (1956), in: *Rationalism in Politics and Other Essays* (Indianapolis, IN: Liberty Classics, 1991). Cf. Gertrude Himmelfarb, "Michael Oakeshott: The Conservative Disposition," in: *Marriage and Morals Among the Victorians and Other Essays* (New York: Vintage Books, 1987), and also: Elie Kedourie, "Conservatism and the Conservative Party," "Conservatives and Neo-Conservatives," both in: *The Crossman Confessions and Other Essays* (London/New York: Mansell, 1984).

3. Albert O. Hirschman, *The Rhetoric of Reaction: Perversity, Futility, Jeopardy* (Cambridge, MA/London: The Belknap Press, Harvard University Press, 1991). Cf. Jerry Z. Muller's review, "Albert Hirschman's Rhetoric of Recrimination," *The Public Interest*, No. 104, Summer 1991.

4. Isaiah Berlin, *The Hedgehog and the Fox. An Essay on Tolstoy's View of History* (1953) (London: Weidenfeld & Nicolson, 1988). Isaiah Berlin, "Joseph de Maistre and the Origins of Fascism" (1960), in: *The Crooked Timber of Humanity* (London: John Murray, 1990).

5. Roger Scruton, *The Meaning of Conservatism*, 2nd ed. (London: Macmillan, 1984). See a more recent statement: Roger Scruton, "What Is Right?," *The Times Literary Supplement*, April 3, 1992. Cf. Charles Covell, *The Redefinition of Conservatism: Politics and Doctrine* (Basingstoke/London: Macmillan, 1986), and also Desmond S. King, *The New Right: Politics, Markets and Citizenship* (Basingstoke/London: Macmillan, 1987).

6. Leo Strauss, *Philosophy and Law: Essays Toward the Understanding of Maimonides and His Predecessors*, Preface, (Philadelphia/New York/Jerusalem: The Jewish Publication Society, 1987).

7. Alexander Kojève, "Tyranny and Wisdom," Leo Strauss, "Restatement on Xenophons' *Hiero*" (both 1950), in: Leo Strauss, *On Tyranny*, revised and expanded ed., Victor Gourevitch, Michael S. Roth, eds. (New York/Toronto: The Free Press, 1991).

8. Carl Schmitt, *The Concept of the Political* (1927), tr. George Schwab.

NOTES TO CHAPTER FOUR (pp. 29–46)
An Ideological Might-have-been

1. "Theoretical Problems of 'Economic Anthropology'," in *Philosophy of the Social Sciences*, vol. 6, 1974.

2. See for instance Yu. V. Bromley, *Sovremennye etnicheskiye procesy v SSSR* (Contemporary Ethnic Processes in the USSR), Moscow, 1975.

3. Semenov's ideas on this are found in *Istoriya pervobytnogo obshchestva. Obshchiye voprosy. Problemy antroposotsiogenesa* (History of Primitive Society: Several Issues. Problems of Anthropo-Sociogenesis), ed. Yu. V. Bromley, A. I. Pershitz, Yu. Semenov. Moscow, 1983.

4. Cf. R. C. Tucker, *Philosophy and Myth in Karl Marx*, Cambridge, 1961.

5. K. R. Popper, *The Open Society and its Enemies*, London, 1962.

6. H. Lubasz, "The Aristotelian Dimension in Marx," *Times Higher Education Supplement*, January 1977.

7. W. V. O. Quine, *Ontological Relativity and other Essays*, New York and London, 1969.

8. K. R. Popper, *Objective Knowledge*, Oxford, 1972.

9. Semonov's ideas on this are available in English. See especially Y. Semenov, "The Theory of Socioeconomic formations and world history" in E. Gellner (ed.), *Soviet and Western Anthropology*, London/New York, 1970.

10. *Problemy Istorii Dokapitalisticheskikh Obshchestv* (Problems of the History of pre-capitalist societies), ed. L. V. Danilova and others, Nauka, Moscow, 1968, especially the first essay, by L. V. Danilova, "Diskussionnye Problemy Teorii Dokapitalisticheskikh Obshchestv" ("Contentious Problems in the Theory of Pre-capitalist Societies").

11. Roman Szporluk, *Communism and Nationalism: Karl Marx versus Friedrich List*, Oxford University Press, New York, Oxford, 1988.

12. *Problemy Istorii Dokapitalisticheskikh Obshchestv* (Problems of the History of Pre-capitalist Societies), L. V. Danilova (editor) and others, Nauka, Moscow, 1968.

13. R. G. Collingwood, *Autobiography*, Oxford, 1939.

NOTES TO CHAPTER FIVE (pp. 47–62)
Philosophy and Ideology: The Case of Poland

1. As witness his *Positivist Philosophy: From Hume to the Vienna Circle*, tr. N. Guterman, Harmondsworth: Penguin, 1972.

2. Kołakowski was divested of his teaching post at Warsaw University after March 1968 in the course of an anti-Jewish and anti-intellectual purge. This turned out to have been with good reason, from the viewpoint of the authorities, as in 1966, on the 10th anniversary of October '56, Kołakowski, together with K. Pomian, devastatingly criticized Gomułkan socialism and served thereafter as a *maître à penser* for the March student rebels. Going beyond the scope of *philosophy* strictly conceived, we may mention also the name of the economist Włodzimierz Brus (as of some years teaching in England). Brus, also an orthodox Marxist in the early Fifties, gave at Warsaw University in the autumn of 1967 a series of informal lectures in which he stirred up the numerous, especially young, sympathizers of "Revisionism" among his audience by questioning a very important dogma of the orthodoxy, namely, that *state* ownership of the means of production is identical with the *social* ownership of them, hitherto held up as an ideal of the "socialist" society. This thought would later recur in the social teaching of Pope John Paul II and be crucially important for criticizing Communism on its own terms.

3. For firsthand, detailed information on the Lvov-Warsaw school see: Zbigniew Jordan, *Philosophy and Ideology: The Development of Philosophy and Marxism-Leninism in Poland since the Second World War*, Dordrecht: Reidel, 1963. And especially: Jan Woleński, *Logic and Philosophy in the Lvov-Warsaw School*, Dordrecht: Reidel, 1989. Cf. also the informative article by Barry Smith: "Kasimir Twardowski: An Essay on the Borderlines of Ontology, Psychology and Logic," in: K. Szaniawski, (ed.), *The Vienna Circle and the Philosophy of the Lvov-Warsaw School*, Dordrecht/Boston/Lancaster: Kluwer, 1989, pp. 313–73.

4. No doubt under the influence of Lenin's redefinition of the term "ideology" (in *What is to be Done?*), for whom this term began to signify almost any political program whatsoever.

5. In my (hitherto unpublished) doctoral dissertation *Zarys filozoficznej teorii ideologii* ("An Outline of a Philosophical Theory of Ideology"), Lublin/Gdańsk, 1991 (The Catholic University of Lublin).

6. The addition in italics is necessary in order to exclude cases where some privileges of a particular group *are* justified with recourse to what has to be done for the sake of the larger society (e.g., by means of something like the Rawlsian "difference principle"), or at least are universally believed to be so justified.

7. In the above-mentioned dissertation.

8. A very interesting description of the then still officially Communist Hungarian society in terms of game theory is presented by Elemér Hankiss in his *Társaddalmi csapdák* (in Hungarian: "Social Traps"), Budapest: Magvetö Kiadó, 1979.

9. Only after 1918 was Poland to reappear as an independent state.

10. These outbursts are usually referred to by the names of months in which they started; thus the landmarks of Polish post-war history are *October* (1956), *March* (1968), *December* (1970), *August* (1980), and *December* (1981), perhaps also *June* (1989), when semi-free Parliamentary elections ousted the Communists from power.

11. Where one factor, or another unit of social organizations, was on strike to support the cause of another unit.

NOTE TO CHAPTER SIX (pp. 63–66)
Marxism and the Professionalisation of Philosophy

1. For a more detailed picture see my paper "Philosophy inside Communism: the Case of Poland," *Studies in Eastern European Thought* (forthcoming).

NOTES TO CHAPTER SEVEN (pp. 67–102)
Philosophy, "Parallel Polis" and Revolution: The Case of Czechoslovakia

1. Václav Bĕiohradský, "Post-komunismus v SSSR" (post-Communism in the USSR—in Czech), *Přítomnost* 9/91, Prague, p. 3. The Czech philosoher and sociologist Václav Bĕlohradský was born in Prague in 1944 and studied at the Philosophical Faculty of the Charles University. After the Soviet occupation of Czechoslovakia in 1968 Bĕiohradský emigrated to Italy, where, in 1973, he was made Professor of Sociology at the University of Genova.

2. Karel Čapek, *Spisy* XX., *Hovory's T. G. Masarykem* (Collected Works XX., Discussions with T. G. Masaryk—in Czech), Prague 1990, p. 517. The Czech philosopher and politician Tomas Garrigue Masaryk (1850–1937), "Father of the Nation," was the first President of the Czechoslovak Republic. He studied at Vienna University, particularly under Brentano and especially Brentano's ethical views made a deep impression on Masaryk's thought. After becoming Professor of Philosophy at the Czech-speaking University in Prague in 1882, Masaryk established the so-called "Realist Party," a political organization of critical intellectuals. During World War I Masaryk emigrated to Paris (later to London), where he founded the Czech National Council. In his capacity as leader of the national liberation movement of the Czechs and Slovaks he became also the commander of the Free Czechoslovak Army (Czechoslovak Legions) which (unsuccessfully) tried to re-establish democracy in Russia in 1918–1920. In his political activity, Masaryk aimed always to realize the ideals of humanism and democracy.

3. "It may indeed prove to be far the most difficult and not the least important task for human reason rationally to comprehend its own limitations." F. A. von Hayek, *The Counter-Revolution of Science*, Liberty Press, Indianapolis 1979, p. 162.

4. See Rudolf Haller, *Fragen zu Wittgenstein und Aufsätze zur österreichischen Philosophie*, Rodopi B. V., Amsterdam 1986, p. 44.

5. See Barry Smith, "Austrian Economics and Austrian Philosophy," in: W. Grassl and B. Smith (eds.), *Austrian Economics, Historical and Philosophical Background*, Croom Helm, London & Sydney, 1986, pp. 1–36.

6. See Franz Mehring, *Die Lessing-Legende*, J. H. W. Dietz Nachf., Stuttgart, 1922, I.8.

7. See Václav Bělohradský, "Je Masarykovo pojetí Německa ještě aktuální?," (Is Masaryk's conception of Germany still topical?—in Czech), *Přítomnost*, Prague, June 6th, 1990, pp. 16–17.

8. See Edmund Husserl, *Die Krisis der europäischen Wissenschaften und die transzendentale Phänomenologie*, Ergänzende Texte, Beilage III., in: Husserliana Bd. VI., Martinus Nijhoff, Haag 1954.

9. See Martin Heidegger, *Sein und Zeit*, Max Niemeyer Verlag, Tübingen, 1977, pp. 270–95.

10. See Václav Bělohradský, "Je Masarykovo pojetí Německa ještě aktuální?," p. 16.

11. See Jacques Bergier, Louis Pauwels, *Le Matin des Magiciens*, Gallimard, Paris 1960, part II.

12. The anti-étatist thinking of the representatives of the Czech National Revival (Ján Kollár, Pavel Josef Šafařík, František Palacký) was influenced by some ideas of J. G. Herder; according to Herder, the state is an artificial entity, while the nation is a natural form of unity rising from the family; the most natural state is the state of one nation with one national character. Herder hoped that all artificial state complexes will break down in such a way that the ideal of humanity will be brought into existence in the form of national states. (See J. G. Herder, *Ideen zur Philosophie der Geschichte der Menschheit*, IX, 4) The impact of Herder's concept of nation is explicit e.g., in Palacký, who claimed that the *raison d'être* of Austria consists in its becoming a federation of free, autonomous nations having equal rights and mutually influencing each other in order to develop a higher cultural, economic and social unity.

13. See Jan Patočka, "O smysl dneška" (About the sense of our time—in Czech), *Rozmluvy*, 18 Church Hill, Purley, Surrey, 1987, pp. 87–104.

14. Patočka argues that Brentano's conception of intentionality was inspired not only by Aristotle and the Scholastics, but also by Bolzano's concept of the "judgement in a subjective sense." Jan Patočka, "O smysl dneška," p. 108.

15. Franz Brentano, *Vom Ursprung sittlicher Erkenntnis*, F. Meiner, Leipzig 1921, pp. 27–28. (This work hs been translated into English as: *The Origin of our Knowledge of Right and Wrong*, London: Routledge & Kegan Paul, 1969.)

16. In this connection, the excellent work of Rio Preisner must be mentioned, too. See R. Preisner, "Kritika totalitarismu" (Criticism of Totalitarianism—in Czech), *Rozmluvy*, 18 Church Hill, Purley, Surrey, 1984. But, Preisner's fundamental criticism of both totalitarianism and modern liberalism was not so influential as Havel's and Bělohradský's ideas because of its strict Christian orientation.

17. See Václav Bělohradský, "Krize eschatologie neosobnosti" (Personality Crisis

in Secular Eschatology—in Czech), *Rozmluvy*, London 1982, pp. 4–12. The English version of this work of Bělhoradský was published in Genoa in 1982.

18. See Daniel Bell, *The End of Ideology*, The Free Press of Glencoe, 1960; Václav Bělohradský, *Prirozeny svět jako politický problém* (The Life-World as Political Problem—in Czech), Prague 1991, pp. 179–92. The Italian version of this book by Bělohradský was published under the title: *Il mondo della vita: un problema politico* in Milan in 1981.

19. See Václav Havel, "Moc bezmocnych" (The Power of the Powerless—in Czech), in: Havel's "O lidskou identitu," *Rozmluvy*, Prague 1990, pp. 55–71 (Chapters I–VI). Havel's essay was published also as part of an English collection entitled *The Power of the Powerless*, London, Hutchinson, 1985.

20. The Czech philosopher Jan Patočka (1907–1977) studied first at the Czech-speaking branch of the Charles University and later at the Sorbonne (under Koyré and Husserl) and at the University of Freiburg under Husserl and Heidegger. He started to teach phenomenological and existential philosophy in 1945, but after the Communist coup of 1948 he was removed from his university teaching post and assigned to a series of clerical occupations. In 1968 he was made Professor of Philosophy at the Charles University, but in 1970 he was once more expelled from the University and banned from all publication. Patočka nevertheless held private seminars in his home and produced a series of samizdat publications. The fusion of Patočka's thought and practice came in 1977 when, together with Hayek, he drafted and signed the human rights manifesto Charter 77. In consequence of this, Patočka was detained and subjected to extended police interrogation as a result of which, on 13 March 1977, he died of a cerebral hemmorrhage.

21. See Václav Bělohradský, "Je Masarykovo pojetí Německa ještě aktuální?," p. 16.

22. This study was published in: Jan Patočka, *Negativní platonismus* (Negative Platonism—in Czech), Praha 1990, pp. 59–220.

23. *Ibid.*, p. 206.

24. *Ibid.*, p. 207.

25. See Jan Patočka, *O smysl dneška*, pp. 18–19. (Patočka's work *O smysl dneška* consists of 9 essays which were written in the 1960s.)

26. Patočka is fully aware of the fact that not every orientation towards the world is connected with a striving for authenticity. See *O smysl dneška*, p. 19.

27. See Jan Patočka, *Ketzerische Essais über die Philosophie der Geschichte*, Klett-Cotta, Stuttgart 1988, chapter 1.

28. *Ibid.*, chapter 2.

29. *Ibid.*, chapter 3.

30. See Václav Havel, "Příběh a totalita" (Story and Totality—in Czech), in: Havel's *Do ràznych stran*, Prague 1990, pp. 116–37.

31. See Jan Patočka, *Ketzerische Essais über die Philosophie der Geschichte*, chapter 6.

32. See František Kautman, *Masaryk, Šalda, Patočka*, Prague 1990, p. 79.

33. See Václav Havel, *The Power of the Powerless*, chapter III.

34. *Ibid.*, chapter VII.

35. *Ibid.*, chapter VIII.

36. *Ibid.*, chapter VII.

37. Notwithstanding the fact that Havel performed "small work" practically, his theoretical interpretation of Masaryk's conception is not very exact. For Havel iden-

tified "small work" with good and faithful professional work. (*The Power of the Powerless*, chapter XIV.) This misinterpretation had necessarily to lead to doubt being cast upon the relevance of "small work" to the anti-totalitarian movement. However, Havel concludes that good and faithful professional work must necessarily enter into conflict with Communist pseudo-political management of all spheres of living, which implies that it is able to turn itself into "living in truth" or even "dissent."

38. See Václav Havel, *Listy Olze* (*Letters to Olga*—in Czech), Atlantis, Brno 1990, p. 221 (letter Nr. 95).

39. *Ibid.*, p. 254 (letter Nr. 109).

40. *Ibid.*, p. 359 (letter Nr. 144).

41. *Ibid.*, p. 348 (letter Nr. 141).

42. *Ibid.*, p. 335 (letter Nr. 137).

43. *Ibid.*, p. 359 (letter Nr. 144).

44. This idea can be found in Marx's well-known conception of "Weltlich-werden der Philosophie." See Karl Marx-Friedrich Engels *Gesamtausgabe* (MEGA), Erste Abteilung, Band 1, Dietz Verlag, Berlin 1975, p. 68.

45. See Václav Havel, *The Power of the Powerless*, chapter 13.

46. *Ibid.*, chapter XV.

47. *Ibid.*, chapter XVII.

48. *Ibid.*, chapter XVIII.

49. *Ibid.*, chapter XXI.

50. See Rio Preisner, *Kritika totalitarismu*, p. 314.

51. Timothy Garton Ash employs the term "refolution" to describe that reform from above which arises under revolutionary pressure from below. See his *The Uses of Adversity*, Random House, New York 1989, the chapter "Refolution."

52. See Ralf Dahrendorf, *Úvahy o revoluci v Evropě* (the Czech translation of Dahrendorf's essay *Reflections on the Revolution in Europe*, Chatto & Windus, London 1990), Prague 1991, p. 29.

53. Josef Šafařík, *Sedm listů Melinovi* (*Seven Letters to Melin*—in Czech), Prague 1948, p. 252.

54. See Ludvík Vaculík, "Odkud síla" (*From Where the Power is*—in Czech), *Lidové noviny*, Prague, November 1989 (extraordinary edition), p. 6.

NOTES TO CHAPTER EIGHT (pp. 103–134)
Visions from the Ashes:
Philosophical Life in Bulgaria from 1945 to 1992

1. Cf. R. Tzanoff, "Bulgarian Philosophy," *The Encyclopedia of Philosophy*, Vol. 1 (New York/London: Macmillan, 1967), pp. 423–24; G. Schischkoff, "Philosophie in Bulgarien," *Zeitschrift für philosophische Forschung*, Bd. 27 (1972), Heft 2, pp. 246–55; B. Peichev, "Recent Contributions to Bulgaristics and to the History of Philosophy," *Southeastern Europe* 2 (1975), pp. 199–203; A. Ignatow, "Philosophie der Arriergarde: Die Auseinandersetzungen zwischen Dogmatikern und Revisionisten in Bulgarien," *Studies in Soviet Thought* 16 (1976),

nos. 1–2, pp. 27–66; and M. Buchvarov, "Philosophical Thought in Bulgaria," *Southeastern Europe* 8 (1981), nos. 1–2, pp. 279–94.

2. Ignatow, *op. cit.*, p. 28.

3. Cf. J. Lacroix, *Le Personnalisme: Tableau de la philosophie contemporaine* (Paris: Fischbacher, 1957), p. 419; J.-P. Sartre, *Search for a Method*, tr. H. Barnes (New York: Knopf, 1963), which begins with an assertion of this dominance; and W. McBride, *Sartre's Political Theory* (Bloomington: Indiana University Press, 1991),which discusses this state of affairs virtually *passim*.

4. Ignatow, *op. cit.*, p. 28.

5. Cf. A. Dendaine, "L'origine de l'hérésic médiévale," *Rivista di storia della chiesa i Italia* VI (1952) 1, pp. 47–73; E. Werner, "Neue Lösungsversuche des Bogomilenproblems," *Zeitschrift für Geisteswissenschaft* III (1955/56), pp. 773–802; A. Lombard, *Pauliciens, Bulgares, et Bons-hommes en Orient et en Occident* (Geneva/Basel, 1879); A. Boschkov, *La peinture bulgare*, tr. K. Todorov (Recklinghausen: A. Bougers, 1974); M. Arnaudov, *Sketches in Bulgarian Folklore*, 2 vols. (in Bulgarian) (Sofia, 1968/69); etc. Throughout this article and these footnotes, Bulgarian titles will be rendered in English translation.

6. Cf. O. Martin, "La Fraternité blanche universelle et l'instructeur du monde," in Zam Bhotiva, *Lumiére de Shambhala* (Paris: Telesma, 1990), pp. 1–28; O. Martin, *Le Soleil de Shambhala et l'école divine du Maître St. Jean* (Paris: Telesma, 1991), pp. 34–35; *'Le testament des couleurs' par le Maître Peter Deunov* (Paris: Telesma, 1987); F. Theodosy, *'Les paroles sacrées du maître' par le Maître Peter Deunov* (Paris: Telesma, 1988); *'L'art du chant divin'*, *méthode de développement spirituel et d'union cosmique suivant l'enseignement des maîtres: Peter Deunov et O. Aivanhov* (Paris: Telesma, 1989); etc.

7. N. Raynov was the author of more than 20 published novels, of a32-volume series of unpublished novels about the history of the human race, of more than 30 volumes of stories and legends, of a 12-volume history of art, and of several monographs on architecture, the decorative arts, etc., as well as of innumerable articles. Of particular philosophical interest are his essays on mysticism and disbelief and on man and *Übermensch*, collected in *Today and Tomorrow* (Sofia, 1925); the articles "Messiah and Superstitions" and "Prejudices concerning Theosophy," published in the theosophical journal, *Orpheus* (1925, nos. 3–4 and 5–6), which he founded and edited; his "Foreword" to his Bulgarian translation of Porphyry's *Cave of the Nymphs*; as well as his previously-mentioned *History of Art*. A revival of interest in his work is currently underway in Bulgaria.

8. The issue of the relationship between Stalinist "Marxism" and the Marxism of Marx has of course been the object of countless books and articles in Western countries over several decades. One of these efforts, still (we think) worthwhile, was the book by the American co-author of the present article, W. McBride, *The Philosophy of Marx* (London: Hutchinson/New York: St. Martin's, 1977). The same author also dealt with the general phenomenon of the relationship (in fact, the virtually inevitable gap) between philosophers' conceptions of social ideals and real societies supposedly modeled after them in his article, "The Practical Relevance of Practical Philosophy: Philosophers' Impact on History," originally published in *Philosophy in Context* 13 (1983), pp. 31–44, and reprinted in J. C. Nyíri, ed., *Perspectives on Ideas and Reality* (Budapest, 1990), pp. 66–84. See also I. Raynova, "Philosophy as Critique of Reality: Marx against Stalin," *Filosofska Misul* (*FM*) 1991, no. 2, pp. 22–25 (in Bulgarian),· to appear in French in "Critique et

différence," *Actes du XXIII-éme Congrés de l'Association des Sociétés de Philosophie de Langue Française*, Tunis, 1990.

9. This is not quite precise, since the National Front that took power in September 1944 consisted of a coalition of the Bulgarian Workers' party, the Bulgarian People's Agrarian Union, the Zveno National Union, the Radical Party, and the "independent intellectuals." This parliamentary arrangement and coalition government lasted, as we shall see, until 1948.

10. *FM* (1945, nos. 1/2), pp. 3-4.

11. The first version of this crucially important work by T. Pavlov was published in the Soviet Union in 1936. It is based on a study of Deborin's 1928 work, *Dialectical Materialism and the Theory of Reflections*, about certain theses of which Pavlov raises questions. Deborin was the official director of the "philosophical front" in the USSR.

12. "The Scientific Notion of Democracy and Certain Questions of Our Time," *FM* (1945), no. 1/2, pp. 5-55.

13. These were the Bulgarian Communist Party and the official Bulgarian People's Agrarian Union.

14. "Comrade G. Dimitrov on the Role and Tasks of the Journal *Filosofska Misul*," *FM* (1946, no. 3), p. 7.

15. *Ibid.*, p. 8.

16. T. Pavlov, "The Road and Perspectives of Scientific Bulgarian Thought," *FM* 1947, no. 1, pp. 3-26.

17. This work of 458 manuscript pages, along with another, *Dialectics and Sophistics* (541 ms. pp.), was never published, as a result, quite clearly, of Pavlov's intervention. It should also be noted that the Pavlov-Michaltschev polemics are traceable back to the 1920s, when Pavlov's first publications appeared and were strongly criticized in *Filosofski Pregled* (FP). This inspired Pavlov to write his book, *Rehmkeism and Materialism* (1930), which was in turn ridiculed in FP (1930/31).

18. A few years later Lepeschinskaja's "experiments," like those of Lysenko, were to fall into total disrepute.

19. Cf. D. Spassov, "The Discussion of the 'New' Work of Academician Michaltschev, Traditional Logic and its Materialist Argumentation," *FM* 1953, no. 2, pp. 125-45, and the attacks by the participants themselves that are published in the *Yearbook of the University of Sofia*, Vol. 48, no. 1, pp. 135-298.

20. Cf. L. Sivilov, "The Accursed Dialectic," *FM* 1991, no. 1, p. 86.

21. E. Panova, "Against Fetishization of Objective Social Necessity," *FM* 1954, no. 5, pp. 95-101.

22. Editorial note at the beginning of D. Spassov's article, "On the Character of Elementary Logical Laws," *FM* 1954, no. 3, p. 42.

23. *Ibid.*, p. 55.

24. T. Pavlov, *Reflection Theory* (Sofia, 1945), p. 391.

25. Z. Oschavkov, *Historical Materialism and Sociology* (Sofia, 1957), p. 215.

26. Cf. S. Michailov and N. Stefanov, "On the Specificity of Philosophical and Sociological Knowledge of Society," *FM* 1958, no. 5; K. Vassilev, *Introduction to the Philosophy of History* (Sofia, 1962); etc.

27. A. Popov, "On the Nature and Object of Historical Materialism," *FM* 1958, no. 2, pp. 26-42.

28. N. Nikolov, "Is There a Difference between Historical Materialism and Marxist Sociology?," *FM* 1961, no. 5.

29. According to Oschavkov, "The object of Marxist-Leninist philosophy is the relationship among history, being, social being, and thought, consciousness, social consciousness, the most general forms and laws of the development of nature, society, and thought, the most general method of knowledge and change."—*op. cit.*, p. 15. This does appear to encompass a good deal of reality.

30. D. Spassov, "A Failed Attempt at Developing Marxism," *FM* 1959, no. 1, pp. 109–21.

31. P.-E. Mitev, *From the Social Problem to the Discovery of a World Concept* (Sofia, 1984), pp. 39–40.

32. 32. Cf. A. Danailov, "A Tragic Page," *Utschitelsko delo*, April 20, 1989, p. 6. This article analyzes the directives first given by T. Pavlov in *FM* 1948, no. 3, then reaffirmed at the Fifth Congress of the Bulgarian Communist Party and finally at the Lysenkoist biology conference of April 4–8, 1948, at which all those who had strayed from the true faith were forced to repentance and self-criticism.

33. G. Vekilov, *Science and Dogmatism* (Sofia, 1963), p. 31.

34. This book is in fact a summary of Iribadzhakov's fight against Lysenkoism, begun in 1959. (Cf. *FM* 1959, no. 6.)

35. N. Iribadzhakov, *Philosophy and Biology* (Sofia, 1967), pp. 123–315. For a synopsis of the fate of Lysenkoism in the USSR, including its astonishing temporary revival by Khrushchev, see Loren Graham, *Science and Philosophy in the Soviet Union* (New York: Alfred A. Knopf, 1972), pp. 195–251.

36. A. Polikarow, "Über einige Fragen des Kampfes gegen die zeitgenössische idealistische Philosophie," *Deutsche Zeitschrift für Philosophie* 1960, no. 11, p. 1351.

37. K. Darkovski, "On N. Iribadzhakov's Book, *Modern Criticisms of Marxism*, and Some Questions about the Struggle against Contemporary Bourgeois Philosophy," *FM* 1962, no. 1, pp. 78–86.

38. Cf. I. Markov, "Marxism, Criticism, and Careerism," *FM* 1961, no. 6.

39. Cf. "Letter to the Central Committee of the Bulgarian Communist Party," *FM* 1963, no. 3, pp. 3–4; and "For a Scientific and Intransigent Critique of Contemporary Bourgeois Philosophy," *FM* 1963, no. 3, pp. 5–13.

40. So, for example, I. Raynova, coauthor of this article, once having been labelled "anti-Marxist," had to fight for three years with her Philosophy Department subdivision, formerly called "Criticism of Contemporary Bourgeois Philosophy," before being able, in January 1989, to defend her dissertation, "Directions of Anthropologism in France: Existentialism—Personalism."

41. After one of his many references to Pearson, in which Lenin cites articles from *Mind* and *Revue Philosophique* in support of his contention that Pearson is an idealist, he turns his attention to the founder and first editor of *The Monist*, Paul Carus, whom he cites (from Volumes XV and XIII) for his belief that 'all truth is divine and God reveals himself in science as he does in history' and, in conclusion, calls "a leader of a gang of American literary fakers who are engaged in doping the people with religious opium." *Materialism and Empirio-criticism* (New York: International, 1927), pp. 228–29. Does the history of philosophy move in circles rather than spirals, after all?

42. T. Pavlov, *Reflection Theory*, p. 44.

43. A. Polikarov, *Matter and Knowledge* (Sofia, 1961), pp. 153–61; cf. also his article, "Once Again on Reflection as a Property of All Matter," *FM* 1962, no. 5.

44. A. Gavrilov, *On the Question of the Nature of Consciousness* (Sofia, 5th ed., 1984), pp. 155–97.

45. B. Mountian, "Reflection," in *Foundations of Marxist Philosophy* (Sofia, 1979).

46. J. Jelev, I. Djadjev, and P. Uvakow, "Über die philosophische Bestimmung der Materie," *Deutsche Zeitschrift für Philosophie*, 1964, no. 5, pp. 633–55.

47. Cf. *FM* 1967, no. 1, p. 24.

48. The criticism of *Fascism* centered around its alleged lack of analytic basis in the categories of historical materialism and in class analysis, as well as around the charge that Zhelev had identified fascism with totalitarianism by collecting and copying the well-known positions of K. Friedrich, Z. Brzezinski, L. Shapiro, K. Popper, H. Arendt, and others. Cf. M. Iankov, "For a Scientific, Marxist-Leninist Class Analysis of Fascism," *FM* 1982, no. 12, pp. 69–73.

49. Cf. D. Spassov, *Dogmatism and Anti-Dogmatism in Philosophy* (Sofia, 1984), pp. 6 and 26–27.

50. Cf. (all published in Sofia) D. Spassov, *Fundamental Problems of Mathematical Logic* (1955); *The New and the Old in Logic* (1958); *A Philosophical Introduction to Symbolic Logic* (1962); *From the Logical Point of View* (1965); *Analysis of Knowledge* (1969); *The Philosophy of Linguistics against Linguistic Philosophy* (1970); *Symbolic Logic* (1975); *Unity and Diversity* (1977); and *From Logic to Sociology* (1980); A. Bankov, *Thought and Logic* (1960); and *Logic of Scientific and Artistic Creation* (1974); A. Deikov, *Philosophy of Empiricist Logic* (1977); and *Logic* (1978); H. Eschkenhazy, *On Logical Paradoxes* (1977); N. Merdzhanov, *Inductive Methods in Contemporary Logic* (1975) etc.

51. Cf. (all published in Sofia) R. Radev, *On Arabic History* (1966); *Critique of Neo-Thomism* (1970); *The Philosophy of the Hellenistic Age* (1973); *Epicurus* (1976); *Socrates* (1980); *Ancient Philosophy* (an anthology) (1981); *The Latin Aristotle: Peter Abelard* (1982); and *History of Ancient Philosophy*, 2 vols. (1983/84); K. Kanev, *Satveda: The First Hindu Philosophical Doctrine of Being* (1976); *Jawaharlal Nehru—Philosophy and Humanism* (1983); and *Yoga* (1984); S. Boyanov, *The Philosophy of G. Bruno* (1969); *The Great German Thinkers* (1975); and *Humanism in the Western European Renaissance: Italy and France* (1980); E. Panova, *Fundamental Positions in Philosophy from Bacon to Marx* (1968); and *Kant and Analytic Metaphysics* (1987); I. Stefanov, *Kant and the Problem of the Dialectic* (1981); *Fichte's Dialectic* (1982); and *Neo-Kantian Philosophy* (1987); S. Levy, *Between Lebensphilosophie and Existentialism* (1967); and *Humanism and the Crisis of Liberal Consciousness: Miguel de Unamuno and Philosophy* (1979); and A. Litchev, *Philosophy in Search of Man* (1978).

52. Cf. (all published in Sofia) L. Dramaliev, *Morality: Essence and Specificity* (1972); K. Neschev, *Tact* (1974); *Fundamental Problems of the Moral End* (1975); *Eudaimonism* (1977); *The Moral Ideal* (1978); and *Ethics* (1980); D. Stankov, *Morality as a Normative System* (1976); and *The Moral Culture* (1977); D. Georgiev, *Ethical Knowledge, Worldview, Values* (1977); A. Andonov, *Free and Unfree Man* (1977); etc.

53. See I. Passy, *The Tragic* (1963); *On Beauty and Art* (1966); *Philosophical and Literary Studies* (1968); *Aesthetic Studies* (1970); *The Comic* (1972); *Kant's Aesthetics* (1976); *French Moralists* (1978); *Essays* (1981); *Classical German Aesthetics* (1982); *Metaphor* (1983); and *At the Origins of Modern Aesthetics* (1987);

D. Avramov, *Aesthetics of Modern Art* (1969); A. Natev, *End or End-in-Itself of Art* (1960); *Art and Society* (1961); *Between the Doubtful and the Indubitable* (1961); *Art and Cultural Craft* (1974); and *The Turning-Points in Art* (1982); E. Nikolov, *Phenomenology and Aesthetics* (1965); *Aesthetics of Television* (1985); *Culture: A Descriptive Essay* (1987); and *Philosophy of Communication* (1988); I. Tzoneva, *Aesthetics: Kant, Schelling, Hegel* (1984); etc.

54. Tzoneva, *op. cit.*, p. 167.

55. I. Tzoneva, "Defense of Philosophical Aesthetics," *FM* 1989, no. 9, pp. 86–87.

56. Cf. I. Raynova, "The Second Canadian-Bulgarian Meeting," *FM* 1988, no. 4, p. 109; I. Raynova, "Philosophers and Culture," *Problemi na kulturata*, 1987, no. 6.

57. This is a relative term, since it refers not so much to actual age as to a certain new attitude, which is also to be found in some individuals who are in their forties or even fifties—e.g., I. Tzoneva, I. Stefanov, P.-E. Mitev, *et al.*

58. Cf. "The Success of a Solitary Battle," *Sofia News*, February 15–28, 1990, p. 2.

59. Cf. I. Raynova, "Dismantle Philosophy?," *Sofia News*, June 21, 1990, p. 4; "Calm Your Temper, Mr. Sendov" (open letter to the President of the Academy of Sciences signed by I. Raynova, I. Katzarski, M. Todorova, I. Vassileva, I. Hristov, R. Stupov), *Kultura*, September 28, 1990, p. 2.

60. Cf. his assessment of Bulgarian politics in 1990, "Bulgaria: The Romantic Period of the Opposition Continues," in *Praxis International* 10, nos. 3/4 (October 1990–January 1991), pp. 306–17.

61. Cf., for example, M. Vesneva, *Extrasensory Knowledge* (Sofia, 1991), pp. 128–35; M. Konstantinov and H. Madjarov, *The New Culture in the Age of Aquarius* (Sofia, 1991), pp. 16–17; I. Raynova, *From the Philosophy of Existence to Post-Personalism* (Sofia, 1991); and I. Raynova, *From Husserl to Ricoeur: The Phenomenological Approach to Human Being* (Sofia, 1992). A work in progress by the American coauthor of this article, tentatively entitled Philosophy in the Post-Marxist Era in Eastern Europe: Observations and Projections, will focus primarily, particularly in its second half, on related issues of values in a post-Marxist world, of social roles (especially of women), and of the role of religion. A planned final chapter is to be entitled "Ultimate Things: The Death and Rebirth of Materialism?" or, alternatively, "From One Materialism to Another?"

NOTES TO CHAPTER NINE (pp. 135–164)
The Crisis of Continuity in Post-Soviet Russian Philosophy

1. The author wishes to acknowledge the generous grant of the *Fond national suisse de la recherche scientifique* which made possible *in situ* research for this paper.

2. While it was the custom formerly to write about "Soviet" philosophy and most often to mean by this philosophy in the Russian language, be it produced by Russians or nationals of other cultures in the Soviet Union, in what follows I limit myself to philosophy in post-Soviet Russia, above all Moscow.

3. With the demise of the Communist Party, its ideological and propaganda sectors have been disbanded and the Institute of Marxism-Leninism, whose task it was to edit and publish the works of the "classics" (Marx, Engels, and Lenin) as well as to promote the study of the heritage, has been closed.

4. At least two "universities" have been established, partly with the support of outside financial assistance: The Russian State Humanitarian University (sometimes called the "Afanasyev University" with reference to its leading light, the historian Ju. N. Afanasyev who is engaged first of all in promoting a recovery of the national identity; cf. the two volumes entitled *Nase otecestvo. Opyt politiceskoj istorii,* Moscow, "Terra," 1991), and the Russian Open University.

5. In 1961 T. J. Blakeley published *Soviet Scholasticism* in which he reconstructed the "internal logic" of mainstream Soviet philosophical practice. One wonders what post-Soviet philosophers think of that book today.

6. Ivin has collected a whole array of characteristics associated with the dogmatic scholastic mentality: authoritarianism, retrospectiveness and traditionalism, conservatism, a predetermined refusal of innovation, anonymity, commentary, rhetoricity, fundamentalism, cumulativism, hierarchicalism, symbolism, an evaluative approach, schematism, system-building, etc. He is inspired in part by his studies of Thomas Kuhn and accounts of Medieval philosophizing, e.g., De Wolf, Gilson, and G. G. Majorov (*Formirovanie srednevekovoj filosofii: Latinskaja patristika,* Moscow, 1979).

7. See the discussion of the Stalinist input to this trait of the Soviet mind in Pechenev 1990. He writes (p. 62) that Stalin, in his article "Anarchism or Socialism?," argued that Marxism is premised on "a conception of society in which the condition of the freedom of the individual is the liberation of the *masses*" (emphasis in the original). One might also read this in light of Marx's declaration in "On the Jewish Question" (1844) that political emancipation is possible only when an individual aligns his "*forces propres*" with the "*force sociale.*"

8. It would be vain to pretend that there were no exceptions to this general absence of discussion on foundational matters. One recent Western study documents and discusses one such exception in full: Bakhurst 1991. However, it seems fair to say that Soviet thought has stood in the shadow of a certain positivism inherited from Engels and Lenin: from the former the theory of universal dialectical laws, from the latter the dual definition of "matter"—as objective reality, i.e., in epistemological terms, and as the stuff the physical sciences study. Hence, ontological questions boil down to applications of the dialectical laws to scientific discoveries in objectively existing domains of "matter"—as certified by the epistemological characterization thereof—thus rendering 'the metaphysical' implications of ontology virtually obsolete.

9. Cf. Swiderski, 1979a.

10. One recent critic, former dean of the philosophy department of Moscow State University, laments the 'provincialism' of Soviet philosophy: "Essentially what we did was to exclude Marxist philosophy from the wider context of development of world philosophy. Moreover, there is paradox in the fact that we contrived to exclude our own philosophy from the wider context of development of Marxist philosophy in the world and turned it into a provincial philosophy with its own problems, categories, anxieties, etc." (Panin 1990, p. 170).

11. A sign of this anonymity is found in the circumstance that, in the Soviet Union, only two "official," i.e., extra-academic, professional journals existed, viz.,

Voprosy filosofii [Questions of Philosophy] and *Filosofskie nauki* [Philosophical Sciences], both of which stood under the aegis of the Central Committee of the Communist Party. The contest for space in the pages of these journals (the press runs of *Voprosy filosofii* sometimes reached eighty and ninety thousand per issue) was won by those who adopted the "house style."

12. I have not been able to take into account here the discussion just published by Politizdat in Moscow under the title *Filosofskoe soznanie: dramatizm obnovlenija* (The Philosophical Consciousness: The Drama of Renewal), edited by N. I. Lapin.

13. While I know no text by Bochenski in which he articulates this thesis, it was a central theme of his discussions in lectures given at the University of Fribourg in the Winter Semester of 1971.

14. Panin (1990, p. 170) writes about the "de-existentialization" of Soviet philosophy. "We even came to the point where ethics was considered a peripheral science. In this sense it seems to me that the authors [of the textbook—EMS] were correct to elevate the humanist problematic to the highest level."

15. This turning was evidenced in the protracted debates prior to the appearance of the textbook about the "real meaning" of the "great basic question of philosophy"—what is primary, being or thinking, spirit or nature? In many discussion pieces, articles, and even letters published at the end of the eighties, the tendency was to disparage the traditional formulation of the "basic question." Away from the sacrosanct formula "materialism" (primacy of being, i.e., nature) vs. "idealism" (primacy of spirit, i.e., thinking) to a reformulation in terms of such conceptual pairs as "man—the world of man," or "consciousness—objectivized consciousness," all of which played on semantic correlations intrinsic to the conceptual framework of human experience constituted in interaction governed by cultural rules, symbols, etc.

16. Much of what follows is based on impressions formed in the course of discussions I held with philosophers in Moscow in November 1991.

17. The names most often cited are: E. Il'enkov, M. Mamardasvili, B. Grusin, B. Scedrovickij, A. Zinov'ev, as well as Bibler and Bakhtine.

18. The history of the "sixties generation" has yet to be written; that it is a subject of significance is testified by one of the more influential younger philosophers today, V. Podoroga, who confided to me that the real philosophical life was in the hands of this "generation," and that without their example and encouragement he would have abandoned philosophy.

19. Oleg Drobnickij is credited with the advances made in moral-value theory, cf. the collection in Charcev 1966.

20. The step to culture theory was certainly aided by the international renown of J. Lotman's school in Tartu as well as by the studies of the Moscow structuralist group. To be sure, there were other sources, always present in the underground, in particular Bakhtine and Vygotsky.

21. Human agency in the sense of a philosophical theory of action is not the immediate subject of the theory of activity (*teorija dejatel'nosti*) pursued by A. N. Leont'ev, Luria and other psychologists, partly under the influence of V. S. Vygotsky's theories.

22. Admittedly, not everyone was timid. An exception, occurring at the highest level, in the journal of the Central Committee of the Party, *Kommunist*, was the preprint of E. Ju. Solov'ev's contribution to the new textbook; Solov'ev 1988.

23. Bochenski showed that, far from being a neat synthesis of German

philosophy, British and French Socialist doctrine, and political economic theory, as Lenin contended, Marxism-Lennism was a concoction of scientific materialism, positivism, Hegelianism, Russian social democratic political theory, and Lenian-Stalinian "bolshevism": Bochenski 1958. Cf. also Kolakowski 1977.

24. The original discussion was organized in 1989 under the auspices of the club "Free Word" (*Svobodnoe slovo*) by a philosopher Valentin Tolstykh. It brought together philosophers, sociologists, artists, and cinematographers. The collection, comprisng some 25 contributions, has yet to be published in its entirety. "Is Marxism Dead?" is an extract from that discussion published in *Voprosy filosofii* 1990, 10, pp. 19–57 (recently made available in English translation in *Soviet Studies in Philosophy*, 1991, 30, 2, pp. 7–75). "The Emancipation of the Spirit" (*Osvobozdenie ducha*), Moscow, Politizdat (recently reconstituted under the name "Epokha"), edited by Tolstykh and A. A. Gusejnoy, contains parts of the first discussion together with texts presented at other meetings of the Club of the Free Word. Another discussion of note centred around a polemic by A. Tsipko "Protivorecija ucenija Karla Marksa" ("The Contradictions in the Doctrine of K. Marx") in *VMGU: Social'no-politiceskie issledovanija* 1990, 2, 77–84; the discussion appeared in the fifth issue for 1990 of the same year under the title "Marksizm: problemy, protivorecija, perspektivy" ("Marxism: Problems, Contradictions, Perspectives"), pp. 3–71. Finally, *VLGU* 1991, 5 contains an uneven and somewhat unfocused discussion.

25. As if in preparation for such an eventuality, a soon to be published philosophical novel by the émigré professor, Aleksandr Pjatigorsky (*Filosofija odnogo pereulka*, Moscow, Progress, 1992), extols the virtues of a business man who conducts his existence philosophically and thus brings out, far better than the professor who relies on the abstractions of systems, the many and varied dimensions of consciousness.

26. I take it that the reader understands that not everything that may be said about philosophy in Russia is exhausted by the listing that follows. The most evident absence is the burgeoning interest in the history of philosophy and the philosophy thereof as well as the recovery of thinkers like Losev, Asmus, Il'enkov, *et al.*, who philosophized in a manner hardly congenial to mainstream Marxist-Leninists (among other things: they, especially Losev, carried out foundational research virtually incompatible with the ontology of dialectical materialism). That said, however, I must at the very least report that attitudes in Russia to the study of the history of philosophy are mixed. During the height of the Brezhnevian "stagnation" when, as Ivin phrases it, many souls migrated into noncontroversial areas, viz. those in which foundational issues were of little importance, the history of philosophy became an area of prime attractiveness to younger and older researchers alike. Today, however, when the need for well-versed and competent philosophers is crucial, these "historians" have yet to show their mettle and thus overcome the reputation that has grown up around them—they are sometimes regarded as "specialists," often in the manner of intellectual historians applying methods of little direct importance to philosophical analysis and argument.

27. Historians of philosophy are increasingly well served today by the publication in a special series prepared by the editorial board of *Voprosy filosofii* of the classics of Russian thought. The journal has been especially active in promoting this revival; hardly an issue goes by in which there is not a text of some figure from the past often introduced and even annotated by an expert.

28. A new journal bearing the title *Paralleli (Rossija-vostok-zapad)* has been founded by a historian, A. Kara-Murza, which has the task of getting to the bottom of the Russian cultural identity by means of cross-cultural comparativist studies. In this connection, mention should be made of two other new journals both entitled *Logos*, one from Leningrad/St. Petersburg, the other from Moscow, both of which see their tasks as continuing the tradition of the first *Logos*, published in Russia in the years 1910–1914.

29. As if to confirm the "Soviet" essence of the anthropocentric turn in its final stage, it is interesting to note that none of its leading figures, at least on the basis of the texts known to me, cited the personalism of the Russian tradition, and indeed, as I have argued, they were more inclined to conceive the category of the person in Kantian—or Schelerian—terms.

30. To investigate such issues a research centre has been founded, "Rossijskaja civilizacja: puti vyzivanija" (Russian Civilization: paths to Survival) under the combined direction of several younger historians of ideas and philosophy: A. V. Rubcov, S. L. Cizkov, A. Kara-Murza, L. Poljakov, and B. Oresin. The institutional backing for the centre comes from one of the more active publishing houses, Progress.

31. The Bibler school is becoming well-remarked because Bibler is publishing extensively (cf. Bibler 1990a, b, c) and because his associates are held in esteem, e.g., A. Akhutin, but also T. Dlugac and V. Neretina.

32. The group seems to be headed by Valery Podoroga who is the director of a research "laboratory" in the Institute of Philosophy ("The laboratory of post classical investigations in philosophy: Literature, Art, and Politics") and includes N. Avtonomova, E. Nadtocij, M. Riklin, S. Zimovec, N. Klimenkova; their texts are not readily accessible as for the most part they appear in internal offset and mimeograph publications of the Institute of Philosophy. But Podoroga is more visible; cf. Podoroga 1991a, b. Another grouping which overlaps to some extent with the first was called the All-Union Association of Young Philosophers within the USSR Philosophical Society; it sponsored *Totalitarizm* (1989), edited by the very active A. Kara-Murza and, among others, L. Poljakov.

33. Riklin (1991, p. 7) refers to Bakhtine's school including V. N. Volosinov (often thought to be Bakhtine) and P. N. Medvedev who applied his theory of language to the Marxian theory of social consciousness and arrived at the conclusion that the being of the social is determined by social consciousness, i.e., ideology, or simply culture.

34. These and other themes are treated in internal publications of the IF, such as *Soznanie* (1990) and *Totalitarizm i Soznanie* (1990).

35. "Wenn man die kritische Transzendentallehre unter dem Blickpunkt der neuesten philosophischen Entwicklung im Westen betrachtet, kann man sehen, das ihr Schöpfer nicht so sehr an noch einer welterklärenden Konzeption gearbeitet hat, als vielmehr an den universellen Voraussetzungen des modernen philosophischen Konsensus. Das ist die beste Basis eine pluralistische Korrelation unterschiedlicher Weltanschauungen, die sich von den Ansprüchen auf geistigen Hegemonismus losgesagt haben, und sozusagen nach dem Prinzip der Ergänzung aufeinander hinweisen. Aber aus diesem Grunde wird Kant zum aktuellen politischen Denker, dessen Grundsätze den gegenwärtigen Bedürfnissen nach Konvergenz und Dialog entsprechen." (Solov'ëv 1991b, p. 23)

36. Translations of standard Western studies on these themes are virtually nonexistent. However, a project is under way to establish a new philosophy journal in 1992 with the provocative title *Put'* (The Path)—provocative because it takes the same

name as that of the journal edited until 1945 by N. Berdjaev in Paris as the organ of Russian (mainly religious) philosophy—a main purpose of which will be to publish translations; an accompanying book series is also planned for the same purpose. I owe this information to the editor and leading spirit of this project, Anatoli Jakovlev.

37. The department is chaired by V. I. Kovalenko and the chair of political philosophy has been entrusted to Victor V. Il'in.

NOTES TO CHAPTER TEN (pp. 165–170)
The New European Philosophy

1. The distinction is based above all on the radically different role of texts and authorities in the two traditions. On the one hand are those philosophical cultures which are based on training in argument and in certain associated technical methods and whose primary concern is the finding of solutions to problems of certain clearly demarcated sorts. On the other hand are those philosophical cultures which are marked by the presence of "masters" and "initiates" and whose primary concern is the development of the philosophy of a given school (philosophizing *through* Kant, or Hegel, or Heidegger, and so on). See my "Textual Deference," *American Philosophical Quarterly*, 28 (1991), 1–13.

2. See L. B. Puntel, "The History of Philosophy in Contemporary Philosophy: The View from Germany," *Topoi*, 10 (1991), 147–54.

3. See on this the useful work of Luc Ferry and Alain Renaut, *La pensée 68: Essai sur l'anti-humanisme contemporain*, Paris: Gallimard, 1985 (Eng. trans. *French Philosophy of the Sixties. An Essay on Antihumanism*, Amherst, MA: The University of Massachusetts Press, 1990).

4. On the Central European roots of analytic philosophy see Michael Dummett, *Ursprünge der analytischen Philosophie*, Frankfurt a. M.: Suhrkamp, 1987.

5. Through his pupil, Husserl, Brentano of course also crucially influenced post-war French philosophy. On Brentano's early influence see, e.g., R. Haller, *Studien zur Österreichischen Philosophie*, Amsterdam: Rodopi, 1979 and J. C. Nyíri, ed., *From Bolzano to Wittgenstein: The Tradition of Austrian Philosophy*, Vienna: Hölder-Pichler-Tempsky, 1986.

6. See my "Austrian origins of Logical Positivism," in B. Gower, ed., *Logical Positivism in Perspective*, London/Sydney: Croom Helm (1987), Totowa, NJ: Barnes and Noble (1988), 35–68 and in K. Szaniawski, ed., *The Vienna Circle and the Lvov-Warsaw School*, Dordrecht/Boston/Lancaster: Kluwer (1989) 19–53.

7. See K. Mulligan, ed., *Speech Act and Sachverhalt: Reinach and the Foundations of Realist Phenomenology*, Dordrecht/Boston/Lancaster: Nijhoff, 1987.

8. The history of philosophy, too, can be seen as being allied with exact or analytic philosophy in this wider sense, namely insofar as it is carried out in a clear and rigorous fashion.

9. The year of publication of Carl Menger's *Grundsätze der Volkswirtschaftslehre* (Vienna: Braumüller, Eng. trans. *Principles of Economics*, New York and London: New York University Press, 1976), a work which initiated the so-called

"Austrian School of Economics." See W. Grassl and B. Smith, eds., *Austrian Economics. Historical and Philosophical Background*, London and Sydney: Croom Helm, 1986.

10. See Deborah A. Redman, *Economics and the Philosophy of Science*, New York and Oxford: Oxford University Press, 1991.